The Muses' Library

POEMS OF BEN JONSON

BEN. IOHNSONII. ✳ VERA EFFIGIES DOCTISSIMI POETARVM ANGLORVM

Ro: Vaughan fecit.

Johnsoni typus, ecce!qui furoris.
Antistes sacer, Enthei Camenis,
Vindex Ingeny recens Sepulti,
Antiquæ reparator vnus artis.

Desuncta Pater Eruditionis,
Et Scenæ veteris novator audax.
Nec fœlix minus, aut minus politus,
Cui solus similis, Figura, Vivet.

O could there be an art found out that might
Produce his shape soe lively as to Write. AbҌ

POEMS

OF

BEN JONSON

edited

with an introduction

by

GEORGE BURKE
JOHNSTON

HARVARD UNIVERSITY PRESS

CAMBRIDGE, MASSACHUSETTS

First published in U.S.A. 1955
by Harvard University Press
Cambridge, Massachusetts

Printed in Great Britain
by Butler & Tanner Ltd
Frome and London

CONTENTS

CONTENTS

CONTENTS

THE FORREST

THE UNDER-WOOD

CONTENTS

CONTENTS

CONTENTS

CONTENTS

xiii

CONTENTS

MISCELLANY

CONTENTS

CONTENTS

CONTENTS

ACKNOWLEDGEMENTS

I ACKNOWLEDGE with gratitude the following courtesies:

The Modern Language Association of America granted funds for microfilming and photostating books and manuscripts.

Harcourt, Brace and Company granted permission to reprint the passages from T. S. Eliot's 'Ben Jonson' in *Selected Essays 1913–1932* and the critical passage on 'To the Memory of my Beloved, the Author Mr. William Shakespeare' in Hazelton Spencer's *Art and Life of William Shakespeare*.

The William Andrews Clark Memorial Library of the University of California gave permission to reprint 'To Lucy Countess of Bedford' (*Miscellany* V) from Jonson's *Cynthias Revels*, 1601.

The Library of Harvard University gave permission to reproduce and print from Jonson's manuscript of the 'Epitaph on Cecilia Bulstrode' (*Miscellany* XVIII), which is from the bequest of Miss Amy Lowell.

The Henry E. Huntington Library and Art Gallery granted permission to print the following pieces from the books named in the explanatory notes to each piece: *Miscellany* II, XV, XX, XXV, XXVIII, LVII.

The Director of the Folger Shakespeare Library gave permission to reprint the following pieces: *The Under-wood* XXIV; *Miscellany* III, VI–VIII, XII, XIX, XXIII, XXXI, XXXIII, XXXIV, XXXVIII, XL–XLII, XLIV, XLVI, XLVII, XLIX, L, LIV–LVI, LIX–LXI.

The Delegates of the Clarendon Press, Oxford, have granted permission to print the following from *Ben Jonson*, edited by C. H. Herford, Percy Simpson, and Evelyn Simpson, Oxford 1925–52: *The Forrest* XII, lines 93–100; *Miscellany* I, XI, XXII, XXIV, XXVI, XXX, XXXIX, XLIII, LI–LIII, LXII–LXVII.

ACKNOWLEDGEMENTS

However, my debt to this great monument of scholarship, more lasting than bronze, cannot be paid with a mere acknowledgement of permission to reprint certain pieces: for more than two decades it has increased my knowledge and appreciation of Jonson. It is the firm foundation of present and future Jonsonian scholarship.

My friends James G. McManaway, August H. Mason, William Lee Sandidge, and Henry W. Wells gave helpful criticism on the Introduction. The Columbia University Press allowed me to draw freely on my *Ben Jonson: Poet* in preparing the Introduction and Explanatory Notes.

GEORGE BURKE JOHNSTON

Virginia Polytechnic Institute
June 1953

INTRODUCTION

INTRODUCTION

MANY of the great Elizabethan and Jacobean writers are only walking shadows. Their works are distinct and vigorous; the authors veiled in mystery or obscurity. It is not so with Ben Jonson. His familiar, rugged face looks intently from several authentic portraits; many of his books, autographed and sometimes annotated, survive; extant letters and dedications add touches of human reality; staunch friends and violent enemies built up a vivid picture to which he himself contributed. Although he has been dead for three centuries and more, he still arouses an intense partisanship which colours the critical conception of his writings, and even tends to obscure their variety.

In spite of the personal impression Jonson made on his own and following ages, biographical facts, particularly about his early life, are not numerous; and many questions about him, both biographical and literary, remain unanswered.[1] He was born in 1572 or 1573, possibly on 11 June. There are conflicting accounts of the death of his father. John Taylor, the Water Poet, writing in 1637, placed the death of the father, whom he called a reverend Preacher, 'when Ben was 17 years of age'. In 1680 Izaak Walton wrote to John Aubrey that the father's death occurred when Ben was in the sixth form at Westminster School. The Drummond *Conversations*, 1618–19, state that the father's death occurred a month before the son's birth. This account, since it purports to come from Jonson himself, has been generally accepted. All the accounts agree that after the death of Ben's father, his mother married a bricklayer, and that for a while young Ben practised his stepfather's trade. Taylor's account is more circumstantial than most, blaming the stepfather for commanding his stepson to come home from his learned studies to go to work. Gibes about bricklaying followed the poet to the end of his career.

His eventual choice of a literary career was no doubt largely influenced by the time in which he lived. There was a real demand for poetry, especially dramatic poetry. The burst of poetic energy in the sixteenth century has been credited in part to England's grammar schools. Certainly education had a large share in the literary careers of the shoemaker's son from Canterbury, the citizen's son from Stratford, and the bricklayer's stepson from London. Marlowe was the only one of the three who received a University education; but Shakespeare was trained in an excellent school in Stratford, and Jonson studied at Westminster School under William Camden, one of the finest scholars of the day. Neither Marlowe nor Shakespeare disclosed the man who first fired him with love of learning; but Ben Jonson showed in written tributes to his master how great he felt his debt to be. This debt was not only knowledge of the classical languages and literatures, important as that knowledge was; for Camden was also a student of his own country's history, language, and literature. If John Cotton, Hugh Holland, and Ben Jonson are fair examples, he shared that enthusiasm with his pupils.

After leaving Westminster School, probably in 1588, Jonson was a bricklayer, a soldier, and a travelling actor. The exact chronology of events between his departure from the school and his first appearance in Philip Henslowe's *Diary* in 1597 is uncertain, but there have been plausible conjectures. The military duty in Flanders has been assigned to either 1591–92 or 1596. His marriage probably took place on 14 November 1594, in the Church of St. Magnus the Martyr by London Bridge. The identification of the Benjamine Johnson who married Anne Lewis as Benjamin Jonson the poet was made by Mark Eccles, and has been accepted by the editors of the Oxford *Jonson*. A daughter of this marriage, Mary, died at the age of six months. C. H. Herford suggested 1596 as her death-year, but Percy Simpson proposes 1598 or later. In 1596, Benjamin, Junior, was born, if we reckon backward from 1603, the death date of the seven-year-old son, as recorded by Drummond. The untimely deaths of these children were treated with tenderness in Jonson's poems. No other children of the poet can be identified with certainty.

The earliest entry about Jonson in Philip Henslowe's diary refers to him as 'Bengemen Johnson player'. Dekker's attacks in *Satiromastix* (1602) on Jonson as actor may have a husk of exaggeration, but without a kernel of truth the satire would have been pointless. Dekker specified two of Jonson's roles: 'mad Ieronimoes part', played on the road, and Zulziman, played in Paris Garden. Hieronimo, in Kyd's *Spanish Tragedy*, was one of the great acting roles of the period, a role performed by the superbactors Edward Alleyn and Richard Burbage. John Aubrey, possibly influenced by Dekker's attacks, said that Jonson was a poor actor but an excellent instructor. His early retirement from acting has been taken as confirmation of his failure. If he was a failure, his acting in such a role as Hieronimo needs to be explained away; and Herford and Simpson suggested that the role was performed with a weak travelling company, probably Pembroke's Men, and not with one of the powerful London companies. Ben had, however, one important qualification of a good actor: Margaret, Duchess of Newcastle, reported that her husband considered Ben Jonson the only man he ever heard read well.

Jonson's relations with Kyd's *Spanish Tragedy* were not confined to acting. For several years, beginning in 1597, Henslowe recorded payments to Benjamin

Jonson for plots, plays, or parts of plays. Two of these payments (1601 and 1602) were for additions to 'Jeronymo', surely *The Spanish Tragedy*. Some scholars have denied Jonson's authorship of the printed additions to this play, basing the denial on the presence of a splendour of imagination apparently beyond Jonson's powers, at least so early in his career, and the absence of dramatic fitness, a quality which his works rarely lack. Others reason that external evidence assigns additions to Jonson; that the extant additions are not assigned to any other writer; and finally, that since limits to Jonson's imagination and ability are not easily fixed, the additions are probably his. As for the lack of dramatic fitness, the additions might be the work of his days as travelling actor of Hieronimo, passages which he had tried out in the provinces and found successful enough to sell to Henslowe, with or without rewriting. However, whether the disputed passages are by Jonson or not, he was connected with the old play both as actor and play-dresser, and like Shakespeare he must have learned much stagecraft from Kyd.

In 1597 Jonson and two other actors were imprisoned for their part in *The Isle of Dogs*, written chiefly by Thomas Nashe. Of the three actors, Robert Shaw, Gabriel Spencer, and Benjamin Jonson, one was accused of being 'maker of part of the said play'. Jonson is the logical actor-author. Another of the three, Gabriel Spencer, had a lurid, if brief, career: in 1596 he had killed one James Feake with a rapier, and in 1598 he was himself killed with a rapier by Ben Jonson. Spencer's death led to Jonson's second recorded brush with the law, which very nearly ended his life; however, he was able to plead benefit of clergy, which any Latinist could do, and saved himself by reading his 'neck verse', with which Dekker later taunted him in *Satiromastix*.

This fortunate escape helped to make the year 1598 the first of several exceptionally memorable ones in Jonson's career. In that year Francis Meres recorded him as one of 'our best for Tragedie', not mentioning him as a comic writer; but the early tragedies seem to be lost beyond recovery. However, the year marked the production of his first play known to be a success, the comedy *Every Man in his Humour*, still recognized as one of his most delightful works. This play began his long and successful connexion with the theatrical company of Burbage and Shakespeare. This company produced five of Jonson's plays during Shakespeare's active career, and four after his retirement. However, Jonson did not identify himself exclusively with one theatrical company.

Between *Every Man out of his Humour* (1599) and *Sejanus* (1603) he took part in the War of the Theatres. Exactly how and when this bloodless conflict started is still matter for Wars of the Scholars. Apparently Jonson took offence at some character in one of John Marston's plays, and Marston took offence at one or more characters in Jonson's plays. It was once fashionable to identify almost every character in numerous plays with some Elizabethan dramatist; but a moderate reaction has set in, and present-day critics are not likely to seek for Chapman, Shakespeare, or others in most plays once considered part of the War. It is agreed that two plays constitute the main battles of this conflict: Jonson's *Poetaster* (1601) and Dekker's *Satiromastix* (1601). *Poetaster* is laid in Augustan Rome; but Crispinas and Demetrius in the play are evident caricatures of John Marston and Thomas Dekker, and Dekker said that Captain Tucca was modelled on one Captain Hannam. That is perhaps as far as the interpreter needs to go in personal identifications. The play has been variously interpreted as a personal satire, as a defence of poetry, and as a moral satire aimed at fashionable Ovidian eroticism. It is probably all three. For many years, however, the personal satire was stressed to the exclusion of other elements in the play, and probably still receives undue emphasis. Even now Jonson's Horace is sometimes called 'Jonson'. Horace is unquestionably Jonson's spokesman in *Poetaster*, but the dramatist gave his creation traits of the historical Horace. Dekker himself pointed out differences between the English and the Roman poet. Dekker's counter-attack in *Satiromastix* is a satirical assault which may be enjoyed with or without malice. The attack on Jonson seems an afterthought added to an independent play. Horace, Crispinas, Demetrius, and Captain Tucca are lifted bodily from *Poetaster*. Apparently neither Dekker nor his audience was troubled by the appearance of ancient Romans at the court of William Rufus; however, the names only are Roman. Dekker's Horace is an outrageous but effective caricature of Jonson, calculated to move laughter even in the most loyal member of the Tribe of Ben.

In an anonymous university play, *The Return from Parnassus*, Part Two (c. 1602), William Kemp and Richard Burbage were presented discussing the state of the drama. Kemp praised 'our fellow Shakespeare' as superior to the university writers and Jonson, adding: 'O, that Ben Jonson is a pestilent fellow! He brought up Horace giving the poets a pill, but our fellow Shakespeare hath given him a purge that made him bewray his credit.' *Poetaster* was not produced by Burbage's company, but *Satiromastix* was; hence one explanation of Shakespeare's part in the War of the Theatres has been that the production of *Satiromastix* was the famous 'purge', given Jonson by Shakespeare. Perhaps Shakespeare acted Horace, and struck off Jonson's mannerisms and voice so well that the unknown authors of *The Return from Parnassus* referred to this rather than to a literary composition.[2] Those who assume that the purge was literary have proposed Jacques in *As You Like It* (1599) or Ajax in *Troilus and Cressida* (1602) as caricatures of Jonson. But whatever part Shakespeare played in the War, no serious rift developed between him and Jonson; for when the latter resolved to turn from comedy and to sing 'high, and aloofe, safe from the wolves black jaw, and the dull asses hoofe', Shakespeare produced and acted in *Sejanus*, the resultant tragedy. Except for the disgruntled Jonson, who turned his back on comedy for a short time, the participants in the War of the Theatres apparently did not take it very seriously. The feud may have been more commercial than emotional, for it seems to have stimulated theatrical attendance.

The year 1603 was another of the first magnitude in Jonson's career: *Sejanus*, according to the Oxford editors, marked the real turning-point in his dramatic technique and led to the great comedies of his maturity. The year also laid the foundations for the series of court masques. When Elizabeth died and James I came to the throne, a new era of extravagant court entertainment began. Jonson opened his career as masque writer for the court with *The Entertainment at Althrope*, welcoming the Queen and the Prince 'on Satturday being the 25. of June 1603. as they came first into the Kingdome'. Perhaps the beginning had already been made with *A Panegyre on the Happie Entrance of James, our Soveraigne, to His First high Session of Parliament* (March 1603). Although the *Panegyre* is a poem and not a true masque, it has affinities with the masque form, including a summary of an oration by Themis, the personification of Law. This ambitious piece undoubtedly helped Jonson to get his foothold as court poet and masque writer for the royal family. Two other poems probably belong to this year: the touching epigram on the death of the child Benjamin, and the 'Ode. *Allegorike*', prefixed to Hugh Holland's *Pancharis*. The 'Ode' is a worthy predecessor to the best and most famous of Jonson's commendatory poems, 'To the Memory of my Beloved, the Author Mr. William Shakespeare'.

Except for the third recorded imprisonment of Jonson, which was due to satirical passages in *Eastward Hoe*, the ensuing decade held an almost uninterrupted series of triumphs for him in drama, masque, and poetry, accompanied by growing prestige in the theatre, at court, and in literary circles. During this period he was thrown in company with other outstanding writers, especially dramatists. The successful but uneasy collaboration on masque productions with Inigo Jones flourished and led to acquaintance with notable musicians and artists. With this collaboration the masque form reached its height, although its great period was relatively brief. Seeds for the bitter enmity between the poet and the architect were undoubtedly planted early in their association, but the growth was a long one, not reaching complete fruition until the last decade of Jonson's life. Probably by 1612 or 1613 the first collection of the non-dramatic poetry, *Epigrams*, Book One, was completed. In his dedication to William Herbert, Earl of Pembroke, Jonson called these epigrams 'the ripest of my studies'. These usually brief pieces bear testimony to the friendly associations of the author with England's nobility, abundantly borne out by the lists of the noble actors in his court masques. Even members of the royal family were willing members of a number of his casts. Among his patrons in these years were Lucy, Countess of Bedford, daughter of Sir John Harington; Elizabeth, Countess of Rutland, daughter of Sir Philip Sidney; and Mary, Lady Wroth, niece of Sir Philip Sidney. In 1612–13 he went abroad with the son of Sir Walter Raleigh, and in 1614 contributed a commendatory poem to Sir Walter's *History of the World*. This triumphant period was rounded out by the publication of the first folio edition of his *Works* in 1616, the year of the death of William Shakespeare and Francis Beaumont.

The importance of Jonson's 1616 Folio can hardly be overestimated; it is difficult to choose the perfect epithet for it. Until the publication of this book, plays had little literary standing, and were usually printed in cheap quartos; hence the idea of considering plays 'works' aroused some ridicule. Jonson's Folio, however, was not only the first of the dramatic folios; in many respects it was the best. All the other dramatic folios before the Restoration appeared after the death of their authors; Jonson's, of course, is the only one edited and corrected by its author. Its literary merit is worthy of the care bestowed on it. Aside from its own merits, however, it was a valuable precursor, for its success led to the publication of other dramatic collections including the great Shakespeare Folio in 1623, which has been adored '*almost t'idolatrie*', and the Beaumont and Fletcher Folio of 1647.

After 1616 the shadows lengthened. *The Devil Is an Ass*, acted in that year, was the first of the plays to fall under Dryden's damning phrase 'dotages'. Perhaps its failure was one cause of Jonson's prolonged absence from the stage, which did not end until the production of *The Staple of News* in 1626.

The period of absence from the stage, however, was by no means barren of incident or literary output. In 1618 Ben took his famous journey on foot to Scotland, during which he paid his much-discussed visit to Drummond of Hawthornden. The recorded *Conversations* between Jonson and Drummond contain biographical information not found elsewhere, and are perhaps primarily responsible for the nineteenth- and twentieth-century conceptions of Jonson the man.

Many Jonsonians agree with William Hazlitt that Drummond 'has not done himself or Jonson any credit by his account of their conversation'.[3] Possibly because of this feeling, the *Conversations* have been attacked as forgeries, though the term is a misnomer, for the manuscript of Sir Robert Sibbald (1641–1722) is frankly a copy of a lost original, not a pretended original. Sibbald's copy is now almost universally considered an authentic version of Drummond's lost manuscript. The editors of the Oxford *Ben Jonson* advanced the theory that Drummond wrote down his memoranda 'day by day, just as they occurred'; but a reasonable case can be made for interpreting them as later reminiscences. For instance, according to the *Conversations* both Oxford and Cambridge conferred the degree of Master of Arts on Jonson; the register of the University of Oxford dates the conferring of the degree 17 July 1619, about six months after the visit to Drummond. Either Jonson had been notified of the award several months before it was actually conferred, or Drummond added the information after Jonson had left. To the best of my knowledge no record of the Cambridge degree, aside from the *Conversations*, has been discovered. An important factor to be weighed in interpreting the *Conversations* is Ben Jonson himself. Drummond's statement that drink was one of the elements in which his guest lived is an indication that the latter was in his cups throughout his visit. Perhaps some of the inaccuracies in the *Conversations* stem from the condition of the source; perhaps Jonson's opinions and anecdotes were coloured by a desire to shock or ridicule his host, who may have appeared unduly prim to the Rabelaisian bard. The *Conversations* are interesting and useful, but are not worthy of profound trust.

Perhaps Jonson's dramatic powers had failed by 1623; but two of his most interesting poems belonged to that year. Certainly decay is not evident in the poem to the memory of Shakespeare, to which Hazelton Spencer paid this superlative compliment:

'Ben's was the noblest tribute, and remains so. For unlike Arnold and Browning, Jonson knew Shakespeare, man as well as book, and his praise is discriminating, and of all the Elizabethan and Jacobean writers he was best qualified by critical bent and creative fire to appraise a peerless colleague worthily. He rose superbly to a great opportunity. The lines which follow are doubly a tribute to Shakespeare, whose memory evoked the best occasional poem in our language.' [4]

The Shakespeare Folio was evidently a major event in Jonson's life. Some less than kind interpreters have suggested that his interest in the Folio was primarily financial, and his fine poem, therefore, insincere. The second of the major poems of 1623 was brought about by a less happy and auspicious event than the publication of Shakespeare's book. In the latter part of 1623 a fire destroyed many of Jonson's books and manuscripts, including a poetic narrative of his 'Journey into Scotland'. As a partial compensation for the lost works he left his 'Execration upon Vulcan', which survives in atleast six manuscripts and two printed versions. The Oxford editors' analysis of the variant readings in this poem is a valuable contribution to the understanding of Jonson's methods of writing.

A third event in 1623, very recently discovered and not yet thoroughly interpreted, may disclose Jonson in an entirely new career. C. J. Sisson has found a record of testimony delivered by Ben Jonson on behalf of Lady Raleigh in a law-suit brought against Sir Peter Vanlore. The testimony describes Jonson as 'of Gresham Colledge in London' and gives his age as '50

yeares & upwards'. Sisson suggests that Jonson may
have been a deputy professor of rhetoric at the College
at some time during the period between 1619, when
he returned from Scotland, and 1626, when he returned to the stage. Percy Simpson finds this credible,
though neither scholar has committed himself to a
positive statement as yet. The theory is tempting, for
Jonson was respected in his own time as a teacher of
both acting and writing, and his pupils (in an informal
sense) included Francis Beaumont, Robert Herrick,
Nathan Field, Richard Brome, and others. Brome was
for a time his servant, and aroused the indignation of
his master by being a theatrical success at the time of
the failure of *The New Inn*; but apparently the indignation was short-lived.

The final period of the old poet's life had its share of
misery. At least six petitions of debt were filed against
him from 1626 to 1634. He was stricken with palsy and
then paralysis. After his long years as the favoured
court poet of King James, he was for a time totally
neglected by King Charles. Inigo Jones triumphed
over him in their extended quarrel about the relative
importance of spectacle and literature in the masque.
His plays met with failure on the stage and with
lampoons from hostile pens; and although he lashed
at his enemies, he was himself conscious of the decline
of his power. But the picture was not entirely black:
most of the Sons of Ben remained loyal; the failure of
The New Inn recalled him to the attention of the King,
and restored him to royal favour; he wrote many
laureate pieces for the royal family; his other patrons
included Sir Kenelm and Lady Venetia Digby and
William Cavendish, Earl of Newcastle. Lady Venetia's
death led to Jonson's most ambitious attempt at
original non-dramatic verse. The Earl of Newcastle
was responsible for the writing and preservation of
many of his literary efforts including several letters, the

most interesting of which is the account of a dream
worked into a half-serious allegory. In the dream a
pet fox given to the poet by a well-wisher—stroking
a live fox was considered a remedy for palsy—had a
heated argument with the poet and finally advised him
to look in his cellar. On doing this he found the house
undermined by moles (*wants*, a dialectical form of
moles). The letter ended with an appeal to Newcastle
for relief from the *wants* which were as real in the
waking hours as in the dream. Judging from the
numerous works written for the Earl, the appeal was
heard and relief granted. Margaret Cavendish, the
Earl's second wife, who wrote a biography of her
husband, gave Lord Warden of the Forest of Sher-
wood and Lord-Lieutenant of Nottinghamshire as two
of his numerous titles, granted by King Charles I.
There could hardly be a better explanation of Jonson's
choice of the theme of Robin Hood for the frag-
mentary *Sad Shepherd*, possibly his last dramatic composition. *The King's Entertainment at Welbeck* (1633)
also has references to tales of Robin Hood, and speaks
of the King's host as the Lord-Lieutenant of Nottinghamshire and Darbyshire.

Jonson's strong religious vein, evident in his sacred
poems in the 1616 Folio, grew stronger, apparently, in
his infirm last years. The Oxford *Jonson* contains two
pictures of his old age illustrating this; the first in im-
pudent lines by Nicholas Oldisworth, warning the old
man that future ages might take him for a bishop
instead of a poet; the second in Walton's note to
Aubrey, telling of a visitor who found the infirm poet
lamenting the guilt of profaning the Scriptures in his
plays. But more telling than either of these traditional
sketches is the long 'Elegy on my Muse', the final
surviving poem of *Eupheme*, composed on the death of
Lady Venetia Digby. This piece shows evidence of
many of Jonson's 'humble Gleanings in Divinitie'.

In this poem old age, sickness, poverty, and approaching death do not seem able to o'er-crow his spirit; and in the forty or more years of his poetic career, he had built a sound structure well fitted to last for centuries. Immediately after his death in 1637 the Sons of Ben compiled a memorial volume called *Jonsonus Virbius*.

Our knowledge of Jonson's reading rests on more copious facts than our knowledge of his life. Lists of books known to be his appear in the first and the last volumes of the Oxford *Jonson*; in his numerous footnotes to plays and masques and in quotations in his *Grammar* he referred to much of his reading; later scholars have unearthed many sources of his translated or adapted notes in the *Discoveries*. His young admirer Lucius Cary, Lord Falkland, summed up his reading with the following sweeping statement:

> *His learning such, no author old nor new,*
> *Escap'd his reading that deserv'd his view,*
> *And such his judgment, so exact his test,*
> *Of what was best in books, as what books best,*
> *That had he join'd those notes his labours took,*
> *From each most prais'd and praise-deserving book,*
> *And could the world of that choice treasure boast,*
> *It need not care though all the rest were lost:*
> *And such his wit, he writ past what he quotes,*
> *And his productions far exceed his notes.*[5]

Even with allowance for hyperbole, this passage indicates the breadth and sweep of Jonson's reading; and this breadth of reading should be taken into account in the study of his works. In addition to the classics, he was widely read in the medieval and renaissance literature of Western Europe, especially in that of his own country. Quotations and references in his works indicate his knowledge of the English poets from Chaucer to his own contemporaries, and of English prose-writers from More to Bacon.

His active and vigorous life and his wide reading are crucial matters for the appreciation and understanding of Jonson's poems, even in the limited sense of the word, excluding the dramatic works. In addition, no part of his work may safely be neglected in the study of this limited portion. Plays, masques, and prose essays frequently illuminate passages in the poems. The magnitude of Jonson's accomplishment is not manifest unless all his works are considered; nevertheless, even the poems demonstrate remarkable scope and variety. In length they range from two-line epigrams to the 680-line translation of *The Art of Poetry*; or, leaving aside the translation, to the more than two hundred lines of 'An Execration upon Vulcan' and the 'Elegy on my Muse'. Subject-matter is quite as varied as length. The coarseness of some of the poems is offset by many examples of tenderness, noble friendliness, and religious fervour. One characteristic of Jonson's variety is that he often treated a poetic convention seriously in one work and satirized or burlesqued it in another. It is, of course, possible to enjoy both the serious treatment and the burlesque; and it is not a necessary part of the enjoyment to struggle with the question of which treatment mirrors the poet's heart most clearly.

Although Jonson's expressed preference for the heroic couplet has led to the impression that he limited himself as did his literary grandson Pope, he actually practised considerable metrical variety. His songs and hymns were written in various meters, and he tried his hand at Italian and English sonnets, stanzaic and Pindaric odes, quatrains, *terza rima*, and even the popular tumbling verse and Skeltonic leashes. Many of his pieces, especially his odes, are in elaborate and complicated forms. He was consistent in using rhyme in his poems; every one in the Folios of 1616 and 1640 is rhymed. The only unrhymed poem included in the present collection is a fragment from *England's Parnassus*, probably a dramatic fragment. Yet the poet's playful 'Fit of Rime against Rime', crying out against this 'rack of finest wits', has been accepted at its face value. In common with other rhymers, Jonson sometimes descended to hackneyed echoes, upon which Swinburne fell with fury; but the poet who never used a hackneyed rhyme would be fantastic indeed. On the other hand, the comical feminine rhymes in certain poems, notably 'The Famous Voyage', foreshadowed the practice of Butler, Byron, Browning, and Gilbert.

Jonson has often been limited and labelled in dogmatic critical passages; but he refuses to remain confined, and splits the neat packages in sundry places. Certain adjectives, however, continue to cling to him from century to century: aside from the famous and inevitable *rare*, appear *rugged, solid, colossal, learned*, and *classical*; another, *great*, has often been used by men not given to indiscriminate praise. Vines may obscure the structure which they adorn, and some Jonsonians have been wise in stripping away adjectives to take a fresh view of their author. Even now, however, it is customary to make certain generalizations on his classicism, coarseness, realism, and preference for pedestrian rather than winged words, and then to qualify generalizations with specific examples from allegedly exceptional lyrics. Since this book contains the bulk of his poems, material for both generalizations and exceptions is available to the reader, and comment can be brief.

Drummond stated that Jonson excelled in translation; this view was held not only by his contemporaries in general, but apparently by Jonson himself, for he defended with fury his translated passages in *Catiline* against those who preferred his more original passages in the play. Modern critics have not shared this estimate of the value of the translations. Swinburne complained that 'a worse translator than Ben Jonson never committed a double outrage on two languages at once'; of *The Art of Poetry* he said: 'The translation is one of those miracles of incompetence, incongruity, and insensibility, which must be seen to be believed.'[6] C. H. Herford was not so uncomplimentary to the translations, and he recognized the virtue of Jonson's mastery of the original language; but he joined Swinburne in condemning *The Art of Poetry*, and in lamenting the loss of Jonson's commentary on the text. But the fault condemned by the modern writers, the literalism of the translations, seems to have been the virtue admired by his contemporaries. In his 'Englished' works he performed a real service for his readers: he gave them as nearly as he could what the original text contained. In a translation he did not mix Dictys Cretensis or Dares Phrygius with Homer, or a medieval *exemplum* with Ovid. Better literal translations available to-day have caused his real service to scholarship to be forgotten, while his failure to make great poetry of literal translation has been too well remembered.

Of course, literal translation was not the only use he made of classical subject-matter. He frequently adapted classical works to refer to individuals or situations in his own day, a practice in which he was followed by Dryden, Pope, and Samuel Johnson among others. The 'Epigram of Inigo Jones' is little more than an Englishing of an epigram of Martial, adapted to the idiosyncrasies of the King's Surveyor; but much of its effectiveness is due to its accurate rendering of the Latin original in terse English, especially in the final line: 'Thy forehead is too narrow for my brand.' Many of Jonson's pieces apparently from classical sources have been altered not only in setting or in characters but also, and more importantly, in spirit: the final work is so different from the original that it has become a new work. As John Addington Symonds demonstrated in *The Academy*, 1884, almost every line of the 'Song to Celia' ('Drink to Me Only with Thine Eyes') has its counterpart in the *Epistles* of Philostratus. However, the poem is not a translation but a synthesis of scattered passages. Although only one conceit is not borrowed from Philostratus, the piece is a unified poem, and its glory is Jonson's. It has remained alive and popular for over three hundred years, and it is safe to say that no other work by Jonson is so well known. Willa McClung Evans advanced the opinion that this poem was written for a melody already in existence, and that the happy marriage of words and music was responsible for its excellence.[7] Several of Jonson's other popular pieces were written to be sung, but whether the music helped shape the poems or was composed for them after they were written is uncertain.

Only one of Jonson's longer poems has found favour with the anthologists: 'To the Memory of my Beloved, the Author Mr. William Shakespeare'. The greatness of Shakespeare himself has had so much to do with the admiration of the poem that it is not easy to consider the poem objectively; but the lines stand out sharply in the volumes of praise devoted to Shakespeare. Hazelton Spencer's generous comment on the 'Shakespeare' has already been quoted. The poem is also admired for its brief and telling epithets: thundering Æschylus, tart Aristophanes, neat Terence, witty Plautus, Marlowe's mighty line, insolent Greece and haughty Rome. Only once did Jonson go astray: in 'sporting Kyd', a bad pun, perhaps all the more tempting because of his early experiences with *The Spanish Tragedy*.

Jonson praised in verse Chapman, Fletcher, some of the Sons of Ben, and many other figures. Perhaps the two commendatory poems most appropriate for comparison with the 'Shakespeare' are the 'Ode *Allegorike*', 1603, and 'The Vision of Ben Jonson on the Muses of his Friend M. Drayton', 1627. The former was written to his schoolmate and friend Hugh Holland, who contributed verses to the Jonson and the Shakespeare Folios. Drayton, though somewhat neglected in our day, is by no means so obscure a figure as Holland. Both the 'Ode *Allegorike*' and the 'Drayton' are longer and more deliberately poetic, and carry more sustained allegory than the 'Shakespeare'. The 'Ode *Allegorike*' deals with the flight of the Black Swan, Holland, over the British Isles, and in oblique and fanciful language prophesies that the Black Swan and the Thames will replace Leda's white Adulterer and Eridanus among the constellations, to the grief of 'the choise of Europes pride'. The oblique and the fanciful are omitted in the blunt statement in the 'Shakespeare':

> *Triumph, my Britaine, thou hast one to showe,*
> *To whom all Scenes of Europe homage owe.*

The conceit of the swan changed to a constellation is caught up and condensed in the ten concluding lines of the 'Shakespeare'. The poem has other borrowings, including other self-borrowings, but they are equally transfigured. One striking feature is that no specific work by Shakespeare is mentioned. Shakespeare is compared with ancients and moderns and granted equality or superiority, but no *Hamlet* or *Lear* is compared with an *Oresteia* or *Œdipus*, or with a *Spanish Tragedy* or *Faustus*. Appropriately the comparisons are between dramatic poets, except for Chaucer and Spenser as the aristocracy of English letters. This method of comparison for praise was followed also in the 'Drayton', though here the authors chosen are narrative and lyric poets instead of dramatists. The poem is a masque-like vision: 'It was no Dreame! I was awake, and saw!' The trumpet of Fame ushers in a procession of Drayton's works. Along with the other two poems the 'Drayton' illustrates typical practices of its author: writing for a specific occasion, drawing on his copious reading, repeating and altering his own themes. Personal friendship may well have had a share in all three poems. There is evidence that Jonson and Holland were friends, though not necessarily intimate friends; there must have been suspicion that Jonson and Drayton were not friends, or there would have been no need for them to protest so much. The sincerity of their friendship is still contested. More interest and more controversy is excited by the question of the friendship of Jonson and Shakespeare. Shakespeare does not abide our question here any more than he does in numerous other relationships, but Jonson left a definite statement in the *Discoveries*:

. . . for I lov'd the man, and doe honour his memory (on this side Idolatry) as much as any.

Perhaps the finer lines, the compression, the noble austerity, and the merit of the 'Shakespeare' were the gifts of the goddess Fortune; perhaps they resulted from their author's greater care and interest in the subject; perhaps they mean more to us largely because Shakespeare means more to us. At any rate, the poem portrays its author fully as much as it does its subject, and it repays serious study and becomes richer with continued rereading.

Three other longer poems, rarely if ever printed in anthologies, are valuable in a broader understanding of the poet: 'The Famous Voyage', 'An Execration upon Vulcan', and the 'Elegy on my Muse'. The first of these is perhaps the coarsest and most unsavoury of all the poems. Swinburne must have had it in mind when he characterized the *Epigrams* as metrical

emetics; most scholars have turned from it with under-
standable disgust. Nevertheless, it was printed in the
selective and carefully-edited 1616 Folio, and must be
taken into account. It is a burlesque Odyssey down
Fleet Ditch, paralleling the visit of Æneas to Hades so
closely that Book VI of the *Æneid* is an almost in-
dispensable commentary. It is a suggestive coincidence
that the ghost of Don Andrea in *The Spanish Tragedy*
also describes a visit to Hades. Don Andrea's trip may
have influenced Jonson's choice of theme, for *The
Spanish Tragedy* was fair game to the satirist. The
material in the poem is drawn from literature (ancient,
medieval, and modern) and from contemporary events
and individuals. One character in the poem is Old
Bankes the juggler, 'grave tutor to the learned horse',
Morocco. The combined souls of Bankes and
Morocco have transmigrated into the body of a cat
floating in the stream. This cat with its sudden appearance and its friendly advice, almost inevitably recalls
the Cheshire Cat, but one would hardly dare suggest
literary ancestry. The 'Voyage' ends with a learned
pun:

> *And I could wish for their eterniz'd sakes,*
> *My Muse had plough'd with his, that sung A-jax.*

The final line surely refers on one level to Homer, on
another to Sir John Harington, author of *The Meta-
morphosis of Ajax*, and father of Jonson's patron,
Lucy Countess of Bedford.

'An Execration upon Vulcan' has much in common
with the 'Voyage', but it has received more praise and
aroused less disgust. It is a valuable autobiographical
document, including a list of lost works in progress or
completed at the time of the fire. Also it displays its
author in a pleasant light at a difficult time. It includes
both literary and personal satire, with especial attention to early news-men. Like the 'Voyage', it has

malodorous sections and introduces disreputable contemporaries. Vulcan is treated with flippant disrespect,
particularly as a companion of alchemists, who often
bore Jonson's satiric lash. In a manner typical of
Jonson's practice, the 'Execration' is closely bound up
with other works of his, particularly with the masques
Mercury Vindicated from the Alchemists, *News from
the New World*, and *Neptune's Triumph*, and with the
play *The Staple of News*. But it stands independently
as one of Jonson's most interesting poems.

The 'Elegy on my Muse', longest of the original
poems in itself, is part of a still more ambitious poetic
scheme as one of 'ten lyric pieces' of *Eupheme*. Only
four of the poems in *Eupheme* are complete in the
Folio; the rest are partially or totally lost. Lady
Venetia Digby, subject of the poems, died in 1633, and
Jonson used as an epigraph on the 'Elegy' a line from
Statius's 'Epicedion in Priscillam', apologizing for the
long delay in bringing consolation to the bereaved
husband; Herford, therefore, believed the poem Jonson's last considerable effort in verse, and not too unworthy a conclusion to his poetic career. The opening
of the poem is as personal as the epigrams on the
death of his children. The main body of it shows the
same turning from worldly to spiritual things noted by
friends and scoffers in his last years; but it is by no
means a Jonsonian rarity as a religious poem, for he
wrote religious pieces throughout his long career. The
'Elegy' is devoted to the characterization of Lady
Venetia as perfect wife and mother, housekeeper,
charitable giver, and saintly devotee. There is no suggestion of her colourful, gossip-stained youth.

Samuel Johnson, in his classic comparison of
Dryden and Pope, said: 'Dryden is read with frequent
astonishment, and Pope with perpetual delight.' In
this, Jonson is more like Dryden: many modern
readers will be unable to find perpetual delight in the

often uneven poems. However, many of the brief epigrams which seem flat to tastes whetted by the Romantics show sound thought and skilful expression. Even these and other so-called failures of the poet help to construct the complete picture of Jonson. In this introduction, with its mere sampling of the poems, I have tried to show the availability of the frequent astonishment. The poems as a whole do not have the stature of the great comedies; but to borrow Ben's image, lilies have their beauties as well as oaks, and to stretch it farther, much may be said for onions and thistles.

The reader, then, is invited to enter Jonson's lesser theatre, 'where Cato, if he liv'd, might enter without scandal'. The invitation cannot be couched in the terms of Jonson's invitation at the beginning of the Shakespeare Folio ('Looke not on his Picture, but his Booke'); for the force of Rare Ben—his impact on his own and succeeding centuries—makes it difficult to turn the eyes completely from the Picture. But the Booke is entitled to the major share of attention.

I have retained the spelling of the original editions, but I have substituted s for ∫, and modernized i and j and u and v. Poems not by Jonson, or very doubtfully his, are marked with an asterisk in the text and notes.

CRITICAL COMMENTS

CRITICAL COMMENTS

I

In the meantime I must desire you to take notice, that the greatest man of the last age (Ben. Johnson) was willing to give place to [the Ancients] in all things: He was not onely a professed Imitator of Horace, but a learned Plagiary of all the others; you track him every where in their Snow: If Horace, Lucan, Petronius Arbiter, Seneca, and Juvenal had their own from him, there are few serious thoughts which are new in him; you will pardon me therefore if I presume he lov'd their fashion when he wore their cloathes.

...As for Johnson, to whose Character I am now arriv'd, if we look at him while he was himself, (for his last Playes were but his dotages) I think him the most learned and judicious Writer which any Theater ever had. He was a most severe Judge of himself as well as others. One cannot say he wanted wit, but rather that he was frugal of it. In his works you find little to retrench or alter. Wit and Language, and Humour also in some measure we had before him; but something of Art was wanting to the Drama till he came. He manag'd his strength to more advantage then any who preceded him. You seldome find him making Love in any of his Scenes, or endeavouring to move the Passions; his genius was too sullen and saturnine to do it gracefully, especially when he knew he came after those who had performed both to such an height. He was deeply conversant in the Ancients, both Greek and Latine, and he borrow'd boldly from them: There is scarce a Poet or Historian among the Roman Authours of those times whom he has not translated in *Sejanus* and *Catiline*. But he has done his Robberies so openly, that one may see he fears not to be taxed by any Law. He invades Authours like a Monarch, and what would be theft in other Poets, is onely victory in him. With the spoils of these Writers he so represents old Rome to us, in its Rites, Ceremonies, and Customs, that if one of their Poets had written either of his Tragedies we had seen less of it then in him. If there was any fault in his Language, 'twas that he weav'd it too closely and laboriously in his serious Playes: perhaps too, he did a little too much Romanize our Tongue, leaving the words which he translated almost as much Latine as he found them: wherein though he learnedly followed the Idiom of their language, he did not enough comply with ours. If I would compare him with Shakespeare, I must acknowledge him the more correct Poet, but Shakespeare the greater wit. Shakespeare was the Homer, or Father of our Dramatick Poets; Johnson was the Virgil, the pattern of elaborate writing; I admire him, but I love Shakespeare.

JOHN DRYDEN, *Of Dramatick Poesie,*
An Essay, 1668

II

But as to his [Shakspeare's] want of learning, it may be necessary to say something more: ... I am inclined to think this opinion proceeded originally from the zeal of the partizans of our Author and Ben Johnson; as they endeavoured to exalt the one at the expense of the other. It is ever the nature of parties to be in extremes; and nothing is so probable, as that because Ben Johnson had much the more learning, it was said on the one hand that Shakspeare had none at all; and because Shakspeare had much the most wit and fancy, it was retorted on the other, that Johnson wanted both. Because Shakspeare borrowed nothing, it was said that Ben Johnson borrowed every thing. Because Johnson did not write extempore, he was reproached

1

with being a year about every piece; and because Shakspeare wrote with ease and rapidity, they cried he never once made a blot. Nay, the spirit of opposition ran so high, that whatever those of the one side objected to the other, was taken at the rebound, and turned into praises; as injudiciously as their antagonists before had made them objections. . . .

But however this contention might be carried on by the partizans on either side, I cannot help thinking these two great poets were good friends, and lived on amicable terms, and in offices of society with each other. It is an acknowledged fact, that Ben Johnson was introduced upon the stage, and his first works encouraged by Shakspeare. And after his death, that Author writes *To the Memory of his beloved Mr. William Shakspeare,* which shews as if the friendship had continued through life. I cannot for my own part find any thing *invidious* or *sparing* in those verses, but wonder Mr. Dryden was of that opinion. He exalts him not only above all his contemporaries, but above Chaucer and Spenser, whom he will not allow to be great enough to be ranked with him; and challenges the names of Sophocles, Euripides, and Æschylus, nay all Greece and Rome at once, to equal him; and (which is very particular) expressly vindicates him from the imputation of wanting art, not enduring that all his excellencies should be attributed to nature. It is remarkable too, that the praise he gives to him in his *Discoveries* seems to proceed from a personal kindness; he tells us, that he loved the man, as well as honoured his memory; celebrates the honesty, openness, and frankness of his temper; and only distinguishes, as he reasonably ought, between the real merit of the Author, and the silly and derogatory applauses of the Players. Ben Johnson might indeed be sparing in his commendations (though certainly he is not so in this instance) partly from his own nature, and partly from judgment. For men of judgment think they do any man more service in praising him justly, than lavishly.

ALEXANDER POPE, *Preface to the Works of Shakspeare*, 1725

III

I am inclined to consider 'The Fox' as the greatest of Ben Jonson's works. But his smaller works are full of poetry.

... In Ben Jonson you have an intense and burning art. Some of his plots, that of 'The Alchemist', for example, are perfect. Ben Jonson and Beaumont and Fletcher would, if united, have made a great dramatist indeed, and yet would not have come near Shakspere; but no doubt Ben Jonson was the greatest man after Shakspere in that age of dramatic genius.

SAMUEL TAYLOR COLERIDGE, *Table Talk*, June 24, 1827; February 17, 1833

IV

If poets may be divided into two exhaustive but not exclusive classes,—the gods of harmony and creation, the giants of energy and invention,—the supremacy of Shakespeare among the gods of English verse is not more unquestionable than the supremacy of Jonson among its giants. Shakespeare himself stands no higher above Milton and Shelley than Jonson above Dryden and Byron.... No giant ever came so near to the ranks of the gods: were it possible for one not born a god to become divine by dint of ambition and devotion, this glory would have crowned the Titanic labours of Ben Jonson. There is something heroic and magnificent in his lifelong dedication of all his gifts and all his powers to the service of the art he had elected as the business of all his life and the aim of all his aspiration. And the result also was magnificent: the flowers of his growing have every quality but one which belongs to the rarest and finest among flowers: they have colour, form, variety, fertility, vigour: the one thing they want is fragrance. Once or twice only in all his indefatigable career of toil and triumph did he achieve what was easily and habitually accomplished by men otherwise unworthy to be named in the same day with him; by men who would have avowed themselves unworthy to unloose the latchets of his shoes. That singing power which answers in verse to the odour of a blossom, to the colouring of a picture, to the flavour of a fruit,—that quality without which they may be good, commendable, admirable, but cannot be delightful,—was not, it should seem, a natural gift of this great writer's: hardly now and then could his industry attain to it by some exceptional touch of inspiration or of luck.... But Ben, as a rule,—a rule which is proved by the exception—was one of the singers who could not sing; though, like Dryden, he could intone most admirably; which is more—and much more—than can truthfully be said for Byron.

ALGERNON CHARLES SWINBURNE, *A Study of Ben Jonson*, 1889

V

The reputation of Jonson has been of the most deadly kind that can be compelled upon the memory of a great poet. To be universally accepted; to be damned by the praise that quenches all desire to read the book; to be afflicted by the imputation of virtues which excite the least pleasure; and to be read only by historians and antiquaries—this is the most perfect conspiracy of approval. For some generations the reputation of Jonson has been carried rather as a liability than as an asset in the balance-sheet of English literature.... We have no difficulty in seeing what brought him to this pass; how, in contrast, not with Shakespeare, but with Marlowe, Webster, Donne, Beaumont, and Fletcher, he has been paid out with reputation instead of enjoyment. He is no less a poet than these men, but his poetry is of the surface.

... The artistic result of *Volpone* is not due to any effect that Volpone, Mosca, Corvino, Corbaccio, Voltore have upon each other, but simply to their combination into a whole. And these figures are not personifications of passions; separately, they have not even that reality, they are constituents. It is a similar indication of Jonson's method that you can hardly pick out a line of Jonson's and say confidently that it is great poetry; but there are many extended passages to which you cannot deny that honour.... Jonson is the legitimate heir of Marlowe.... And if Marlowe is a poet, Jonson is also.

THOMAS STEARNS ELIOT, *Selected Essays,*
1917–1932

EPIGRAMMES
AND
THE FORREST

1616

EPIGRAMMES.

I.

BOOKE.

The Author B. I.

LONDON,

M. DC. XVI.

TO THE GREAT EXAMPLE OF HONOR
AND VERTUE, THE MOST NOBLE
WILLIAM, EARLE OF PEMBROKE,
L. CHAMBERLAYNE, &C.

MY LORD. While you cannot change your merit, I dare not change your title: It was that made it, and not I. Under which name, I here offer to your Lo: the ripest of my studies, my *Epigrammes*; which, though they carry danger in the sound, doe not therefore seeke your shelter: For, when I made them, I had nothing in my conscience, to expressing of which I did need a cypher. But, if I be falne into those times, wherein, for the likenesse of vice, and facts, every one thinks anothers ill deeds objected to him; and that in their ignorant and guiltie mouthes, the common voyce is (for their securitie) *Beware the Poet*, confessing, therein, so much love to their diseases, as they would rather make a partie for them, then be either rid, or told of them: I must expect, at your Lo: hand, the protection of truth, and libertie, while you are constant to your owne goodnesse. In thankes whereof, I returne you the honor of leading forth so many good, and great names (as my verses mention on the better part) to their remembrance with posteritie. Amongst whom, if I have praysed, unfortunately, any one, that doth not deserve; or, if all answere not, in all numbers, the pictures I have made of them: I hope it will be forgiven me, that they are no ill pieces, though they be not like the persons. But I foresee a neerer fate to my booke, then this: that the vices therein will be own'd before the vertues (though, there, I have avoyded all particulars, as I have done names) and that some will be so readie to discredit me, as they will have the impudence to belye themselves. For, if I meant them not, it is so. Nor, can

5

I hope otherwise. For, why should they remit any thing of their riot, their pride, their selfe-love, and other inherent graces, to consider truth or vertue; but, with the trade of the world, lend their long eares against men they love not: and hold their deare Mountebanke, or Jester, in farre better condition, then all the studie, or studiers of humanitie? For such, I would rather know them by their visards, still, then they should publish their faces, at their perill, in my Theater, where Cato, if he liv'd, might enter without scandall.

Your Lo: most faithfull honorer,

BEN. JONSON.

EPIGRAMMES

I

To the Reader

PRAY thee, take care, that tak'st my booke in hand,
To reade it well: that is, to understand.

II

To my Booke

IT will be look'd for, booke, when some but see
Thy title, *Epigrammes*, and nam'd of mee,
Thou should'st be bold, licentious, full of gall,
Wormewood, and sulphure, sharpe, and tooth'd
    withall;
Become a petulant thing, hurle inke, and wit,
As mad-men stones: not caring whom they hit.
Deceive their malice, who could wish it so.
And by thy wiser temper, let men know
Thou art not covetous of least selfe fame,
Made from the hazard of anothers shame: 10
Much lesse with lewd, prophane, and beastly phrase,
To catch the worlds loose laughter, or vaine gaze.
He that departs with his owne honesty
For vulgar praise, doth it too dearely buy.

III

To my Booke-seller

THOU, that mak'st gaine thy end, and wisely well,
Call'st a booke good, or bad, as it doth sell,

Use mine so, too: I give thee leave. But crave
For the lucks sake, it thus much favour have,
To lye upon thy stall, till it be sought;
Not offer'd, as it made sute to be bought;
Nor have my title-leafe on posts, or walls,
Or in cleft-sticks, advanced to make calls
For termers, or some clarke-like serving-man,
Who scarse can spell th'hard names: whose knight
    lesse can.   10
If, without these vile arts, it will not sell,
Send it to Bucklers-bury, there 'twill, well.

IV

To King James

How, best of Kings, do'st thou a scepter beare!
How, best of Poets, do'st thou laurell weare!
But two things, rare, the Fates had in their store,
And gave thee both, to shew they could no more.
For such a *Poet*, while thy dayes were greene,
Thou wert, as chiefe of them are said t'have beene.
And such a Prince thou art, wee daily see,
As chiefe of those still promise they will bee.
Whom should my *Muse* then flie to, but the best
Of Kings for grace; of *Poets* for my test?   10

V

On the Union

When was there contract better driven by Fate?
Or celebrated with more truth of state?
The world the temple was, the priest a king,
The spoused paire two realmes, the sea the ring.

VI

To Alchymists

IF all you boast of your great art be true;
Sure, willing povertie lives most in you.

VII

On the New Hot-house

WHERE lately harbour'd many a famous whore,
A purging bill, now fix'd upon the dore,
Tells you it is a hot-house: So it ma',
And still be a whore-house. Th'are *Synonima*.

VIII

On a Robbery

RIDWAY rob'd Duncote of three hundred pound,
Ridway was tane, arraign'd, condemn'd to dye;
But, for this money was a courtier found,
Beg'd Ridwayes pardon: Duncote, now, doth crye,
Rob'd both of money, and the lawes reliefe,
The courtier is become the greater thiefe.

IX

To All, to Whom I Write

MAY none, whose scatter'd names honor my booke,
For strict degrees of ranke, or title looke:

9

'Tis 'gainst the manners of an Epigram:
And, I a Poet here, no Herald am.

X

To my lord Ignorant

THOU call'st me Poet, as a terme of shame:
But I have my revenge made, in thy name.

XI

On some-thing, that walkes some-where

AT court I met it, in clothes brave enough,
To be a courtier; and lookes grave enough,
To seeme a statesman: as I neere it came,
It made me a great face, I ask'd the name.
A lord, it cryed, buried in flesh, and blood,
And such from whom let no man hope least good,
For I will doe none: and as little ill,
For I will dare none. Good Lord, walke dead still.

XII

On Lieutenant Shift

SHIFT, here, in towne, not meanest among squires,
That haunt Pikt-hatch, Mersh-Lambeth, and White-
    fryers,
Keepes himselfe, with halfe a man, and defrayes
The charge of that state, with this charme, god payes.
By that one spell he lives, eates, drinkes, arrayes
Himselfe: his whole revennue is, god payes.

10

The quarter day is come; the hostesse sayes,
Shee must have money: he returnes, god payes.
The taylor brings a suite home; he it 'ssayes,
Lookes o're the bill, likes it: and say's, god payes. 10
He steales to ordinaries; there he playes
At dice his borrow'd money: which, god payes.
Then takes up fresh commoditie, for dayes;
Signes to new bond, forfeits: and cryes, god payes.
That lost, he keepes his chamber, reades Essayes,
Takes physick, teares the papers: still god payes..
Or else by water goes, and so to playes;
Calls for his stoole, adornes the stage: god payes.
To every cause he meets, this voyce he brayes:
His onely answere is to all, god payes.   20
Not his poore cocatrice but he betrayes
Thus: and for his letcherie, scores, god payes.
But see! th'old baud hath serv'd him in his trim,
Lent him a pockie whore. Shee hath paid him.

XIII

To Doctor Empirick

WHEN men a dangerous disease did scape,
Of old, they gave a cock to Æsculape;
Let me give two: that doubly am got free,
From my diseases danger, and from thee.

XIV

To William Camden

CAMDEN, most reverend head, to whom I owe
All that I am in arts, all that I know,
(How nothing's that?) to whom my countrey owes

The great renowne, and name wherewith shee goes,
Then thee the age sees not that thing more grave,
More high, more holy, that shee more would crave.
What name, what skill, what faith hast thou in things!
What sight in searching the most antique springs!
What weight, and what authoritie in thy speech!
Man scarse can make that doubt, but thou canst
    teach.   10
Pardon free truth, and let thy modestie,
Which conquers all, be once over-come by thee.
Many of thine this better could, then I,
But for their powers, accept my pietie.

XV

On Court-worme

ALL men are wormes: But this no man. In silke
'Twas brought to court first wrapt, and white as
    milke;
Where, afterwards, it grew a butter-flye:
Which was a cater-piller. So t'will dye.

XVI

To Brayne-Hardie

HARDIE, thy braine is valiant, 'tis confest,
Thou more; that with it every day, dar'st jest
Thy selfe into fresh braules: when, call'd upon,
Scarse thy weekes swearing brings thee of, of one.
So, in short time, th'art in arrerage growne
Some hundred quarrells, yet dost thou fight none;
Nor need'st thou: for those few, by oath releast,
Make good what thou dar'st doe in all the rest.

Keepe thy selfe there, and thinke thy valure right,
He that dares damne himselfe, dares more then
fight.   10

XVII

To the learned Critick

MAY others feare, flie, and traduce thy name,
As guiltie men doe magistrates: glad I,
That wish my poems a legitimate fame,
Charge them, for crowne, to thy sole censure hye.
And, but a sprigge of bayes given by thee,
Shall out-live gyrlands, stolne from the chast tree.

XVIII

To my meere English Censurer

To thee, my way in Epigrammes seemes new,
When both it is the old way, and the true.
Thou saist, that cannot be: for thou hast seene
Davis, and Weever, and the best have beene,
And mine come nothing like. I hope so. Yet,
As theirs did with thee, mine might credit get:
If thou'ldst but use thy faith, as thou didst then,
When thou wert wont t'admire, not censure men.
Pr'y thee beleeve still, and not judge so fast,
Thy faith is all the knowledge that thou hast.   10

XIX

On Sir Cod the perfumed

THAT Cod can get no widow, yet a knight,
I sent the cause: Hee wooes with an ill sprite.

XX

To the same Sir Cod

TH'EXPENCE in odours is a most vaine sinne,
Except thou could'st, Sir Cod, weare them within.

XXI

On reformed Gam'ster

LORD, how is Gam'ster chang'd! his haire close cut!
His neck fenc'd round with ruffe! his eyes halfe shut!
His clothes two fashions of, and poore! his sword
Forbidd' his side! and nothing, but the word
Quick in his lips! who hath this wonder wrought?
The late tane bastinado. So I thought.
What severall wayes men to their calling have!
The bodies stripes, I see, the soule may save.

XXII

On my first Daughter

HERE lyes to each her parents ruth,
Mary, the daughter of their youth:

Yet, all heavens gifts, being heavens due,
It makes the father, lesse, to rue.
At six moneths end, shee parted hence
With safetie of her innocence;
Whose soule heavens Queene, (whose name shee
  beares)
In comfort of her mothers teares,
Hath plac'd amongst her virgin-traine:
Where, while that sever'd doth remaine,   10
This grave partakes the fleshly birth.
Which cover lightly, gentle earth.

XXIII

To John Donne

DONNE, the delight of Phœbus, and each Muse,
Who, to thy one, all other braines refuse;
Whose every worke, of thy most earely wit,
Came forth example, and remaines so, yet:
Longer a knowing, then most wits doe live;
And which no affection praise enough can give!
To it, thy language, letters, arts, best life,
Which might with halfe mankind maintayne a strife.
All which I meant to praise, and, yet, I would;
But leave, because I cannot as I should!   10

XXIV

To the Parliament

THERE'S reason good, that you good lawes should
  make:
Mens manners ne're were viler, for your sake.

XXV

On Sir Voluptuous Beast

WHILE Beast instructs his faire, and innocent wife,
In the past pleasures of his sensuall life,
Telling the motions of each petticote,
And how his Ganimede mov'd, and how his goate,
And now, her (hourely) her owne cucqueane makes,
In varied shapes, which for his lust shee takes:
What doth he else, but say, leave to be chast,
Just wife, and, to change me, make womans hast.

XXVI

On the same Beast

THEN his chast wife, though Beast now know no
   more,
He'adulters still: his thoughts lye with a whore.

XXVII

On Sir John Roe

IN place of scutcheons, that should decke thy herse,
Take better ornaments, my teares, and verse.
If any sword could save from Fates, Roe's could;
If any Muse out-live their spight, his can;
If any friends teares could restore, his would;
If any pious life ere lifted man
To heaven; his hath: O happy state! wherein
Wee, sad for him, may glorie, and not sinne.

XXVIII

On Don Surly

DON SURLY, to aspire the glorious name
Of a great man, and to be thought the same,
Makes serious use of all great trade he knowes.
He speakes to men with a Rhinocerotes nose,
Which hee thinkes great; and so reades verses,too:
And, that is done, as he saw great men doe.
H'has tympanies of businesse, in his face,
And, can forget mens names, with a great grace.
He will both argue, and discourse in oathes,
Both which are great. And laugh at ill made clothes;
That's greater, yet: to crie his owne up neate.   11
He doth, at meales, alone, his pheasant eate,
Which is maine greatnesse. And, at his still boord,
He drinkes to no man: that's, too, like a lord.
He keepes anothers wife, which is a spice
Of solemne greatnesse. And he dares, at dice,
Blaspheme god, greatly. Or some poore hinde beat,
That breathes in his dogs way: and this is great.
Nay more, for greatnesse sake, he will be one
May heare my Epigrammes, but like of none.   20
Surly, use other arts, these only can
Stile thee a most great foole, but no great man.

XXIX

To Sir Annual Tilter

TILTER, the most may'admire thee, though not I:
And thou, right guiltlesse, may'st plead to it, why?
For thy late sharpe device. I say 'tis fit
All braines, at times of triumph, should runne wit.

17

For then, our water-conduits doe runne wine;
But that's put in, thou'lt say. Why, so is thine.

XXX

To Person Guiltie

GUILTIE, be wise; and though thou know'st the
   crimes
Be thine, I taxe, yet doe not owne my rimes:
'Twere madnesse in thee, to betray thy fame,
And person to the world; ere I thy name.

XXXI

On Banck the Usurer

BANCK feeles no lamenesse of his knottie gout,
His monyes travaile for him, in and out:
And though the soundest legs goe every day,
He toyles to be at hell, as soone as they.

XXXII

On Sir John Roe

WHAT two brave perills of the private sword
Could not effect, not all the furies doe,
That selfe-divided Belgia did afford;
What not the envie of the seas reach'd too,
The cold of Mosco, and fat Irish ayre,
His often change of clime (though not of mind)
What could not worke; at home in his repaire
Was his blest fate, but our hard lot to find.

Which shewes, where ever death doth please t'appeare,
Seas, serenes, swords, shot, sicknesse, all are there. 10

XXXIII

To the Same

ILE not offend thee with a vaine teare more,
Glad-mention'd Roe: thou art but gone before,
Whither the world must follow. And I, now,
Breathe to expect my when, and make my how.
Which if most gracious heaven grant like thine,
Who wets my grave, can be no friend of mine.

XXXIV

Of Death

HE that feares death, or mournes it, in the just,
Shewes of the resurrection little trust.

XXXV

To King James

WHO would not be thy subject, James, t'obay
A Prince, that rules by'example, more than sway?
Whose manners draw, more than thy powers
    constraine.
And in this short time of thy happiest raigne,
Hast purg'd thy realmes, as we have now no cause
Left us of feare, but first our crimes, then lawes.
Like aydes 'gainst treasons who hath found before?
And than in them, how could we know god more?

First thou preserved wert, our king to bee,
And since, the whole land was preserv'd for thee.10

XXXVI

To the Ghost of Martial

MARTIAL, thou gav'st farre nobler Epigrammes
To thy Domitian, than I can my James:
But in my royall subject I passe thee,
Thou flatterd'st thine, mine cannot flatter'd bee.

XXXVII

On Chev'rill the Lawyer

No cause, nor client fat, will Chev'rill leese,
But as they come, on both sides he takes fees,
And pleaseth both. For while he melts his greace
For this: that winnes, for whom he holds his peace.

XXXVIII

To Person Guiltie

GUILTIE, because I bad you late be wise,
And to conceale your ulcers, did advise,
You laugh when you are touch'd; and long before
Any man else, you clap your hands, and rore,
And crie good! good! This quite perverts my sense,
And lyes so farre from wit, 'tis impudence.
Beleeve it, Guiltie, if you loose your shame,
I'le loose my modestie, and tell your name.

XXXIX

On Old Colt

FOR all night-sinnes, with others wives, unknowne,
Colt, now, doth daily penance in his owne.

XL

On Margaret Ratcliffe

M ARBLE, weepe, for thou dost cover
A   dead beautie under-neath thee,
R ich, as nature could bequeath thee:
G rant then, no rude hand remove her.
A ll the gazers on the skies
R ead not in faire heavens storie,
E xpresser truth, or truer glorie,
T hen they might in her bright eyes.
R are, as wonder, was her wit;
A nd like Nectar ever flowing: 10
T ill time, strong by her bestowing,
C onquer'd hath both life and it.
L ife, whose griefe was out of fashion,
I n these times. Few so have ru'de
F ate, in a brother. To conclude,
F or wit, feature, and true passion,
E arth, thou hast not such another.

XLI

On Gypsee

GYPSEE, new baud, is turn'd physitian,
And gets more gold, then all the colledge can:

Such her quaint practise is, so it allures,
For what shee gave, a whore; a baud, shee cures.

XLII

On Giles and Jone

WHO sayes that Giles and Jone at discord be?
Th'observing neighbours no such mood can see.
Indeed, poore Giles repents he married ever.
But that his Jone doth too. And Giles would never,
By his free will, be in Jones company.
No more would Jone he should. Giles riseth early,
And having got him out of doores is glad.
The like is Jone. But turning home, is sad.
And so is Jone. Oft-times, when Giles doth find
Harsh sights at home, Giles wisheth he were blind.
All this doth Jone. Or that his long yearn'd life   11
Were quite out-spun. The like wish hath his wife.
The children, that he keepes, Giles sweares are none
Of his begetting. And so sweares his Jone.
In all affections shee concurreth still.
If, now, with man and wife, to will, and nill
The selfe-same things, a note of concord be:
I know no couple better can agree!

XLIII

To Robert Earle of Salisburie

WHAT need hast thou of me? or of my Muse?
Whose actions so themselves doe celebrate?
Which should thy countries love to speake refuse,
Her foes enough would fame thee in their hate.
'Tofore, great men were glad of Poets: Now,

I, not the worst, am covetous of thee.
Yet dare not, to my thought, least hope allow
Of adding to thy fame; thine may to me,
When in my booke, men reade but Cecill's name,
And what I write thereof find farre, and free   10
From servile flatterie (common Poets shame)
As thou stand'st cleere of the necessitie.

XLIV

On Chuffe, Bancks the Usurer's Kinsman

CHUFFE, lately rich in name, in chattels, goods,
And rich in issue to inherit all,
Ere blacks were bought for his owne funerall,
Saw all his race approch the blacker floods:
He meant they thither should make swift repaire,
When he made him executor, might be heire.

XLV

On my first Sonne

FAREWELL, thou child of my right hand, and joy;
My sinne was too much hope of thee, lov'd boy,
Seven yeeres tho'wert lent to me, and I thee pay,
Exacted by thy fate, on the just day.
O, could I loose all father, now. For why
Will man lament the state he should envie?
To have so soone scap'd worlds, and fleshes rage,
And, if no other miserie, yet age?
Rest in soft peace, and, ask'd, say here doth lye
Ben. Jonson his best piece of poetrie.   10
For whose sake, hence-forth, all his vowes be such,
As what he loves may never like too much.

XLVI

To Sir Lucklesse Woo-all

Is this the Sir, who, some wast wife to winne,
A knight-hood bought, to goe a wooing in?
'Tis Lucklesse he, that tooke up one on band
To pay at's day of marriage. By my hand
The knight-wright's cheated then: Hee'll never pay.
Yes, now he weares his knight-hood every day.

XLVII

To the same

SIR LUCKLESSE, troth, for lucks sake passe by one:
Hee that wooes every widdow, will get none.

XLVIII

On Mungril Esquire

HIS bought armes Mung' not lik'd; for his first day
Of bearing them in field, he threw'hem away:
And hath no honor lost our Due'llists say.

XLIX

To Play-wright

PLAY-WRIGHT me reades, and still my verses damnes
He sayes, I want the tongue of Epigrammes;
I have no salt: no bawdrie he doth meane.
For wittie, in his language, is obscene.

Play-wright, I loath to have thy manners knowne
In my chast booke: professe them in thine owne.

L

To Sir Cod

LEAVE Cod, tabacco-like, burnt gummes to take,
Or fumie clysters, thy moist lungs to bake:
Arsenike would thee fit for societie make.

LI

To King James

*Upon the happy false rumour of his death, the
two and twentieth day of March, 1607*

THAT we thy losse might know, and thou our love,
Great heav'n did well, to give ill fame free wing;
Which though it did but panick terror prove,
And farre beneath least pause of such a king,
Yet give thy jealous subjects leave to doubt:
Who this thy scape from rumour gratulate,
No lesse than if from perill; and devout,
Doe beg thy care unto thy after-state.
For we, that have our eyes still in our eares,
Looke not upon thy dangers, but our feares.   10

LII

To Censorious Courtling

COURTLING, I rather thou should'st utterly
Dispraise my worke, then praise it frostily:
When I am read, thou fain'st a weake applause,
As if thou wert my friend, but lack'dst a cause.
This but thy judgement fooles: the other way
Would both thy folly, and thy spite betray.

LIII

To Old-end Gatherer

LONG-GATHERING Old-end, I did feare thee wise,
When having pill'd a booke, which no man buyes,
Thou wert content the authors name to loose:
But when (in place) thou didst the patrons choose,
It was as if thou printed had'st an oath,
To give the world assurance thou wert both;
And that, as puritanes at baptisme doo,
Thou art the father, and the witnesse too.
For, but thy selfe, where, out of motly, 's hee
Could save that line to dedicate to thee?   10

LIV

On Chev'ril

CHEV'RIL cryes out, my verses libells are;
And threatens the starre-chamber, and the barre:
What are thy petulant pleadings, Chev'ril, then,
That quit'st the cause so oft, and rayl'st at men?

LV

To Francis Beaumont

How I doe love thee Beaumont, and thy Muse,
That unto me dost such religion use!
How I doe feare my selfe, that am not worth
The least indulgent thought thy pen drops forth!
At once thou mak'st me happie, and unmak'st;
And giving largely to me, more thou tak'st.
What fate is mine, that so it selfe bereaves?
What art is thine, that so thy friend deceives?
When even there, where most thou praysest mee,
For writing better, I must envie thee.   10

LVI

On Poet-Ape

POORE Poet-Ape, that would be thought our chiefe,
Whose workes are eene the fripperie of wit,
From brocage is become so bold a thiefe,
As we, the rob'd, leave rage, and pittie it.
At first he made low shifts, would pick and gleane,
Buy the reversion of old playes; now growne
To'a little wealth, and credit in the scene,
He takes up all, makes each mans wit his owne.
And, told of this, he slights it. Tut, such crimes
The sluggish gaping auditor devoures;   10
He markes not whose 'twas first: and after-times
May judge it to be his, as well as ours.
Foole, as if halfe eyes will not know a fleece
From locks of wooll, or shreds from the whole peece?

LVII

On Baudes, and Usurers

IF, as their ends, their fruits were so, the same,
Baudrie', and usurie were one kind of game.

LVIII

To Groome Ideot

IDEOT, last night, I pray'd thee but forbeare
To reade my verses; now I must to heare:
For offring, with thy smiles, my wit to grace,
Thy ignorance still laughs in the wrong place.
And so my sharpnesse thou no lesse dis-joynts,
Then thou did'st late my sense, loosing my points.
So have I seene at Christ-masse sports one lost,
And, hood-wink'd, for a man, embrace a post.

LIX

On Spies

SPIES, you are lights in state, but of base stuffe,
Who, when you'have burnt your selves downe to
   the snuffe,
Stinke, and are throwne away. End faire enough.

LX

To William Lord Mounteagle

LOE, what my countrey should have done (have rais'd
An obeliske, or columne to thy name,
Or, if shee would but modestly have prais'd
Thy fact, in brasse or marble writ the same)
I, that am glad of thy great chance, here doo!
And proud, my worke shall out-last common deeds,
Durst thinke it great, and worthy wonder too,
But thine, for which I doo't, so much exceeds!
My countries parents I have many knowne;
But saver of my countrey thee alone.   10

LXI

To Foole, or Knave

THY praise, or dispraise is to me alike,
One doth not stroke me, nor the other strike.

LXII

To Fine Lady Would-bee

FINE Madame Would-bee, wherefore should you
    feare,
That love to make so well, a child to beare?
The world reputes you barren: but I know
Your 'pothecarie, and his drug sayes no.
Is it the paine affrights? that's soone forgot.
Or your complexions losse? you have a pot,

That can restore that. Will it hurt your feature?
To make amends, yo'are thought a wholesome
    creature.
What should the cause be? Oh, you live at court:
And there's both losse of time, and losse of sport 10
In a great belly. Write, then on thy wombe,
Of the not borne, yet buried, here's the tombe.

LXIII

To Robert Earle of Salisburie

WHO can consider thy right courses run,
With what thy vertue on the times hath won,
And not thy fortune: who can cleerely see
The judgement of the king so shine in thee;
And that thou seek'st reward of thy each act,
Not from the publike voyce, but private fact;
Who can behold all envie so declin'd
By constant suffring of thy equall mind;
And can to these be silent, Salisburie,
Without his, thine, and all times injurie?   10
Curst be his Muse, that could lye dumbe, or hid
To so true worth, though thou thy selfe forbid.

LXIV

To the same

Upon the accession of the Treasurer-ship to him

NOT glad, like those that have new hopes, or sutes,
With thy new place, bring I these early fruits
Of love, and what the golden age did hold
A treasure, art: contemn'd in th'age of gold.

30

Nor glad as those, that old dependents bee,
To see thy fathers rites new laid on thee.
Nor glad for fashion. Nor to shew a fit
Of flatterie to thy titles. Nor of wit.
But I am glad to see that time survive,
Where merit is not sepulcher'd alive.   10
Where good mens vertues them to honors bring,
And not to dangers. When so wise a king
Contends t'have worth enjoy, from his regard,
As her owne conscience, still, the same reward.
These (noblest Cecil) labour'd in my thought,
Wherein what wonder see thy name hath wrought?
That whil'st I meant but thine to gratulate,
I'have sung the greater fortunes of our state.

LXV

To my Muse

AWAY, and leave me, thou thing most abhord
That hast betray'd me to a worthlesse lord;
Made me commit most fierce idolatrie
To a great image through thy luxurie.
Be thy next masters more unluckie Muse,
And, as thou'hast mine, his houres, and youth abuse.
Get him the times long grudge, the courts ill will;
And, reconcil'd, keepe him suspected still.
Make him loose all his friends; and, which is worse,
Almost all wayes, to any better course.   10
With me thou leav'st an happier Muse then thee,
And which thou brought'st me, welcome povertie.
Shee shall instruct my after-thoughts to write
Things manly, and not smelling parasite.
But I repent me: Stay. Who e're is rais'd,
For worth he has not, He is tax'd, not prais'd.

LXVI

To Sir Henrie Cary

THAT neither fame, nor love might wanting be
To greatnesse, Cary, I sing that, and thee.
Whose house, if it no other honor had,
In onely thee, might be both great, and glad.
Who, to upbraid the sloth of this our time,
Durst valour make, almost, but not a crime.
Which deed I know not, whether were more high,
Or thou more happie, it to justifie
Against thy fortune: when no foe, that day,
Could conquer thee, but chance, who did betray. 10
Love thy great losse, which a renowne hath wonne,
*To live when Broeck not stands, nor Roor doth
      runne.
Love honors, which of best example bee,
When they cost dearest, and are done most free,
Though every fortitude deserves applause,
It may be much, or little, in the cause.
Hee's valiant'st, that dares fight, and not for pay;
That vertuous is, when the reward's away.

* The Castle and River neere where he was taken.

LXVII

To Thomas Earle of Suffolke

SINCE men have left to doe praise-worthy things,
Most thinke all praises flatteries. But truth brings
That sound, and that authoritie with her name,
As, to be rais'd by her, is onely fame.
Stand high, then, Howard, high in eyes of men,
High in thy bloud, thy place, but highest then,

When, in mens wishes, so thy vertues wrought,
As all thy honors were by them first sought:
And thou design'd to be the same thou art,
Before thou wert it, in each good mans heart.   10
Which, by no lesse confirm'd, then thy kings choice,
Proves, that is gods, which was the peoples voice.

LXVIII

On Play-wright

PLAY-WRIGHT convict of publike wrongs to men,
Takes private beatings, and begins againe.
Two kindes of valour he doth shew, at ones;
Active in's braine, and passive in his bones.

LXIX

To Pertinax Cob

COB, thou nor souldier, thiefe, nor fencer art,
Yet by thy weapon liv'st! Th'hast one good part.

LXX

To William Roe

WHEN Nature bids us leave to live, 'tis late
Then to begin, my Roe: He makes a state
In life, that can employ it; and takes hold
On the true causes, ere they grow too old.
Delay is bad, doubt worse, depending worst;
Each best day of our life escapes us, first.

Then, since we (more then many) these truths know:
Though life be short, let us not make it so.

LXXI

On Court-Parrat

To plucke downe mine, Poll sets up new wits still,
Still, 'tis his lucke to praise me 'gainst his will.

LXXII

To Court-ling

I GRIEVE not, Courtling, thou art started up
A chamber-critick, and dost dine, and sup
At Madames table, where thou mak'st all wit
Goe high, or low, as thou wilt value it.
'Tis not thy judgement breeds the prejudice,
Thy person only, Courtling, is the vice.

LXXIII

To Fine Grand

WHAT is't, fine Grand, makes thee my friendship flye,
Or take an Epigramme so fearefully:
As't were a challenge, or a borrowers letter?
The world must know your greatnesse is my debter.
In-primis, Grand, you owe me for a jest;
I lent you, on meere acquaintance, at a feast.
Item, a tale or two, some fortnight after;
That yet maintaynes you, and your house in laughter.

34

Item, the babylonian song you sing;
Item, a faire greeke poesie for a ring: 10
With which a learned Madame you belye.
Item, a charme surrounding fearefully,
Your *partie-per-pale* picture, one halfe drawne
In solemne cypres, the other cob-web-lawne.
Item, a gulling imprese for you, at tilt.
Item, your mistris anagram, i' your hilt.
Item, your owne, sew'd in your mistris smock.
Item, an epitaph on my lords cock,
In most vile verses, and cost me more paine,
Then had I made 'hem good, to fit your vaine. 20
Fortie things more, deare Grand, which you know
    true,
For which, or pay me quickly', or Ile pay you.

LXXIV

To Thomas Lord Chancelor

WHIL'ST thy weigh'd judgements, Egerton, I heare,
And know thee, then, a judge, not of one yeare;
Whil'st I behold thee live with purest hands;
That no affection in thy voyce commands;
That still th'art present to the better cause;
And no lesse wise, then skilfull in the lawes;
Whil'st thou art certaine to thy words, once gone,
As is thy conscience, which is alwayes one:
The Virgin, long-since fled from earth, I see,
T'our times return'd, hath made her heaven in
    thee. 10

LXXV

On Lippe, the Teacher

I CANNOT thinke there's that antipathy
'Twist puritanes, and players, as some cry;
Though Lippe, at Pauls, ranne from his text away,
T'inveigh 'gainst playes: what did he then but play?

LXXVI

On Lucy Countesse of Bedford

THIS morning, timely rapt with holy fire,
I thought to forme unto my zealous Muse,
What kinde of creature I could most desire,
To honor, serve, and love; as Poets use.
I meant to make her faire, and free, and wise,
Of greatest bloud, and yet more good then great;
I meant the day-starre should not brighter rise,
Nor lend like influence from his lucent seat.
I meant shee should be curteous, facile, sweet,
Hating that solemne vice of greatnesse, pride;   10
I meant each softest vertue, there should meet,
Fit in that softer bosome to reside.
Onely a learned, and a manly soule
I purpos'd her; that should, with even powers,
The rock, the spindle, and the sheeres controule
Of destinie, and spin her owne free houres.
Such when I meant to faine, and wish'd to see,
My Muse bad, *Bedford* write, and that was shee.

LXXVII

To one that desired me not to name him

BE safe, nor feare thy selfe so good a fame,
That, any way, my booke should speake thy name:
For, if thou shame,ranck'd with my friends, to goe,
I'am more asham'd to have thee thought my foe.

LXXVIII

To Hornet

HORNET, thou hast thy wife drest, for the stall,
To draw thee custome: but her selfe gets all.

LXXIX

To Elizabeth Countesse of Rutland

THAT Poets are far rarer births then kings,
Your noblest father prov'd: like whom, before,
Or then, or since, about our Muses springs,
Came not that soule exhausted so their store.
Hence was it, that the destinies decreed
(Save that most masculine issue of his braine)
No male unto him: who could so exceed
Nature, they thought, in all, that he would faine.
At which, shee happily displeas'd, made you:
On whom, if he were living now, to looke,   10
He should those rare, and absolute numbers view,
As he would burne, or better farre his booke.

LXXX

Of Life, and Death

THE ports of death are sinnes; of life, good deeds:
Through which, our merit leads us to our meeds.
How wilfull blind is he then, that would stray,
And hath it, in his powers, to make his way!
This world deaths region is, the other lifes:
And here, it should be one of our first strifes,
So to front death, as men might judge us past it.
For good men but see death, the wicked tast it.

LXXXI

To Proule the Plagiary

FORBEARE to tempt me, Proule, I will not show
A line unto thee, till the world it know;
Or that I'have by two good sufficient men,
To be the wealthy witnesse of my pen:
For all thou hear'st, thou swear'st thy selfe didst
    doo.
Thy wit lives by it, Proule, and belly too.
Which, if thou leave not soone (though I am loth)
I must a libell make, and cosen both.

LXXXII

On Cashierd Capt. Surly

SURLY's old whore in her new silkes doth swim:
He cast, yet keeps her well! No, shee keeps him.

LXXXIII

To a Friend

To put out the word, whore, thou do'st me woo,
Throughout my booke. 'Troth put out woman too.

LXXXIV

To Lucy Countesse of Bedford

MADAME, I told you late how I repented,
I ask'd a lord a buck, and he denyed me;
And, ere I could aske you, I was prevented:
For your most noble offer had supply'd me.
Straight went I home; and there most like a Poet,
I fancied to my selfe, what wine, what wit
I would have spent: how every Muse should know it,
And Phœbus-selfe should be at eating it.
O Madame, if your grant did thus transferre mee,
Make it your gift. See whither that will beare mee. 10

LXXXV

To Sir Henry Goodyere

GOODYERE, I'am glad, and gratefull to report,
My selfe a witnesse of thy few dayes sport:
Where I both learn'd, why wise-men hawking follow,
And why that bird was sacred to Apollo.
Shee doth instruct men by her gallant flight,
That they to knowledge so should toure upright,
And never stoupe, but to strike ignorance:
Which if they misse, they yet should re-advance

39

To former height, and there in circle tarrie,
Till they be sure to make the foole their quarrie. 10
Now, in whose pleasures I have this discerned,
What would his serious actions me have learned?

LXXXVI

To the same

WHEN I would know thee Goodyere, my thought
    lookes
Upon thy wel-made choise of friends, and bookes;
Then doe I love thee, and behold thy ends
In making thy friends bookes, and thy bookes
    friends:
Now, I must give thy life, and deed, the voice
Attending such a studie, such a choice.
Where, though't be love, that to thy praise doth
    move,
It was a knowledge, that begat that love.

LXXXVII

On Captaine Hazard the Cheater

TOUCH'D with the sinne of false play, in his punque,
Hazard a month forsware his; and grew drunke,
Each night, to drowne his cares: But when the gaine
Of what she had wrought came in, and wak'd his
    braine,
Upon th'accompt, hers grew the quicker trade.
Since when, hee's sober againe, and all play's made.

LXXXVIII

On English Mounsieur

WOULD you beleeve, when you this Mounsieur see,
That his whole body should speake french, not he?
That so much skarfe of France, and hat, and fether,
And shooe, and tye, and garter should come hether,
And land on one, whose face durst never bee
Toward the sea, farther then halfe-way tree?
That he, untravell'd, should be french so much,
As french-men in his companie, should seeme dutch?
Or had his father, when he did him get,
The french disease, with which he labours yet?   10
Or hung some Mounsieurs picture on the wall,
By which his damme conceiv'd him clothes and all?
Or is it some french statue? No: 'T doth move,
And stoupe, and cringe. O then, it needs must prove
The new french-taylors motion, monthly made,
Daily to turne in Pauls, and help the trade.

LXXXIX

To Edward Allen

IF Rome so great, and in her wisest age,
Fear'd not to boast the glories of her stage,
As skilfull Roscius, and grave Æsope, men,
Yet crown'd with honors, as with riches, then;
Who had no lesse a trumpet of their name,
Then Cicero, whose every breath was fame:
How can so great example dye in mee,
That, Allen, I should pause to publish thee?
Who both their graces in thy selfe hast more
Out-stript, then they did all that went before: 10

41

And present worth in all dost so contract,
As others speake, but onely thou dost act.
Weare this renowne. 'Tis just, that who did give
So many Poets life, by one should live.

XC

On Mill, my Ladies Woman

WHEN Mill first came to court, the unprofiting foole,
Unworthy such a mistris, such a schoole,
Was dull, and long, ere shee would goe to man:
At last, ease, appetite, and example wan
The nicer thing to tast her ladies page;
And, finding good securitie in his age,
Went on: and proving him still, day by day,
Discern'd no difference of his yeeres, or play.
Not though that haire grew browne, which once was
    amber,
And he growne youth, was call'd to his ladies
    chamber,   10
Still Mill continu'd: Nay, his face growing worse,
And he remov'd to gent'man of the horse,
Mill was the same. Since, both his body and face
Blowne up; and he (too'unwieldie for that place)
Hath got the stewards chaire; he will not tarry
Longer a day, but with his Mill will marry.
And it is hop'd, that shee, like Milo, wull
First bearing him a calfe, beare him a bull.

XCI

To Sir Horace Vere

WHICH of thy names I take, not onely beares
A romane sound, but romane vertue weares,
Illustrous Vere, or Horace; fit to be
Sung by a Horace, or a Muse as free;
Which thou art to thy selfe: whose fame was wonne
In th'eye of Europe, where thy deedes were done,
When on thy trumpet shee did sound a blast,
Whose rellish to eternitie shall last.
I leave thy acts, which should I prosequute
Throughout, might flatt'rie seeme; and to be mute 10
To any one, were envie: which would live
Against my grave, and time could not forgive.
I speake thy other graces, not lesse showne,
Nor lesse in practice; but lesse mark'd, lesse knowne:
Humanitie, and pietie, which are
As noble in great chiefes, as they are rare.
And best become the valiant man to weare,
Who more should seeke mens reverence, then feare.

XCII

The new Crie

ERE cherries ripe, and straw-berries be gone,
Unto the cryes of London Ile adde one;
Ripe statesmen, ripe: They grow in every street.
At sixe and twentie, ripe. You shall'hem meet,
And have 'hem yeeld no savour, but of state.
Ripe are their ruffes, their cuffes, their beards, their
    gate,
And grave as ripe, like mellow as their faces,
They know the states of Christendome, not the places:

G   43

Yet have they seene the maps, and bought 'hem too,
And understand 'hem, as most chapmen doe.   10
The councels, projects practises they know,
And what each prince doth for intelligence owe,
And unto whom: They are the almanacks
For twelve yeeres yet to come, what each state lacks.
They carry in their pockets Tacitus,
And the Gazetti, or *Gallo-Belgicus*:
And talke reserv'd, lock'd up, and full of feare,
Nay, aske you, how the day goes, in your eare.
Keepe a starre-chamber sentence close, twelve dayes:
And whisper what a Proclamation sayes.   20
They meet in sixes, and at every mart,
Are sure to con' the catalogue by hart;
Or, every day, some one at Rimee's looks,
Or Bils, and there he buyes the names of books.
They all get Porta, for the sundrie wayes
To write in cypher, and the severall keyes,
To ope' the character. They'have found the sleight
With juyce of limons, onions, pisse, to write.
To breake up seales, and close 'hem. And they know,
If the States make peace, how it will goe   30
With England. All forbidden bookes they get.
And of the poulder-plot, they will talke yet.
At naming the French King, their heads they shake,
And at the Pope, and Spaine slight faces make.
Or 'gainst the Bishops, for the Brethren, raile,
Much like those Brethren; thinking to prevaile
With ignorance on us, as they have done
On them: And therefore doe not onely shunne
Others more modest, but contemne us too,
That know not so much state, wrong, as they doo.   40

XCIII

To Sir John Radcliffe

How like a columne, Radcliffe, left alone
For the great marke of vertue, those being gone
Who did, alike with thee, thy house up-beare,
Stand'st thou, to shew the times what you all were?
Two bravely in the battaile fell, and dy'd,
Upbraiding rebells armes, and barbarous pride:*
And two, that would have falne as great, as they,
The Belgick fever ravished away.
Thou, that art all their valour, all their spirit,
And thine owne goodnesse to encrease thy merit,   10
Then whose I doe not know a whiter soule,
Nor could I, had I seene all Natures roule,
Thou yet remayn'st, un-hurt in peace, or warre,
Though not unprov'd: which shewes, thy fortunes are
Willing to expiate the fault in thee,
Wherewith, against thy bloud, they'offenders bee.

* In Ireland.

XCIV

To Lucy, Countesse of Bedford, with Mr. Donnes Satyres

LUCY, you brightnesse of our spheare, who are
Life of the Muses day, their morning-starre!
If workes (not th'authors) their owne grace should
    looke,
Whose poemes would not wish to be your booke?
But these, desir'd by you, the makers ends
Crowne with their owne. Rare poemes aske rare
    friends.

45

Yet, Satyres, since the most of mankind bee
Their un-avoided subject, fewest see:
For none ere tooke that pleasure in sinnes sense,
But, when they heard it tax'd, tooke more offence.
They, then, that living where the matter is bred,   11
Dare for these poemes, yet, both aske, and read,
And like them too; must needfully, though few,
Be of the best: and 'mongst those, best are you.
Lucy, you brightnesse of our spheare, who are
The Muses evening, as their morning-starre.

XCV

To Sir Henrie Savile

IF, my religion safe, I durst embrace
That stranger doctrine of Pythagoras,
I should beleeve, the soule of Tacitus
In thee, most weighty Savile, liv'd to us:
So hast thou rendred him in all his bounds,
And all his numbers, both of sense, and sounds.
But when I read that speciall piece, restor'd,
Where Nero falls, and Galba is ador'd,
To thine owne proper I ascribe then more;
And gratulate the breach, I griev'd before: 10
Which Fate (it seemes) caus'd in the historie,
Onely to boast thy merit in supply.
O, would'st thou adde like hand, to all the rest!
Or, better worke! were thy glad countrey blest,
To have her storie woven in thy thred;
Minervaes loome was never richer spred.
For who can master those great parts like thee,
That liv'st from hope, from feare, from faction
    free;
That hast thy brest so cleere of present crimes,
Thou need'st not shrinke at voyce of after-times;   20

Whose knowledge claymeth at the helme to stand;
But, wisely, thrusts not forth a forward hand,
No more then Salust in the Romane state!
As, then, his cause, his glorie emulate.
Although to write be lesser then to doo,
It is the next deed, and a great one too.
We need a man that knowes the severall graces
Of historie, and how to apt their places;
Where brevitie, where splendor, and where height,
Where sweetnesse is requir'd, and where weight; 30
We need a man, can speake of the intents,
The councells, actions, orders, and events
Of state, and censure them: we need his pen
Can write the things, the causes, and the men.
But most we need his faith (and all have you)
That dares nor write things false, nor hide things
    true.

XCVI

To John Donne

Who shall doubt, Donne, where I a Poet bee,
When I dare send my Epigrammes to thee?
That so alone canst judge, so'alone dost make:
And, in thy censures, evenly, dost take
As free simplicitie, to dis-avow,
As thou hast best authoritie, t'allow.
Reade all I send: and, if I find but one
Mark'd by thy hand, and with the better stone,
My title's seal'd. Those that for claps doe write,
Let pui'nees, porters, players praise delight, 10
And, till they burst, their backs, like asses load:
A man should seeke great glorie, and not broad.

XCVII

On the new Motion

SEE you yond' Motion? Not the old Fa-ding,
Nor Captayne Pod, nor yet the Eltham-thing;
But one more rare, and in the case so new:
His cloke with orient velvet quite lin'd through,
His rosie tyes and garters so ore-blowne,
By his each glorious parcell to be knowne!
He wont was to encounter me, aloud,
Where ere he met me; now hee's dumbe, or proud.
Know you the cause? H'has neither land, nor lease,
Nor baudie stock, that travells for encrease,   10
Nor office in the towne, nor place in court,
Nor 'bout the beares, nor noyse to make lords sport.
He is no favourites favourite, no deare trust
Of any Madames, hath neadd squires, and must.
Nor did the king of Denmarke him salute,
When he was here. Nor hath he got a sute,
Since he was gone, more then the one he weares.
Nor are the Queenes most honor'd maides by th'eares
About his forme. What then so swells each lim?
Onely his clothes have over-leaven'd him.   20

XCVIII

To Sir Thomas Roe

THOU hast begun well, Roe, which stand well too,
And I know nothing more thou hast to doo.
He that is round within himselfe, and streight,
Need seeke no other strength, no other height;
Fortune upon him breakes her selfe, if ill,
And what would hurt his vertue makes it still.

That thou at once, then, nobly maist defend
With thine owne course the judgement of thy
    friend,
Be alwayes to thy gather'd selfe the same:
And studie conscience, more then thou would'st
    fame.   10
Though both be good, the latter yet is worst,
And ever is ill got without the first.

XCIX

To the same

THAT thou hast kept thy love, encreast thy will,
Better'd thy trust to letters; that thy skill,
Hast taught thy selfe worthy thy pen to tread,
And that to write things worthy to be read:
How much of great example wert thou, Roe,
If time to facts, as unto men would owe?
But much it now availes, what's done, of whom:
The selfe-same deeds, as diversly they come,
From place, or fortune, are made high, or low,
And even the praisers judgement suffers so.   10
Well, though thy name lesse then our great ones bee,
Thy fact is more: let truth encourage thee.

C

On Play-wright

PLAY-WRIGHT, by chance, hearing some toyes I'had
    writ,
Cry'd to my face, they were th'elixir of wit:
And I must now beleeve him: for, to day,
Five of my jests, then stolne, past him a play.

49

CI

Inviting a friend to supper

To night, grave sir, both my poore house, and I
Doe equally desire your companie:
Not that we thinke us worthy such a ghest,
But that your worth will dignifie our feast,
With those that come; whose grace may make that
    seeme
Something, which, else, could hope for no esteeme.
It is the faire acceptance, Sir, creates
The entertaynment perfect: not the cates.
Yet shall you have, to rectifie your palate,
An olive, capers, or some better sallade   10
Ushring the mutton; with a short-leg'd hen,
If we can get her, full of egs, and then,
Limons, and wine for sauce: to these, a coney
Is not to be despair'd of, for our money;
And, though fowle, now, be scarce, yet there are
    clarkes,
The skie not falling, thinke we may have larkes.
Ile tell you more, and lye, so you will come:
Of partrich, pheasant, wood-cock, of which some
May yet be there; and godwit, if we can:
Knat, raile, and ruffe too. How so ere, my man   20
Shall reade a piece of Virgil, Tacitus,
Livie, or of some better booke to us,
Of which wee'll speake our minds, amidst our
    meate;
And Ile professe no verses to repeate:
To this, if ought appeare, which I not know of,
That will the pastrie, not my paper, show of.
Digestive cheese, and fruit there sure will bee;
But that, which most doth take my Muse, and mee,
Is a pure cup of rich Canary-wine,
Which is the Mermaids, now, but shall be mine: 30

Of which had Horace, or Anacreon tasted,
Their lives, as doe their lines, till now had lasted.
Tabacco, Nectar, or the Thespian spring,
Are all but Luthers beere, to this I sing.
Of this we will sup free, but moderately,
And we will have no Pooly', or Parrot by;
Nor shall our cups make any guiltie men:
But, at our parting, we will be, as when
We innocently met. No simple word,
That shall be utter'd at our mirthfull boord,   40
Shall make us sad next morning: or affright
The libertie, that wee'll enjoy to night.

CII

To William Earle of Pembroke

I DOE but name thee Pembroke, and I find
It is an Epigramme, on all man-kind;
Against the bad, but of, and to the good:
Both which are ask'd, to have thee understood.
Nor could the age have mist thee, in this strife
Of vice, and vertue; wherein all great life
Almost, is exercis'd: and scarse one knowes,
To which, yet, of the sides himselfe he owes.
They follow vertue, for reward, today:
To morrow vice, if shee give better pay: 10
And are so good, and bad, just at a price,
As nothing else discernes the vertue' or vice.
But thou, whose noblesse keeps one stature still,
And one true posture, though besieg'd with ill
Of what ambition, faction, pride can raise;
Whose life, ev'n they, that envie it, must praise;
That art so reverenc'd, as thy comming in,
But in the view, doth interrupt their sinne;

51

Thou must draw more: and they, that hope to see
The common-wealth still safe, must studie thee.   20

CIII

To Mary Lady Wroth

How well, faire crowne of your faire sexe, might
   hee,
That but the twi-light of your sprite did see,
And noted for what flesh such soules were fram'd,
Know you to be a Sydney, though un-nam'd?
And, being nam'd, how little doth that name
Need any Muses praise to give it fame?
Which is, it selfe, the imprese of the great,
And glorie of them all, but to repeate!
Forgive me then, if mine but say you are
A Sydney: but in that extend as farre   10
As lowdest praisers, who perhaps would find
For every part a character assign'd.
My praise is plaine, and where so ere profest,
Becomes none more then you, who need it least.

CIV

To Susan Countesse of Montgomery

Were they that nam'd you, prophets? Did they see,
Even in the dew of grace, what you would bee?
Or did our times require it, to behold
A new Susanna, equall to that old?
Or, because some scarce thinke that storie true,
To make those faithfull, did the Fates send you?
And to your Scene lent no lesse dignitie
Of birth, of match, of forme, of chastitie?

Or, more then borne for the comparison
Of former age, or glorie of our one,   10
Were you advanced, past those times, to be
The light, and marke unto posteritie?
Judge they, that can: Here I have rais'd to show
A picture, which the world for yours must know,
And like it too; if they looke equally:
If not, 'tis fit for you, some should envy.

CV

To Mary Lady Wroth

MADAME, had all antiquitie beene lost,
All historie seal'd up, and fables crost;
That we had left us, nor by time, nor place,
Least mention of a Nymph, a Muse, a Grace,
But even their names were to be made a-new,
Who could not but create them all, from you?
He, that but saw you weare the wheaten hat,
Would call you more then Ceres, if not that:
And, drest in shepheards tyre, who would not say:
You were the bright Œnone, Flora, or May?   10
If dancing, all would cry th'Idalian Queene,
Were leading forth the Graces on the greene:
And, armed to the chase, so bare her bow
Diana'alone, so hit, and hunted so.
There's none so dull, that for your stile would aske,
That saw you put on Pallas plumed caske:
Or, keeping your due state, that would not cry,
There Juno sate, and yet no Peacock by.
So are you Natures Index, and restore,
I'your selfe, all treasure lost of th'age before.   20

CVI

To Sir Edward Herbert

IF men get name, for some one vertue: Then,
What man art thou, that art so many men,
All-vertuous Herbert! on whose every part
Truth might spend all her voyce, Fame all her art.
Whether thy learning they would take, or wit,
Or valour, or thy judgement seasoning it,
Thy standing upright to thy selfe, thy ends
Like straight, thy pietie to God, and friends:
Their latter praise would still the greatest bee,
And yet, they, all together, lesse then thee.   10

CVII

To Captayne Hungry

DOE what you come for, Captayne, with your newes;
That's, sit, and eate: doe not my eares abuse.
I oft looke on false coyne, to know't from true:
Not that I love it, more, then I will you.
Tell the grosse Dutch those grosser tales of yours,
How great you were with their two Emperours;
And yet are with their Princes: Fill them full
Of your Moravian horse, Venetian bull.
Tell them, what parts yo'have tane, whence run away,
What States yo'have gull'd, and which yet keepes
        yo'in pay.   10
Give them your services, and embassies
In Ireland, Holland, Sweden, pompous lies,
In Hungary, and Poland, Turkie too;
What at Ligorne, Rome, Florence you did doe:
And, in some yeere, all these together heap'd,
For which there must more sea, and land be leap'd,

If but to be beleev'd you have the hap,
Then can a flea at twise skip i'the Map.
Give your yong States-men, (that first made you
    drunke,
And then lye with you, closer, than a punque,   20
For newes) your Ville-royes, and Silleries,
Janin's, your Nuncio's, and your Tuilleries,
Your Arch-Dukes Agents, and your Beringhams,
That are your wordes of credit. Keepe your Names
Of Hannow, Shieter-huissen, Popenheim,
Hans-spiegle, Rotteinberg, and Boutersheim,
For your next meale: this you are sure of. Why
Will you part with them, here, unthriftely?
Nay, now you puffe, tuske, and draw up your chin,
Twirle the poore chaine you run a feasting in.   30
Come, be not angrie, you are Hungry; eate;
Doe what you come for, Captayne, There's your
    meate.

CVIII

To true Souldiers

STRENGTH of my Countrey, whilst I bring to view
Such as are misse-call'd Captaynes, and wrong you;
And your high names: I doe desire, that thence
Be nor put on you, nor you take offence.
I sweare by your true friend, my Muse, I love
Your great profession; which I once, did prove:
And did not shame it with my actions, then,
No more, then I dare now doe, with my pen.
He that not trusts me, having vow'd thus much,
But's angry for the Captayne, still: is such.   10

55

CIX

To Sir Henry Nevil

Who now calls on thee, Nevil, is a Muse,
That serves nor fame, nor titles; but doth chuse
Where vertue makes them both, and tha.'s in thee:
Where all is faire, beside thy pedigree.
Thou art not one, seek'st miseries with hope,
Wrestlest with dignities, or fain'st a scope
Of service to the publique, when the end
Is private gaine, which hath long guilt to friend.
Thou rather striv'st the matter to possesse,
And elements of honor, then the dresse;   10
To make thy lent life, good against the Fates:
And first to know thine owne state, then the States.
To be the same in roote, thou art in height;
And that thy soule should give thy flesh her weight.
Goe on, and doubt not, what posteritie,
Now I have sung thee thus, shall judge of thee.
Thy deedes, unto thy name, will prove new wombes,
Whil'st others toyle for titles to their tombes.

CX

To Clement Edmonds, on his Cæsars commentaries *observed, and translated*

Not Cæsars deeds, nor all his honors wonne,
In these west-parts, nor when the warre was done,
The name of Pompey for an enemie,
Cato's to boote, Rome, and her libertie,
All yeelding to his fortune, nor, the while,
To have engrav'd these acts, with his owne stile,

56

And that so strong and deepe, as't might be thought,
He wrote, with the same spirit that he fought,
Nor that his worke liv'd in the hands of foes,
Un-argued then, and yet hath fame from those;   10
Not all these, Edmonds, or what else put too,
Can so speake Cæsar, as thy labours doe.
For, where his person liv'd scarce one just age,
And that, midst envy, and parts; then fell by rage:
His deedes too dying, but in bookes (whose good
How few have read! how fewer understood?)
Thy learned hand, and true Promethean art
(As by a new creation) part by part,
In every counsell, stratageme, designe,
Action, or engine, worth a note of thine,   20
T'all future time, not onely doth restore
His life, but makes, that he can dye no more.

CXI

To the same; On the same

Who Edmonds, reades thy booke, and doth not see
What th'antique souldiers were, the moderne bee?
Wherein thou shew'st, how much the latter are
Beholding, to this master of the warre;
And that, in action, there is nothing new,
More, then to varie what our elders knew:
Which all, but ignorant Captaynes will confesse:
Nor to give Cæsar this, makes ours the lesse.
Yet thou, perhaps, shall meet some tongues will
    grutch,
That to the world thou should'st reveale so much,   10
And thence, deprave thee, and thy worke. To those
Cæsar stands up, as from his urne late rose,
By thy great helpe: and doth proclaime by mee,
They murder him againe, that envie thee.

CXII

To a weake Gamster in Poetry

WITH thy small stocke, why art thou ventring still,
At this so subtile sport: and play'st so ill?
Think'st thou it is meere fortune, that can win?
Or thy ranke setting? that thou dar'st put in
Thy all, at all: and what so ere I doe,
Art still at that, and think'st to blow me'up too?
I cannot for the stage a Drama lay,
Tragick, or Comick; but thou writ'st the play.
I leave thee there, and giving way, entend
An Epick poeme; thou hast the same end.   10
I modestly quit that, and thinke to write,
Next morne, an Ode: Thou mak'st a song ere night.
I passe to Elegies; Thou meet'st me there:
To Satyres; and thou dost pursue me. Where,
Where shall I scape thee? in an Epigramme?
O, (thou cry'st out) that is thy proper game.
Troth, if it be, I pitty thy ill lucke;
That both for wit, and sense, so oft dost plucke,
And never art encounter'd, I confesse:
Nor scarce dost colour for it, which is lesse.   20
Pr'y thee, yet save thy rest; give ore in time:
There's no vexation, that can make thee prime.

CXIII

To Sir Thomas Overbury

So Phœbus makes me worthy of his bayes,
As but to speake thee, Overbury, is praise:
So, where thou liv'st, thou mak'st life understood!
Where, what makes others great, doth keepe thee
     good!

I thinke, the Fate of court thy comming crav'd,
That the wit there, and manners might be sav'd:
For since, what ignorance, what pride is fled!
And letters, and humanitie in the stead!
Repent thee not of thy faire precedent,
Could make such men, and such a place repent: 10
Nor may'any feare, to loose of their degree,
Who'in such ambition can but follow thee.

CXIV

To Mrs. Philip Sydney

I MUST beleeve some miracles still bee,
When Sydnyes name I heare, or face I see:
For Cupid, who (at first) tooke vaine delight,
In meere out-formes, untill he lost his sight,
Hath chang'd his soule, and made his object you:
Where finding so much beautie met with vertue,
He hath not onely gain'd himselfe his eyes,
But, in your love, made all his servants wise.

CXV

On the Townes honest Man

YOU wonder, who this is! and, why I name
Him not, aloud, that boasts so good a fame:
Naming so many, too! But, this is one,
Suffers no name, but a description:
Being no vitious person, but the vice
About the towne; and knowne too, at that price.
A subtle thing, that doth affections win
By speaking well o' the company it's in.

Talkes loud, and baudy, has a gather'd deale
Of newes, and noyse, to sow out a long meale.   10
Can come from Tripoly, leape stooles, and winke,
Doe all, that longs to the anarchy of drinke,
Except the duell. Can sing songs, and catches;
Give every one his dose of mirth: and watches
Whose name's un-welcome to the present eare,
And him it layes on; if he be not there
Tell's of him, all the tales, it selfe then makes;
But, if it shall be question'd, under-takes,
It will deny all; and forsweare it too:
Not that it feares, but will not have to doo   20
With such a one. And therein keepes it's word.
'Twill see it's sister naked, ere a sword.
At every meale, where it doth dine, or sup,
The cloth's no sooner gone, but it gets up
And, shifting of it's faces, doth play more
Parts, then th'Italian could doe, with his dore.
Acts old Iniquitie, and in the fit
Of miming, gets th'opinion of a wit.
Executes men in picture. By defect,
From friendship, is it's owne fames architect.   30
An inginer, in slanders, of all fashions,
That seeming prayses, are, yet accusations.
Describ'd, it's thus: Defin'd would you it have?
Then, The townes honest Man's her errant'st knave.

CXVI

To Sir William Jephson

JEPHSON, thou man of men, to whose lov'd name
All gentrie, yet, owe part of their best flame!
So did thy vertue'enforme, thy wit sustaine
That age, when thou stood'st up the master-braine:

Thou wert the first, mad'st merit know her strength,
And those that lack'd it, to suspect at length,
'Twas not entayl'd on title. That some word
Might be found out as good, and not *my Lord.*
That Nature no such difference had imprest
In men, but every bravest was the best: 10
That bloud not mindes, but mindes did bloud adorne:
And to live great, was better, then great borne.
These were thy knowing arts: which who doth now
Vertuously practise must at least allow
Them in, if not, from thee; or must commit
A desperate solœcisme in truth and wit.

CXVII

On Groyne

GROYNE, come of age, his state sold out of hand
For his whore: Groyne doth still occupy his land.

CXVIII

On Gut

GUT eates all day, and lechers all the night,
So all his meate he tasteth over, twise:
And, striving so to double his delight,
He makes himselfe a thorough-fare of vice.
Thus, in his belly, can he change a sin,
Lust it comes out, that gluttony went in.

CXIX

To Sir Raph Shelton

NOT he that flies the court for want of clothes,
At hunting railes, having no guift in othes,
Cries out 'gainst cocking, since he cannot bet,
Shuns prease, for two maine causes, poxe, and debt,
With me can merit more, then that good man,
Whose dice not doing well, to'a pulpit ran.
No, Shelton, give me thee, canst want all these,
But dost it out of judgement, not disease;
Dar'st breath in any ayre; and with safe skill,
Till thou canst finde the best, choose the least ill.   10
That to the vulgar canst thy selfe apply,
Treading a better path, not contrary;
And, in their errors maze, thine owne way know:
Which is to live to conscience, not to show.
He, that, but living halfe his age, dyes such;
Makes the whole longer, then 'twas given him, much.

CXX

Epitaph on S.P. a child of Q. El. Chappel

WEEPE with me all you that read
    This little storie:
And know, for whom a teare you shed,
    Death's selfe is sorry.
'Twas a child, that so did thrive
    In grace, and feature,
As Heaven and Nature seem'd to strive
    Which own'd the creature.
Yeeres he numbred scarse thirteene
    When Fates turn'd cruell,   10

Yet three fill'd Zodiackes had he beene
    The stages jewell;
And did act (what now we mone)
    Old men so duely,
As, sooth, the Parcæ thought him one,
    He plai'd so truely.
So, by error, to his fate
    They all consented;
But viewing him since (alas, too late)
    They have repented.   20
And have sought (to give new birth)
    In bathes to steepe him;
But, being so much too good for earth,
    Heaven vowes to keepe him.

CXXI

To Benjamin Rudyerd

RUDYERD, as lesser dames, to great ones use,
My lighter comes, to kisse thy learned Muse;
Whose better studies while shee emulates,
Shee learnes to know long difference of their states.
Yet is the office not to be despis'd,
If onely love should make the action pris'd:
Nor he, for friendship, to be thought unfit,
That strives, his manners should procede his wit.

CXXII

To the same

IF I would wish, for truth, and not for show,
The aged Saturne's age, and rites to know;

If I would strive to bring backe times, and trie
The world's pure gold, and wise simplicitie;
If I would vertue set, as shee was yong,
And heare her speake with one, and her first
    tongue;
If holiest friend-ship, naked to the touch,
I would restore, and keepe it ever such;
I need no other arts, but studie thee:
Who prov'st, all these were, and againe may bee. 10

CXXIII

To the same

WRITING thy selfe, or judging others writ,
I know not which th'hast most, candor, or wit:
But both th'hast so, as who affects the state
Of the best writer, and judge, should emulate.

CXXIV

Epitaph on Elizabeth, L. H.

WOULD'ST thou heare, what man can say
In a little? Reader, stay.
Under-neath this stone doth lye
As much beautie, as could dye:
Which in life did harbour give
To more vertue, then doth live.
If, at all, shee had a fault,
Leave it buryed in this vault.
One name was Elizabeth,
Th'other let it sleepe with death: 10
Fitter, where it dyed, to tell,
Then that it liv'd at all. Farewell.

CXXV

To Sir William Uvedale

Uv'DALE, thou piece of the first times, a man
Made for what Nature could, or Vertue can;
Both whose dimensions, lost, the world might finde
Restored in thy body, and thy minde!
Who sees a soule, in such a body set,
Might love the treasure for the cabinet.
But I, no child, no foole, respect the kinde,
The full, the flowing graces there enshrin'd;
Which (would the world not mis-call't flatterie)
I could adore, almost t'idolatrie.   10

CXXVI

To his Lady, then Mrs. Cary

RETYR'D, with purpose your faire worth to praise,
'Mongst Hampton shades, and Phœbus grove of
     bayes,
I pluck'd a branch; the jealous god did frowne,
And bad me lay th'usurped laurell downe:
Said I wrong'd him, and (which was more) his love.
I answer'd, Daphne now no paine can prove.
Phœbus replyed. Bold head, it is not shee:
Cary my love is, Daphne but my tree.

CXXVII

To Esme, Lord 'Aubigny

Is there a hope, that Man would thankefull bee,
If I should faile, in gratitude, to thee

To whom I am so bound, lov'd Aubigny?
No, I doe, therefore, call Posteritie
Into the debt; and reckon on her head,
How full of want, how swallow'd up, how dead
I, and this Muse had beene, if thou hadst not
Lent timely succours, and new life begot:
So, all reward, or name, that growes to mee
By her attempt, shall still be owing thee.   10
And, than this fame, I know no abler way
To thanke thy benefits: which is, to pay.

CXXVIII

To William Roe

ROE (and my joy to name) th'art now, to goe
Countries, and climes, manners, and men to know,
T'extract, and choose the best of all these knowne,
And those to turne to bloud, and make thine owne:
May windes as soft as breath of kissing friends,
Attend thee hence; and there, may all thy ends,
As the beginnings here, prove purely sweet,
And perfect in a circle alwayes meet.
So, when we, blest with thy returne, shall see
Thy selfe, with thy first thoughts, brought home
     by thee,   10
We each to other may this voyce enspire;
This is that good Æneas, past through fire,
Through seas, stormes, tempests: and imbarqu'd
     for hell,
Came back untouch'd. This man hath travail'd well.

CXXIX

To Mime

THAT, not a paire of friends each other see,
But the first question is, when one saw thee?
That there's no journey set, or thought upon,
To Braynford, Hackney, Bow, but thou mak'st one;
That scarse the Towne designeth any feast
To which thou'rt not a weeke, bespoke a guest;
That still th'art made the suppers flagge, the drum,
The very call, to make all others come:
Think'st thou, Mime, this is great? or, that they
    strive
Whose noyse shall keepe thy miming most alive, 10
Whil'st thou dost rayse some Player, from the
    grave,
Out-dance the Babion, or out-boast the Brave;
Or (mounted on a stoole) thy face doth hit
On some new gesture, that's imputed wit?
O, runne not proud of this. Yet, take thy due.
Thou dost out-zany Cokely, Pod; nay, Gue:
And thine owne Coriat too. But (would'st thou see)
Men love thee not for this: They laugh at thee.

CXXX

To Alphonso Ferrabosco, on his Booke

To urge, my lov'd Alphonso, that bold fame,
Of building townes, and making wilde beasts tame,
Which Musick had; or speake her knowne effects,
That shee removeth cares, sadnesse ejects,
Declineth anger, perswades clemencie,
Doth sweeten mirth, and heighten pietie,
And is t'a body, often, ill inclin'd,

No lesse a sov'raigne cure, then to the mind;
T'alledge, that greatest men were not asham'd,
Of old, even by her practise to be fam'd;   10
To say, indeed, shee were the soule of heaven,
That the eight spheare, no lesse, then planets
    seaven,
Mov'd by her order, and the ninth more high,
Including all, were thence call'd harmonie:
I, yet, had utter'd nothing on thy part,
When these were but the praises of the Art.
But when I have said, the proofes of all these bee
Shed in thy Songs; 'tis true: but short of thee.

CXXXI

To the same

WHEN we doe give, Alphonso, to the light,
A worke of ours, we part with our owne right;
For, then, all mouthes will judge, and their owne
    way:
The learn'd have no more priviledge, then the lay.
And though we could all men, all censures heare,
We ought not give them taste, we had an eare.
For, if the hum'rous world will talke at large,
They should be fooles, for me, at their owne charge.
Say, this, or that man they to thee preferre;
Even those for whom they doe this, know they erre:
And would (being ask'd the truth) ashamed say, 11
They were not to be nam'd on the same day.
Then stand unto thy selfe, not seeke without
For fame, with breath soone kindled, soone
    blowne out.

CXXXII

To Mr. Josuah Sylvester

IF to admire were to commend, my praise
Might then both thee, thy worke and merit raise:
But, as it is (the Child of Ignorance,
And utter stranger to all ayre of France)
How can I speake of thy great paines, but erre?
Since they can only judge, that can conferre.
Behold! the reverend shade of Bartas stands
Before my thought, and (in thy right) commands
That to the world I publish, for him, this;
Bartas doth wish thy English now were his.   10
So well in that are his inventions wrought,
As his will now be the translation thought,
Thine the originall; and France shall boast,
No more, those mayden glories shee hath lost.

CXXXIII

On the famous Voyage

No more let Greece her bolder fables tell
Of Hercules, or Theseus going to hell,
Orpheus, Ulysses: or the Latine Muse,
With tales of Troyes just knight, our faiths abuse:
We have a Shelton, and a Heyden got,
Had power to act, what they to faine had not.
All, that they boast of Styx, of Acheron,
Cocytus, Phlegeton, our have prov'd in one;
The filth, stench, noyse: save only what was there
Subtly distinguish'd, was confused here.   10
Their wherry had no saile, too; ours had none:
And in it, two more horride knaves, then Charon.

Arses were heard to croake, in stead of frogs;
And for one Cerberus, the whole coast was dogs.
Furies there wanted not: each scold was ten.
And, for the cryes of Ghosts, women, and men,
Laden with plague-sores, and their sinnes, were
    heard,
Lash'd by their consciences, to die, affeard.
Then let the former age, with this content her,   19
Shee brought the Poets forth, but ours th'adventer.

THE VOYAGE IT SELFE

I SING the brave adventure of two wights,
And pitty 'tis, I cannot call 'hem knights:
One was; and he, for brawne, and braine, right able
To have beene stiled of King Arthurs table.
The other was a squire, of faire degree;
But, in the action, greater man then hee:
Who gave, to take at his returne from Hell,
His three for one. Now, lordings, listen well.
    It was the day, what time the powerfull Moone
Makes the poore Banck-side creature wet it'
    shoone,   10
In it' owne hall; when these (in worthy scorne
Of those, that put out moneyes, on returne
From Venice, Paris, or some in-land passage
Of six times to, and fro, without embassage,
Or him that backward went to Berwicke, or which
Did dance the famous Morrisse, unto Norwich)
At Bread-streets Mermaid, having din'd, and merry,
Propos'd to goe to Hol'borne in a wherry:
A harder tasque, then either his to Bristo',
Or his to Antwerpe. Therefore, once more, list ho'.
    A Docke there is, that called is Avernus,   21
Of some Bride-well, and may, in time, concerne us

All, that are readers: but, me thinkes 'tis od,
That all this while I have forgot some god,
Or goddesse to invoke, to stuffe my verse;
And with both bombard-stile, and phrase, rehearse
The many perills of this Port, and how
Sans' helpe of Sybil, or a golden bough,
Or magick sacrifice, they past along!
Alcides, be thou succouring to my song.   30
Thou hast seene hell (some say) and know'st all
    nookes there,
Canst tell me best, how every Furie lookes there,
And art a god, if Fame thee not abuses,
Alwayes at hand, to aide the merry Muses.
Great Club-fist, though thy backe, and bones be
    sore,
Still, with thy former labours; yet, once more,
Act a brave worke, call it thy last adventry:
But hold my torch, while I describe the entry
To this dire passage. Say, thou stop thy nose:
'Tis but light paines: Indeede this Dock's no rose.
   In the first jawes appear'd that ugly monster,   41
Ycleped Mud, which, when their oares did once
    stirre,
Belch'd forth an ayre, as hot, as at a muster
Of all your night-tubs, when the carts doe cluster,
Who shall discharge first his merd-urinous load:
Thorough her wombe they make their famous road,
Betweene two walls; where, on one side, to scar
    men,
Were seene your ugly Centaures, yee call Car-men,
Gorgonian scolds, and Harpyes: on the other   49
Hung stench, diseases, and old filth, their mother,
With famine, wants, and sorrowes many a dosen,
The least of which was to the plague a cosen.
But they unfrighted passe, though many a privie
Spake to'hem louder, then the oxe in Livie;

71

And many a sinke pour'd out her rage anenst'hem;
But still their valour, and their vertue fenc't'hem,
And, on they went, like Castor brave, and Pollux:
Ploughing the mayne. When, see (the worst of all
 lucks)
They met the second Prodigie, would feare a
Man, that had never heard of a Chimæra.   60
One said, it was the bold Briareus, or the beadle,
(Who hath the hundred hands when he doth
 meddle)
The other thoueht it Hydra, or the rock
Made of the trull, that cut her fathers lock:
But, comming neere, they found it but a liter,
So huge, it seem'd, they could by no meanes quite
 her.
Backe, cry'd their brace of Charons: they cry'd, no,
No going backe; on still you rogues, and row.
How hight the place? a voyce was heard, Cocytus.
Row close then slaves. Alas, they will beshite us. 70
No matter, stinkards, row. What croaking sound
Is this we heare? of frogs? No, guts wind-bound,
Over your heads: Well, row. At this a loud
Crack did report it selfe, as if a cloud
Had burst with storme, and downe fell, *ab excelsis*,
Poore Mercury, crying out on Paracelsus,
And all his followers, that had so abus'd him:
And, in so shitten sort, so long had us'd him:
For (where he was the god of eloquence,
And subtiltie of mettalls) they dispense   80
His spirits, now, in pills, and eeke in potions,
Suppositories, cataplasmes, and lotions.
But many Moones there shall not wane (quoth hee)
(In the meane time, let 'hem imprison mee)
But I will speake (and know I shall be heard)
Touching this cause, where they will be affeard
To answere me. And sure, it was th'intent
Of the grave fart, late let in parliament,

Had it beene seconded, and not in fume
Vanish'd away: as you must all presume   90
Their Mercury did now. By this, the stemme
Of the hulke touch'd, and, as by Polypheme
The slie Ulysses stole in a sheepes-skin,
The well-greas'd wherry now had got betweene,
And bad her fare-well sough, unto the lurden:
Never did bottome more betray her burden;
The meate-boate of Beares colledge, Paris-garden,
Stunke not so ill; nor, when shee kist, Kate Arden.
Yet, one day in the yeere, for sweet 'tis voyc't,
And that is when it is the Lord Maiors foist.   100
  By this time had they reach'd the Stygian poole,
By which the Masters sweare, when, on the stoole
Of worship, they their nodding chinnes doe hit
Against their breasts. Here, sev'rall ghosts did flit
About the shore, of farts, but late departed,
White, black, blew, greene, and in more formes
       out-started,
Then all those Atomi ridiculous,
Whereof old Democrite, and Hill Nicholas,
One said, the other swore, the world consists.
These be the cause of those thicke frequent mists
Arising in that place, through which, who goes,   111
Must trie the un-used valour of a nose:
And that ours did. For, yet, no nare was tainted,
Nor thumbe, nor finger to the stop acquainted,
But open, and un-arm'd encounter'd all:
Whether it languishing stucke upon the wall,
Or were precipitated downe the jakes,
And, after, swom abroad in ample flakes,
Or, that it lay, heap'd like an usurers masse,
All was to them the same, they were to passe,   120
And so they did, from Stix, to Acheron:
The ever-boyling floud. Whose bankes upon

73

Your Fleet-lane Furies; and hot cookes doe dwell,
That, with still-scalding steemes, make the place
    hell.
The sinkes ran grease, and haire of meazled hogs,
The heads, houghs, entrailes, and the hides of dogs:
For, to say truth, what scullion is so nastie,
To put the skins, and offall in a pastie?
Cats there lay divers had beene flead, and rosted,
And, after mouldie growne, againe were tosted, 130
Then, selling not, a dish was tane to mince 'hem,
But still, it seem'd, the ranknesse did convince 'hem.
For, here they were throwne in with'the melted
    pewter,
Yet drown'd they not. They had five lives in future.
  But 'mongst these Tiberts, who do'you thinke
    there was?
Old Bankes the juggler, our Pythagoras,
Grave tutor to the learned horse. Both which,
Being, beyond sea, burned for one witch:
Their spirits transmigrated to a cat:
And, now, above the poole, a face right fat 140
With great gray eyes, are lifted up, and mew'd;
Thrise did it spit: thrise div'd. At last, it view'd
Our brave Heroes with a milder glare,
And, in a pittious tune, began. How dare
Your daintie nostrills (in so hot a season,
When every clerke eates artichokes, and peason,
Laxative lettuce, and such windie meate)
Tempt such a passage? when each privies seate
Is fill'd with buttock? And the walls doe sweate
Urine, and plaisters? when the noise doth beate 150
Upon your eares, of discords so un-sweet?
And out-cryes of the damned in the Fleet?
Cannot the Plague-bill keepe you backe? nor bells
Of loud Sepulchres with their hourely knells,
But you will visit grisly Pluto's hall?
Behold where Cerberus, rear'd on the wall

Of Hol'borne (three sergeants heads) lookes ore,
And stayes but till you come unto the dore!
Tempt not his furie, Pluto is away:
And Madame Caesar, great Proserpina,   160
Is now from home. You lose your labours quite,
Were you Jove's sonnes, or had Alcides might.
They cry'd out Pusse. He told them he was Bankes,
That had, so often, shew'd 'hem merry prankes.
They laugh't, at his laugh-worthy fate. And past
The tripple head without a sop. At last,
Calling for Radamanthus, that dwelt by,
A sope-boyler; and Æacus him nigh,
Who kept an ale-house; with my little Minos,
An ancient pur-blind fletcher, with a high nose;   170
They tooke 'hem all to witnesse of their action:
And so went bravely backe, without protraction.
    In memorie of which most liquid deed,
The citie since hath rais'd a Pyramide.
And I could wish for their eterniz'd sakes,
My Muse had plough'd with his, that sung A-JAX.

THE FORREST

I

Why I write not of Love

SOME act of Love's bound to reherse,
I thought to bind him, in my verse:
Which when he felt, Away (quoth hee)
Can Poets hope to fetter mee?
It is enough, they once did get
Mars, and my Mother, in their net:
I weare not these my wings in vaine.
With which he fled me: and againe,
Into my ri'mes could ne're be got
By any arte. Then wonder not,   10
That since, my numbers are so cold,
When Love is fled, and I grow old.

II

To Penshurst

THOU art not, Penshurst, built to envious show,
Of touch, or marble; nor canst boast a row
Of polish'd pillars, or a roofe of gold:
Thou hast no lantherne, whereof tales are told;
Or stayre, or courts; but stand'st an ancient pile,
And these grudg'd at, art reverenc'd the while.
Thou joy'st in better markes, of soyle, of ayre,
Of wood, of water: therein thou art faire.
Thou hast thy walkes for health, as well as sport:
Thy Mount, to which the Dryads doe resort,   10
Where Pan, and Bacchus their high feasts have made,
Beneath the broad beech, and the chest-nut shade;

76

That taller tree, which of a nut was set,
At his great birth, where all the Muses met.
There, in the writhed barke, are cut the names
Of many a Sylvane, taken with his flames.
And thence, the ruddy Satyres oft provoke
The lighter Faunes, to reach thy Ladies oke.
Thy copp's, too, nam'd of Gamage, thou hast there,
That never failes to serve thee season'd deere,   20
When thou would'st feast, or exercise thy friends.
The lower land, that to the river bends,
Thy sheepe, thy bullocks, kine, and calves doe feed:
The middle grounds thy mares, and horses breed.
Each banke doth yeeld thee coneyes; and the topps
Fertile of wood, Ashore, and Sydney's copp's,
To crowne thy open table, doth provide
The purpled pheasant, with the speckled side:
The painted partrich lyes in every field,
And, for thy messe, is willing to be kill'd.   30
And if the high swolne Medway faile thy dish,
Thou hast thy ponds, that pay thee tribute fish,
Fat, aged carps, that runne into thy net.
And pikes, now weary their owne kinde to eat,
As loth, the second draught, or cast to stay,
Officiously, at first, themselves betray.
Bright eeles, that emulate them, and leape on land,
Before the fisher, or into his hand.
Then hath thy orchard fruit, thy garden flowers,
Fresh as the ayre, and new as are the houres.   40
The earely cherry, with the later plum,
Fig, grape, and quince, each in his time doth come:
The blushing apricot, and woolly peach
Hang on thy walls, that every child may reach.
And though thy walls be of the countrey stone,
They'are rear'd with no mans ruine, no mans grone,
There's none, that dwell about them, wish them
        downe;
But all come in, the farmer, and the clowne:

And no one empty-handed, to salute
Thy lord, and lady, though they have no sute.   50
Some bring a capon, some a rurall cake,
Some nuts, some apples; some that thinke they make
The better cheeses, bring 'hem; or else send
By their ripe daughters, whom they would commend
This way to husbands; and whose baskets beare
An embleme of themselves, in plum, or peare.
But what can this (more then expresse their love)
Adde to thy free provisions, farre above
The neede of such? whose liberall boord doth flow,
With all, that hospitalitie doth know!   60
Where comes no guest, but is allow'd to eate,
Without his feare, and of the lords owne meate:
Where the same beere, and bread, and self-same wine,
That is his Lordships, shall be also mine.
And I not faine to sit (as some, this day,
At great mens tables) and yet dine away.
Here no man tells my cups; nor, standing by,
A waiter, doth my gluttony envy:
But gives me what I call, and lets me eate,
He knowes, below, he shall finde plentie of meate,   70
Thy tables hoord not up for the next day,
Nor, when I take my lodging, need I pray
For fire, or lights, or livorie: all is there;
As if thou, then, wert mine, or I reign'd here:
There's nothing I can wish, for which I stay.
That found King James, when hunting late, this way,
With his brave sonne, the Prince, they saw thy fires
Shine bright on every harth as the desires
Of thy Penates had beene set on flame,
To entertayne them; or the countrey came,   80
With all their zeale, to warme their welcome here.
What (great, I will not say, but) sodayne cheare
Did'st thou, then, make 'hem! and what praise was
    heap'd
On thy good lady, then! who, therein, reap'd

The just reward of her high huswifery;
To have her linnen, plate, and all things nigh,
When shee was farre: and not a roome, but drest,
As if it had expected such a guest!
These, Penshurst, are thy praise, and yet not all.
Thy lady's noble, fruitfull, chaste withall.   90
His children thy great lord may call his owne:
A fortune, in this age, but rarely knowne.
They are, and have beene taught religion: Thence
Their gentler spirits have suck'd innocence.
Each morne, and even, they are taught to pray,
With the whole houshold, and may, every day,
Reade, in their vertuous parents noble parts,
The mysteries of manners, armes, and arts.
Now, Penshurst, they that will proportion thee
With other edifices, when they see   100
Those proud, ambitious heaps, and nothing else,
May say, their lords have built, but thy lord dwells.

III

To Sir Robert Wroth

How blest art thou, canst love the countrey, Wroth,
    Whether by choice, or fate, or both;
And, though so neere the citie, and the court,
    Art tane with neithers vice, nor sport:
That at great times, art no ambitious guest
    Of Sheriffes dinner, or Maiors feast.
Nor com'st to view the better cloth of state;
    The richer hangings, or crowne-plate;
Nor throng'st (when masquing is) to have a sight
    Of the short braverie of the night;   10
To view the jewells, stuffes, the paines, the wit
    There wasted, some not paid for yet!

But canst, at home, in thy securer rest,
   Live, with un-bought provision blest;
Free from proud porches, or their guilded roofes,
   'Mongst loughing heards, and solide hoofes:
Along'st the curled woods, and painted meades,
   Through which a serpent river leades
To some coole, courteous shade, which he calls his,
   And makes sleepe softer then it is!   20
Or, if thou list the night in watch to breake,
   A-bed canst heare the loud stag speake,
In spring, oft roused for thy masters sport,
   Who, for it, makes thy house his court;
Or with thy friends; the heart of all the yeere,
   Divid'st, upon the lesser Deere;
In autumne, at the Partrich makes a flight,
   And giv'st thy gladder guests the sight;
And, in the winter, hunt'st the flying hare,
   More for thy exercise, then fare;   30
While all, that follow, their glad eares apply
   To the full greatnesse of the cry:
Or hauking at the river, or the bush,
   Or shooting at the greedie thrush,
Thou dost with some delight the day out-weare,
   Although the coldest of the yeere!
The whil'st, the severall seasons thou has seene
   Of flowrie fields, of cop'ces greene,
The mowed meddowes, with the fleeced sheepe,
   And feasts, that either shearers keepe;   40
The ripened eares, yet humble in their height,
   And furrowes laden with their weight;
The apple-harvest, that doth longer last;
   The hogs return'd home fat from mast;
The trees cut out in log; and those boughes made
   A fire now, that lent a shade!
Thus Pan, and Sylvane, having had their rites,
   Comus puts in, for new delights;

And fills thy open hall with mirth, and cheere,
    As if in Saturnes raigne it were;   50
Apollo's harpe, and Hermes lyre resound,
    Nor are the Muses strangers found:
The rout of rurall folke come thronging in,
    (Their rudenesse then is thought no sinne)
Thy noblest spouse affords them welcome grace;
    And the great Heroes, of her race,
Sit mixt with losse of state, or reverence.
    Freedome doth with degree dispense.
The jolly wassall walkes the often round,
    And in their cups, their cares are drown'd: 60
They thinke not, then, which side the cause shall
      leese,
    Nor how to get the lawyer fees.
Such, and no other was that age, of old,
    Which boasts t'have had the head of gold.
And such since thou canst make thine owne
      content,
    Strive, Wroth, to live long innocent.
Let others watch in guiltie armes, and stand
    The furie of a rash command,
Goe enter breaches, meet the cannons rage,
    That they may sleepe with scarres in age.   70
And shew their feathers shot, and cullors torne,
    And brag, that they were therefore borne.
Let this man sweat, and wrangle at the barre,
    For every price, in every jarre,
And change possessions, oftner with his breath,
    Then either money, warre, or death:
Let him, then hardest sires, more disinherit,
    And each where boast it as his merit,
To blow up orphanes, widdowes, and their states;
    And thinke his power doth equall Fates.   80
Let that goe heape a masse of wretched wealth,
    Purchas'd by rapine, worse then stealth,

And brooding o're it sit, with broadest eyes,
    Not doing good, scarce when he dyes.
Let thousands more goe flatter vice, and winne,
    By being organes to great sinne,
Get place, and honor, and be glad to keepe
    The secrets, that shall breake their sleepe:
And, so they ride in purple, eate in plate,
    Though poyson, thinke it a great fate.   90
But thou, my Wroth, if I can truth apply,
    Shalt neither that, nor this envy:
Thy peace is made; and, when man's state is well,
    'Tis better, if he there can dwell.
God wisheth, none should wracke on a strange
    shelfe:
    To him, man's dearer, then t'himselfe.
And, howsoever we may thinke things sweet,
    He alwayes gives what he knowes meet;
Which who can use is happy: Such be thou.
    Thy morning's, and thy evening's vow   100
Be thankes to him, and earnest prayer, to finde
    A body sound, with sounder minde;
To doe thy countrey service, thy selfe right;
    That neither want doe thee affright,
Nor death; but when thy latest sand is spent,
    Thou maist thinke life, a thing but lent.

IV

To the World

A FAREWELL FOR A GENTLE-WOMAN, VERTUOUS
AND NOBLE

FALSE world, good-night: since thou hast brought
    That houre upon my morne of age,
Hence-forth I quit thee from my thought,
    My part is ended on thy stage.

Doe not once hope, that thou canst tempt
   A spirit so resolv'd to tread
Upon thy throate, and live exempt
   From all the nets that thou canst spread.
I know thy formes are studied arts,
   Thy subtle wayes, be narrow straits;   10
Thy curtesie but sodaine starts,
   And what thou call'st thy gifts are baits.
I know too, though thou strut, and paint,
   Yet art thou both shrunke up, and old,
That onely fooles make thee a saint,
   And all thy good is to be sold.
I know thou whole art but a shop
   Of toyes, and trifles, traps, and snares,
To take the weake, or make them stop:
   Yet art thou falser then thy wares.   20
And, knowing this, should I yet stay,
   Like such as blow away their lives,
And never will redeeme a day,
   Enamor'd of their golden gyves?
Or, having scap'd, shall I returne,
   And thrust my necke into the noose,
From whence, so lately, I did burne,
   With all my powers, my selfe to loose?
What bird, or beast, is knowne so dull,
   That fled his cage, or broke his chaine,   30
And tasting ayre, and freedome, wull
   Render his head in there againe?
If these, who have but sense, can shun
   The engines, that have them annoy'd;
Little, for me, had reason done,
   If I could not thy ginnes avoyd.
Yes, threaten, doe. Alas I feare
   As little, as I hope from thee:
I know thou canst nor shew, nor beare
   More hatred, then thou hast to mee.   40

My tender, first, and simple yeeres
    Thou did'st abuse, and then betray;
Since stird'st up jealousies and feares,
    When all the causes were away.
Then, in a soile hast planted me,
    Where breathe the basest of thy fooles;
Where envious arts professed be,
    And pride, and ignorance the schooles,
Where nothing is examin'd, weigh'd,
    But, as 'tis rumor'd, so beleev'd: 50
Where every freedome is betray'd,
    And every goodnesse tax'd, or griev'd.
But, what we'are borne for, we must beare:
    Our fraile condition it is such,
That, what to all may happen here,
    If't chance to me, I must not grutch.
Else, I my state should much mistake,
    To harbour a divided thought
From all my kinde: that, for my sake,
    There should a miracle be wrought.   60
No, I doe know, that I was borne
    To age, misfortune, sicknesse, griefe:
But I will beare these, with that scorne,
    As shall not need thy false reliefe.
Nor for my peace will I goe farre,
    As wandrers doe, that still doe rome,
But make my strengths, such as they are,
    Here in my bosome, and at home.

v

Song. To Celia

COME my Celia, let us prove,
    While we may, the sports of love;

Time will not be ours, for ever:
He, at length, our good will sever.
Spend not then his guifts in vaine.
Sunnes, that set, may rise againe:
But if once we loose this light,
'Tis, with us, perpetuall night.
Why should we deferre our joyes?
Fame, and rumor are but toyes.   10
Cannot we delude the eyes
Of a few poore houshold spyes?
Or his easier eares beguile,
So removed by our wile?
'Tis no sinne, loves fruit to steale,
But the sweet theft to reveale:
To be taken, to be seene,
These have crimes accounted beene.

VI

To the same

KISSE me, sweet: The warie lover
Can your favours keepe, and cover,
When the common courting jay
All your bounties will betray.
Kisse againe: no creature comes.
Kisse, and score up wealthy summes
On my lips, thus hardly sundred,
While you breath. First give a hundred,
Then a thousand, then another
Hundred, then unto the tother   10
Adde a thousand, and so more:
Till you equall with the store,
All the grasse that Rumney yeelds,
Or the sands in Chelsey fields,

Or the drops in silver Thames,
Or the starres, that guild his streames,
In the silent sommer-nights,
When youths ply their stolne delights.
That the curious may not know
How to tell 'hem, as they flow,   20
And the envious, when they find
What their number is, be pin'd.

VII

Song. That Women are but Mens shaddowes

FOLLOW a shaddow, it still flies you;
Seeme to flye it, it will pursue:
So court a mistris, shee denyes you;
Let her alone, shee will court you.
Say, are not women truely, then,
Stil'd but the shaddowes of us men?
At morne, and even, shades are longest;
At noone, they are or short, or none:
So men at weakest, they are strongest,
But grant us perfect, they're not knowne.   10
Say, are not women truely, then,
Stil'd but the shaddowes of us men?

VIII

To Sicknesse

WHY, Disease, dost thou molest
Ladies? and of them the best?
Doe not men, ynow of rites
To thy altars, by their nights

Spent in surfets: and their dayes,
And nights too, in worser wayes?
Take heed, Sicknesse, what you doe,
I shall feare, you'll surfet too.
Live not we, as, all thy stalls,
Spittles, pest-house, hospitalls,   10
Scarce will take our present store?
And this age will build no more:
'Pray thee, feed contented, then,
Sicknesse; onely on us men.
Or if needs thy lust will tast
Woman-kinde; devoure the wast
Livers, round about the towne.
But, forgive me, with thy crowne
They maintayne the truest trade,
And have more diseases made.   20
What should, yet, thy pallat please?
Daintinesse, and softer ease,
Sleeked limmes, and finest blood?
If thy leanenesse love such food,
There are those, that, for thy sake,
Doe enough; and who would take
Any paines; yea, thinke it price,
To become thy sacrifice.
That distill their husbands land
In decoctions; and are mann'd   30
With ten Emp'ricks, in their chamber,
Lying for the spirit of amber.
That for th'oyle of Talke, dare spend
More then citizens dare lend
Them, and all their officers.
That, to make all pleasure theirs,
Will by coach, and water goe,
Every stew in towne to know;
Dare entayle their loves on any,
Bald, or blinde, or nere so many: 40

And, for thee, at common game,
Play away, health, wealth, and fame.
These, disease, will thee deserve:
And will, long ere thou should'st starve,
On their beds, most prostitute,
Move it, as their humblest sute,
In thy justice to molest
None but them, and leave the rest.

IX

Song. To Celia

DRINKE to me, onely, with thine eyes,
   And I will pledge with mine;
Or leave a kisse but in the cup,
   And Ile not looke for wine.
The thirst, that from the soule doth rise,
   Doth aske a drinke divine:
But might I of Jove's Nectar sup,
   I would not change for thine.
I sent thee, late, a rosie wreath,
   Not so much honoring thee,   10
As giving it a hope, that there
   It could not withered bee.
But thou thereon did'st onely breath,
   And sent'st it backe to mee:
Since when it growes, and smells, I sweare,
   Not of it selfe, but thee.

X

AND must I sing? what subject shall I chuse?
Or whose great name in Poets heaven use?
For the more countenance to my active Muse?

Hercules? alas his bones are yet sore,
With his old earthly labours. T'exact more,
Of his dull god-head, were sinne. Ile implore

Phœbus. No? tend thy cart still. Envious day
Shall not give out, that I have made thee stay,
And foundred thy hot teame, to tune my lay.

Nor will I beg of thee, Lord of the vine,   10
To raise my spirits with thy conjuring wine,
In the greene circle of thy Ivy twine.

Pallas, nor thee I call on, mankinde maid,
That, at thy birth, mad'st the poore Smith affraid,
Who, with his axe, thy fathers mid-wife plaid.

Goe, crampe dull Mars, light Venus, when he
   snorts,
Or, with thy Tribade trine, invent new sports,
Thou, nor thy loosenesse with my making sorts.

Let the old boy, your sonne, ply his old taske,
Turne the stale prologue to some painted maske, 20
His absence in my verse, is all I aske.

Hermes, the cheater, shall not mix with us,
Though he would steale his sisters Pegasus,
And riffle him: or pawne his Petasus.

Nor all the ladies of the Thespian lake,
(Though they were crusht into one forme) could
   make
A beautie of that merit, that should take

My Muse up by commission: No, I bring
My owne true fire. Now my thought takes wing,
And now an Epode to deepe eares I sing.   30

XI

Epode

NOT to know vice at all, and keepe true state,
    Is vertue, and not Fate:
Next, to that vertue, is to know vice well,
    And her blacke spight expell.
Which to effect (since no brest is so sure,
    Or safe, but shee'll procure
Some way of entrance) we must plant a guard
    Of thoughts to watch, and ward
At th'eye and eare (the ports unto the minde)
    That no strange, or unkinde   10
Object arrive there, but the heart (our spie)
    Give knowledge instantly,
To wakefull reason, our affections king:
    Who (in the'examining)
Will quickly taste the treason, and commit
    Close, the close cause of it.
'Tis the securest policie we have,
    To make our sense our slave.
But this true course is not embrac'd by many:
    By many? scarse by any.   20
For either our affections doe rebell,
    Or else the sentinell
(That should ring larum to the heart) doth sleepe,
    Or some great thought doth keepe
Backe the intelligence, and falsely sweares,
    Th'are base, and idle feares
Whereof the loyall conscience so complaines.
    Thus, by these subtle traines,
Doe severall passions invade the minde,
    And strike our reason blinde.   30
Of which usurping rancke, some have thought love
    The first; as prone to move

Most frequent tumults, horrors, and unrests,
    In our enflamed brests:
But this doth from the cloud of error grow,
    Which thus we over-blow.
The thing, they here call Love, is blinde Desire,
    Arm'd with bow, shafts, and fire;
Inconstant, like the sea, of whence 'tis borne,
    Rough, swelling, like a storme: 40
With whom who sailes, rides on the surge of feare,
    And boyles, as if he were
In a continuall tempest. Now, true Love
    No such effects doth prove;
That is an essence farre more gentle, fine,
    Pure, perfect, nay divine;
It is a golden chaine let downe from heaven,
    Whose linkes are bright, and even.
That falls like sleepe on lovers, and combines
    The soft, and sweetest mindes   50
In equall knots: This beares no brands, nor darts,
    To murther different hearts,
But, in a calme, and god-like unitie,
    Preserves communitie.
O, who is he, that (in this peace) enjoyes
    Th'Elixir of all joyes?
A forme more fresh, then are the Eden bowers,
    And lasting, as her flowers:
Richer then Time, and as Time's vertue, rare.
    Sober, as saddest care: 60
A fixed thought, an eye un-taught to glance;
    Who (blest with such high chance)
Would, at suggestion of a steepe desire,
    Cast himselfe from the spire
Of all his happinesse? But soft: I heare
    Some vicious foole draw neare,
That cryes, we dreame, and sweares, there's no such
        thing,
    As this chaste love we sing.

K   91

Peace, Luxurie, thou art like one of those
    Who, being at sea, suppose,   70
Because they move, the continent doth so:
    No, vice, we let thee know
Though thy wild thoughts with sparrowes wings
      doe flye,
    Turtles can chastly dye;
And yet (in this t'expresse our selves more cleare)
    We doe not number, here,
Such spirits as are onely continent,
    Because lust's meanes are spent:
Or those, who doubt the common mouth of fame,
    And for their place, and name,   80
Cannot so safely sinne. Their chastitie
    Is meere necessitie.
Nor meane we those, whom vowes and conscience
    Have fill'd with abstinence:
Though we acknowledge, who can so abstayne,
    Makes a most blessed gayne.
He that for love of goodnesse hateth ill,
    Is more crowne-worthy still,
Then he, which for sinnes penaltie forbeares.
    His heart sinnes, though he feares.   90
But we propose a person like our Dove,
    Grac'd with a Phœnix love;
A beautie of that cleere, and sparkling light,
    Would make a day of night,
And turne the blackest sorrowes to bright joyes:
    Whose od'rous breath destroyes
All taste of bitternesse, and makes the ayre
    As sweet, as shee is fayre.
A body so harmoniously compos'd,
    As if Nature disclos'd   100
All her best symmetrie in that one feature!
    O, so divine a creature
Who could be false to? chiefly, when he knowes
    How onely shee bestowes

The wealthy treasure of her love on him;
    Making his fortunes swim
In the full floud of her admir'd perfection?
    What savage, brute affection,
Would not be fearefull to offend a dame
    Of this excelling frame?   110
Much more a noble, and right generous mind
    (To vertuous moods inclin'd)
That knowes the waight of guilt: He will refraine
    From thoughts of such a straine.
And to his sense object this sentence ever,
    Man may securely sinne, but safely never.

XII

Epistle to Elizabeth Countesse of Rutland

MADAME,
Whil'st that, for which, all vertue now is sold,
And almost every vice, almightie gold,
That which, to boote with hell, is thought worth
    heaven,
And, for it, life, conscience, yea, soules are given,
Toyles, by grave custome, up and downe the court,
To every squire, or groome, that will report
Well, or ill, onely, all the following yeere,
Just to the waight their this dayes-presents beare;
While it makes huishers serviceable men,
And some one apteth to be trusted, then,   10
Though never after; whiles it gaynes the voyce
Of some grand peere, whose ayre doth make rejoyce
The foole that gave it; who will want, and weepe,
When his proud patrons favours are asleepe;
While thus it buyes great grace, and hunts poore fame;
Runs betweene man, and man; 'tweene dame, and
    dame;

Solders crackt friendship; makes love last a day;
Or perhaps lesse: whil'st gold beares all this sway,
I, that have none (to send you) send you verse.
A present, which (if elder writs reherse   20
The truth of times) was once of more esteeme,
Then this, our guilt, nor golden age can deeme,
When gold was made no weapon to cut throtes,
Or put to flight Astrea, when her ingots
Were yet unfound, and better plac'd in earth,
Then, here, to give pride fame, and peasants birth.
But let this drosse carry what price it will
With noble ignorants, and let them still,
Turne, upon scorned verse, their quarter-face:
With you, I know, my offring will find grace.   30
For what a sinne 'gainst your great fathers spirit,
Were it to thinke, that you should not inherit
His love unto the Muses, when his skill
Almost you have, or may have, when you will?
Wherein wise Nature you a dowrie gave,
Worth an estate, treble to that you have.
Beautie, I know, is good, and bloud is more;
Riches thought most: But, Madame, thinke what
    store
The world hath seene, which all these had in trust,
And now lye lost in their forgotten dust.   40
It is the Muse, alone, can raise to heaven,
And, at her strong armes end, hold up, and even,
The soules, shee loves. Those other glorious notes,
Inscrib'd in touch or marble, or the cotes
Painted, or carv'd upon our great-mens tombs,
Or in their windowes; doe but prove the wombs,
That bred them, graves: when they were borne, they
    di'd,
That had no Muse to make their fame abide.
How many equall with the Argive Queene,
Have beautie knowne, yet none so famous seene?   50

Achilles was not first, that valiant was,
Or, in an armies head, that, lockt in brasse,
Gave killing strokes. There were brave men, before
Ajax, or Idomen, or all the store,
That Homer brought to Troy; yet none so live:
Because they lack'd the sacred pen, could give
Like life unto 'hem. Who heav'd Hercules
Unto the starres? or the Tyndarides?
Who placed Jasons Argo in the skie?
Or set bright Ariadnes crowne so high?   60
Who made a lampe of Berenices hayre?
Or lifted Cassiopea in her chayre?
But onely Poets, rapt with rage divine?
And such, or my hopes faile, shall make you shine.
You, and that other starre, that purest light,
Of all Lucina's traine; Lucy the bright.
Then which, a nobler heaven it selfe knowes not.
Who, though shee have a better verser got,
(Or Poet, in the court account) then I,
And, who doth me (though I not him) envy,   70
Yet, for the timely favours shee hath done,
To my lesse sanguine Muse, wherein she'hath wonne
My gratefull soule, the subject of her powers,
I have already us'd some happy houres,
To her remembrance; which when time shall bring
To curious light, to notes, I then shall sing,
Will prove old Orpheus act no tale to be:
For I shall move stocks, stones, no lesse then he.
Then all, that have but done my Muse least grace,
Shall thronging come, and boast the happy place   80
They hold in my strange poems, which, as yet,
Had not their forme touch'd by an English wit.
There like a rich, and golden pyramede,
Borne up by statues, shall I reare your head,
Above your under-carved ornaments,
And show, how, to the life, my soule presents

Your forme imprest there: not with tickling rimes,
Or common-places, filch'd, that take these times,
But high, and noble matter, such as flies
From braines entranc'd, and fill'd with extasies;   90
Moodes, which the god-like Sydney oft did prove,
And your brave friend, and mine so well did love.
Who wheresoere he be, on what dear coast,
Now thincking on you, though to England lost,
For that firme grace he holdes in your regard,
I, that am gratefull for him, have prepar'd
This hasty sacrifice, wherein I reare
A vow as new, and ominous as the yeare,
Before his swift and circled race be run,
My best of wishes, may you beare a sonne.   100

XIII

Epistle. To Katherine, Lady Aubigny

'TIS growne almost a danger to speake true
Of any good minde, now: There are so few.
The bad, by number, are so fortified,
As what th'have lost t'expect, they dare deride.
So both the prais'd, and praisers suffer: Yet,
For others ill, ought none their good forget.
I, therefore, who professe my selfe in love
With every vertue, wheresoere it move,
And howsoever; as I am at fewd
With sinne and vice, though with a throne endew'd;
And, in this name, am given out dangerous   11
By arts, and practise of the vicious,
Such as suspect them-selves, and thinke it fit
For their owne cap'tall crimes, t'indite my wit;
I, that have suffer'd this; and, though forsooke
Of Fortune, have not alter'd yet my looke,

Or so my selfe abandon'd, as because
Men are not just, or keepe no holy lawes
Of nature, and societie, I should faint;
Or feare to draw true lines, 'cause others paint: 20
I, Madame, am become your praiser. Where,
If it may stand with your soft blush to heare,
Your selfe but told unto your selfe, and see
In my character, what your features bee,
You will not from the paper slightly passe:
No lady, but, at some time, loves her glasse.
And this shall be no false one, but as much
Remov'd, as you from need to have it such.
Looke then, and see your selfe. I will not say
Your beautie; for you see that every day: 30
And so doe many more. All which can call
It perfect, proper, pure, and naturall,
Not taken up o'th'doctors, but as well
As I, can say, and see it doth excell.
That askes but to be censur'd by the eyes:
And, in those outward formes, all fooles are wise.
Nor that your beautie wanted not a dower,
Doe I reflect. Some alderman has power,
Or cos'ning farmer of the customes so,
T'advance his doubtfull issue, and ore-flow   40
A Princes fortune: These are gifts of chance,
And raise not vertue; they may vice enhance.
My mirror is more subtile, cleere, refin'd,
And takes, and gives the beauties of the mind.
Though it reject not those of Fortune: such
As bloud, and match. Wherein, how more then
   much
Are you engaged to your happy fate,
For such a lot! that mixt you with a state
Of so great title, birth, but vertue most,
Without which, all the rest were sounds, or lost.   50
'Tis onely that can time, and chance defeat:
For he, that once is good, is ever great.

Wherewith, then, Madame, can you better pay
This blessing of your starres, then by that way
Of vertue, which you tread? what if alone?
Without companions? 'Tis safe to have none.
In single paths, dangers with ease are watch'd:
Contagion in the prease is soonest catch'd.
This makes, that wisely you decline your life,
Farre from the maze of custome, error, strife,   60
And keepe an even, and unalter'd gaite;
Not looking by, or backe (like those, that waite
Times, and occasions, to start forth, and seeme)
Which though the turning world may dis-esteeme,
Because that studies spectacles, and showes,
And after varyed, as fresh objects goes,
Giddie with change, and therefore cannot see
Right, the right way: yet must your comfort bee
Your conscience, and not wonder, if none askes
For truthes complexion, where they all weare
    maskes.   70
Let who will follow fashions, and attyres,
Maintayne their liedgers forth, for forraine wyres,
Melt downe their husbands land, to poure away
On the close groome, and page, on new-yeeres day,
And almost, all dayes after, while they live;
(They finde it both so wittie, and safe to give.)
Let 'hem on poulders, oyles, and paintings, spend,
Till that no usurer, nor his bawds dare lend
Them, or their officers: and no man know,
Whether it be a face they weare, or no.   80
Let 'hem waste body, and state; and after all,
When their owne Parasites laugh at their fall,
May they have nothing left, whereof they can
Boast, but how oft they have gone wrong to man:
And call it their brave sinne. For such there be
That doe sinne onely for the infamie:
And never thinke, how vice doth every houre,
Eate on her clients, and some one devoure.

You, Madame, yong have learn'd to shunne these
   shelves,
Whereon the most of mankinde wracke themselves,
And, keeping a just course, have earely put   91
Into your harbor, and all passage shut
'Gainst stormes, or pyrats, that might charge your
   peace;
For which you worthy are the glad encrease
Of your blest wombe, made fruitfull from above,
To pay your lord the pledges of chast love:
And raise a noble stemme, to give the fame,
To Clifton's bloud, that is deny'd their name.
Grow, grow, faire tree, and as thy branches shoote,
Heare, what the Muses sing about thy roote,   100
By me, their priest (if they can ought divine)
Before the moones have fill'd their tripple trine,
To crowne the burthen which you goe withall,
It shall a ripe and timely issue fall,
T'expect the honors of great 'Aubigny:
And greater rites, yet writ in mysterie,
But which the Fates forbid me to reveale.
Onely, thus much, out of a ravish'd zeale,
Unto your name, and goodnesse of your life,
They speake; since you are truely that rare wife,   110
Other great wives may blush at: when they see
What your try'd manners are, what theirs should bee.
How you love one, and him you should; how still
You are depending on his word, and will;
Not fashion'd for the court, or strangers eyes;
But to please him, who is the dearer prise
Unto himselfe, by being so deare to you.
This makes, that your affections still be new,
And that your soules conspire, as they were gone
Each into other, and had now made one.   120
Live that one, still; and as long yeeres doe passe,
Madame, be bold to use this truest glasse:

Wherein, your forme, you still the same shall finde;
Because nor it can change, nor such a minde.

XIV

Ode. To Sir William Sydney,
on his Birth-day

Now that the harth is crown'd with smiling fire,
    And some doe drinke, and some doe dance,
        Some ring,
        Some sing,
    And all doe strive t'advance
The gladnesse higher:
        Wherefore should I
        Stand silent by,
        Who not the least,
    Both love the cause, and authors of the feast?
Give me my cup, but from the Thespian well,   11
    That I may tell to Sydney, what
        This day
        Doth say,
    And he may thinke on that
Which I doe tell:
      When all the noyse
      Of these forc'd joyes,
        Are fled and gone,
      And he, with his best Genius left alone.   20
This day sayes, then, the number of glad yeeres
    Are justly summ'd, that make you man;
        Your vow
        Must now
    Strive all right wayes it can,
T'out-strip your peeres:
        Since he doth lacke
        Of going backe

Little, whose will
Doth urge him to runne wrong, or to stand
  still.   30
Nor can a little of the common store,
 Of nobles vertue, shew in you;
   Your blood
   So good
 And great, must seeke for new,
And studie more:
  Not weary, rest
  On what's deceast.
   For they, that swell
   With dust of ancestors, in graves but dwell. 40
'Twill be exacted of your name, whose sonne,
 Whose nephew, whose grand-child you are;
   And men
   Will, then,
 Say you have follow'd farre,
When well begunne:
  Which must be now,
  They teach you, how.
   And he that stayes
   To live untill to morrow'hath lost two dayes.
So may you live in honor, as in name, 51
 If with this truth you be inspir'd,
   So may
   This day
 Be more, and long desir'd:
And with the flame
  Of love be bright,
  As with the light
   Of bone-fires. Then
   The Birth-day shines, when logs not burne,
    but men.   60

XV

To Heaven

GOOD, and great God, can I not thinke of thee,
But it must, straight, my melancholy bee?
Is it interpreted in me disease,
That, laden with my sinnes, I seeke for ease?
O, be thou witnesse, that the reynes dost know,
And hearts of all, if I be sad for show,
And judge me after: if I dare pretend
To ought but grace, or ayme at other end.
As thou art all, so be thou all to mee,
First, midst, and last, converted one, and three;   10
My faith, my hope, my love: and in this state,
My judge, my witnesse, and my advocate.
Where have I beene this while exil'd from thee?
And whither rap'd, now thou but stoup'st to mee?
Dwell, dwell here still: O, being every-where,
How can I doubt to finde thee ever, here?
I know my state, both full of shame, and scorne,
Conceiv'd in sinne, and unto labour borne,
Standing with feare, and must with horror fall,
And destin'd unto judgement, after all.   20
I feele my griefes too, and there scarce is ground,
Upon my flesh t'inflict another wound.
Yet dare I not complaine, or wish for death
With holy Paul, lest it be thought the breath
Of discontent; or that these prayers bee
For wearinesse of life, not love of thee.

THE UNDER-WOOD

1640

MARTIAL: *Cineri, gloria sera venit.*

UNDER-WOODS.

CONSISTING OF
DIVERS
POEMS.

By

BEN. IOHNSON.

Martial—— *Cineri, gloria fera venit.*

LONDON.
Printed M. DC. XL.

TO THE READER

WITH the same leave the Ancients call'd that kind of body *Sylva*, or *Hule*, in which there were workes of divers nature, and matter congested; as the multitude call Timber-trees, promiscuously growing, a Wood, or Forrest: so am I bold to entitle these lesser Poems, of later growth, by this of Under-wood, out of the Analogie they hold to the *Forrest*, in my former booke, and no otherwise.

BEN. JONSON.

L

Poems of Devotion

1. THE SINNERS SACRIFICE

To the Holy Trinitie

O HOLY, blessed, glorious Trinitie
Of persons, still one God, in Unitie,
The faithfull mans beleeved Mysterie,
    Helpe, helpe to lift
My selfe up to thee, harrow'd, torne, and bruis'd
By sinne, and Sathan; and my flesh misus'd,
As my heart lies in peeces, all confus'd,
    O take my gift.
All-gracious God, the Sinners sacrifice,
A broken heart thou wert not wont despise,   10
But 'bove the fat of rammes, or bulls, to prize
    An offring meet,
For thy acceptance. O, behold me right,
And take compassion on my grievous plight.
What odour can be, then a heart contrite,
    To thee more sweet?
Eternall Father, God, who did'st create
This All of nothing, gavest it forme, and fate,
And breath'st into 't, life, and light, with state
    To worship thee.   20
Eternall God the Sonne, who not denyd'st
To take our nature; becam'st man, and dyd'st,
To pay our debts, upon thy Crosse, and cryd'st
    All's done in me.
Eternall Spirit, God from both proceeding,
Father and Sonne; the Comforter, in breeding
Pure thoughts in man: with fiery zeale them feeding
    For acts of grace.

Increase those acts, O glorious Trinitie
Of persons, still one God in Unitie;   30
Till I attaine the long'd-for mysterie
   Of seeing your face.
Beholding one in three, and three in one,
A Trinitie, to shine in Unitie;
The gladdest light, darke man can thinke upon;
   O grant it me!
Father, and Sonne, and Holy Ghost, you three
All coeternall in your Majestie,
Distinct in persons, yet in Unitie
   One God to see.   40
My Maker, Saviour, and my Sanctifier,
To heare, to meditate, sweeten my desire,
With grace, with love, with cherishing intire,
   O, then how blest;
Among thy Saints elected to abide,
And with thy Angels, placed side, by side,
But in thy presence, truly glorified
   Shall I there rest?

2. A HYMNE TO GOD THE FATHER

   HEARE mee, O God!
    A broken heart
    Is my best part:
   Use still thy rod,
    That I may prove
    Therein, thy Love.

   If thou hadst not
    Beene sterne to mee,
    But left me free,
   I had forgot   10
    My selfe and thee.

For, sin's so sweet,
   As minds ill bent
   Rarely repent,
Untill they meet
   Their punishment.

Who more can crave
   Then thou hast done:
   That gav'st a Sonne,
To free a slave?   20
   First made of nought;
   With all since bought.

Sinne, Death, and Hell,
   His glorious Name
   Quite overcame,
Yet I rebell,
   And slight the same.

But, I'le come in,
   Before my losse,
   Me farther tosse,   30
As sure to win
   Under his Crosse.

3. A HYMNE ON THE NATIVITIE OF MY SAVIOUR

I SING the birth, was borne to night,
The Author both of Life, and light;
   The Angels so did sound it,
And like the ravish'd Sheep'erds said,
Who saw the light, and were afraid,
   Yet search'd, and true they found it.

The Sonne of God, th'Eternall King,
That did us all salvation bring,
 And freed the soule from danger;
Hee whom the whole world could not take,   10
The Word, which heaven, and earth did make;
 Was now laid in a Manger.

The Fathers wisedome will'd it so,
The Sonnes obedience knew no No,
 Both wills were in one stature;
And as that wisedome had decreed,
The Word was now made Flesh indeed,
 And tooke on him our Nature.

What comfort by him doe wee winne?
Who made himselfe the price of sinne,   20
 To make us heires of glory?
To see this Babe, all innocence;
A Martyr borne in our defence;
 Can man forget this Storie?

II

A Celebration of Charis in Ten Lyrick Peeces

1. HIS EXCUSE FOR LOVING

Let it not your wonder move,
Lesse your laughter; that I love.
Though I now write fiftie yeares,
I have had, and have my Peeres;
Poets, though devine are men:
Some have lov'd as old agen.
And it is not always face,
Clothes, or Fortune gives the grace;

Or the feature, or the youth:
But the Language, and the Truth,   10
With the Ardor, and the Passion,
Gives the Lover weight, and fashion.
If you then will read the Storie,
First, prepare you to be sorie,
That you never knew till now,
Either whom to love, or how:
But be glad, as soone with me,
When you know, that this is she,
Of whose Beautie it was sung,
She shall make the old man young,   20
Keepe the middle age at stay,
And let nothing high decay,
Till she be the reason why,
All the world for love may die.

2. HOW HE SAW HER

I BEHELD her, on a Day,
When her looke out-flourisht May:
And her dressing did out-brave
All the Pride the fields than have:
Farre I was from being stupid,
For I ran and call'd on Cupid;
Love if thou wilt ever see
Marke of glorie, come with me;
Where's thy Quiver? bend thy Bow:
Here's a shaft, thou art to slow!   10
And (withall) I did untie
Every Cloud about his eye;
But, he had not gain'd his sight
Sooner, then he lost his might,
Or his courage; for away
Strait hee ran, and durst not stay,
Letting Bow and Arrow fall,
Nor for any threat, or Call,

Could be brought once back to looke.
I foole-hardie, there up tooke   20
Both the Arrow he had quit,
And the Bow: which thought to hit
This my object. But she threw
Such a Lightning (as I drew)
At my face, that tooke my sight,
And my motion from me quite;
So that there, I stood a stone,
Mock'd of all: and call'd of one
(Which with griefe and wrath I heard)
Cupids Statue with a Beard,   30
Or else one that plaid his Ape,
In a Hercules-his shape.

3. WHAT HEE SUFFERED

After many scornes like these,
Which the prouder Beauties please,
She content was to restore
Eyes and limbes; to hurt me more,
And would on Conditions, be
Reconcil'd to Love, and me:
First, that I must kneeling yeeld
Both the Bow, and shaft I held
Unto her; which Love might take
At her hand, with oath, to make   10
Mee, the scope of his next draught
Aymed, with that selfe-same shaft.
He no sooner heard the Law,
But the Arrow home did draw
And (to gaine her by his Art)
Left it sticking in my heart:
Which when she beheld to bleed,
She repented of the deed,
And would faine have chang'd the fate,
But the Pittie comes too late.   20

Looser-like, now, all my wreake
Is, that I have leave to speake,
And in either Prose, or Song,
To revenge me with my Tongue,
Which how Dexterously I doe
Heare and make Example too.

4. HER TRIUMPH

SEE the Chariot at hand here of Love
   Wherein my Lady rideth!
Each that drawes, is a Swan, or a Dove,
   And well the Carre Love guideth.
As she goes, all hearts doe duty
      Unto her beauty;
And enamour'd, doe wish, so they might
      But enjoy such a sight,
That they still were, to run by her side,
Through Swords, through Seas, whether she
     would ride.   10

Doe but looke on her eyes, they doe light
   All that Loves world compriseth!
Doe but looke on her Haire, it is bright
   As Loves starre when it riseth!
Doe but marke her forhead's smoother
      Then words that sooth her!
And from her arched browes, such a grace
      Sheds it selfe through the face,
As alone there triumphs to the life
All the Gaine, all the Good, of the Elements 20
     strife.

Have you seene but a bright Lillie grow,
   Before rude hands have touch'd it?
Ha' you mark'd but the fall o'the Snow
   Before the soyle hath smutch'd it?

Ha' you felt the wooll o' the Bever?
    Or Swans Downe ever?
Or have smelt o'the bud o' the Brier?
    Or the Nard in the fire?
Or have tasted the bag of the Bee?
O so white! O so soft! O so sweet is she!   30

5. HIS DISCOURSE WITH CUPID

NOBLEST Charis, you that are
Both my fortune, and my Starre!
And doe governe more my blood,
Then the various Moone the flood!
Heare, what late Discourse of you,
Love, and I have had; and true.
'Mongst my Muses finding me,
Where he chanc't your name to see
Set, and to this softer straine;
Sure, said he, if I have Braine,   10
This here sung, can be no other
By description, but my Mother!
So hath Homer prais'd her haire;
So, Anacreon drawne the Ayre
Of her face, and made to rise
Just about her sparkling eyes,
Both her Browes, bent like my Bow.
By her lookes I doe her know,
Which you call my Shafts. And see!
Such my Mothers blushes be,   20
As the Bath your verse discloses
In her cheekes, of Milke, and Roses;
Such as oft I wanton in;
And, above her even chin,
Have you plac'd the banke of kisses,
Where you say, men gather blisses,
Rip'ned with a breath more sweet,
Then when flowers, and West-winds meet.

116

Nay, her white and polish'd neck,
With the Lace that doth it deck,   30
Is my Mothers! Hearts of slaine
Lovers, made into a Chaine!
And betweene each rising breast,
Lyes the Valley, cal'd my nest,
Where I sit and proyne my wings
After flight; and put new stings
To my shafts! Her very Name,
With my Mothers is the same.
I confesse all, I replide,
And the Glasse hangs by her side,   40
And the Girdle 'bout her waste,
All is Venus: save unchaste.
But alas, thou seest the least
Of her good, who is the best
Of her Sex; But could'st thou, Love,
Call to mind the formes, that strove
For the Apple, and those three
Make in one, the same were shee.
For this Beauty yet doth hide,
Something more then thou hast spi'd.   50
Outward Grace weake love beguiles:
Shee is Venus, when she smiles,
But shee's Juno, when she walkes,
And Minerva, when she talkes.

6. CLAYMING A SECOND KISSE BY DESERT

CHARIS guesse, and doe not misse,
Since I drew a Morning kisse
From your lips, and suck'd an ayre
Thence, as sweet, as you are faire,
What my Muse and I have done:
Whether we have lost, or wonne,

If by us, the oddes were laid,
That the Bride (allow'd a Maid)
Look'd not halfe so fresh, and faire,
With th'advantage of her haire,   10
And her Jewels, to the view
Of th'Assembly, as did you!
Or, that did you sit, or walke,
You were more the eye, and talke
Of the Court, to day, then all
Else that glister'd in White-hall;
So, as those that had your sight,
Wisht the Bride were chang'd to night,
And did thinke, such Rites were due
To no other Grace but you!   20
Or, if you did move to night
In the Daunces, with what spight
Of your Peeres, you were beheld,
That at every motion sweld
So to see a Lady tread,
As might all the Graces lead,
And was worthy (being so seene)
To be envi'd of the Queene.
Or if you would yet have stay'd,
Whether any would up-braid   30
To himselfe his losse of Time;
Or have charg'd his sight of Crime,
To have left all sight for you:
Guesse of these, which is the true;
And, if such a verse as this,
May not claime another kisse.

7. BEGGING ANOTHER, ON COLOUR OF MENDING THE FORMER

For Loves-sake, kisse me once againe,
   I long, and should not beg in vaine,

118

Here's none to spie, or see;
     Why doe you doubt, or stay?
  I'le taste as lightly as the Bee,
That doth but touch his flower, and flies away.
    Once more, and (faith) I will be gone.
    Can he that loves, aske lesse then one?
       Nay, you may erre in this,
         And all your bountie wrong: 10
    This could be call'd but halfe a kisse.
What w'are but once to doe, we should doe long.
    I will but mend the last, and tell
    Where, how it would have relish'd well;
       Joyne lip to lip, and try:
         Each suck others breath.
    And whilst our tongues perplexed lie,
Let who will thinke us dead, or wish our death.

8. URGING HER OF A PROMISE

    CHARIS one day in discourse
    Had of Love, and of his force,
    Lightly promis'd, she would tell
    What a man she could love well:
    And that promise set on fire
    All that heard her, with desire.
    With the rest, I long expected,
    When the worke would be effected:
    But we find that cold delay,
    And excuse spun every day,   10
    As, untill she tell her one,
    We all feare, she loveth none.
    Therefore, Charis, you must do't,
    For I will so urge you to't
    You shall neither eat, nor sleepe,
    No, nor forth your window peepe,
    With your emissarie eye,
    To fetch in the Formes goe by:

And pronounce, which band or lace,
Better fits him, then his face; 20
Nay I will not let you sit
'Fore your Idoll Glasse a whit,
To say over every purle
There; or to reforme a curle;
Or with Secretarie Sis
To consult, if Fucus this
Be as good, as was the last:
All your sweet of life is past,
Make accompt unlesse you can,
(And that quickly) speake your Man. 30

9. HER MAN DESCRIBED BY HER OWNE DICTAMEN

Of your Trouble, Ben, to ease me,
I will tell what Man would please me.
I would have him if I could,
Noble; or of greater Blood:
Titles, I confesse, doe take me;
And a woman God did make me,
French to boote, at least in fashion,
And his Manners of that Nation.
Young Il'd have him to, and faire,
Yet a man; with crisped haire 10
Cast in thousand snares, and rings
For Loves fingers, and his wings:
Chestnut colour, or more slack
Gold, upon a ground of black.
Venus, and Minerva's eyes
For he must looke wanton-wise.
Eye-brows bent like Cupids bow,
Front, an ample field of snow;
Even nose, and cheeke (withall)
Smooth as is the Billiard Ball: 20

Chin, as woolly as the Peach;
And his lip should kissing teach,
Till he cherish'd too much beard,
And make Love or me afeard.
He would have a hand as soft
As the Downe, and shew it oft;
Skin as smooth as any rush,
And so thin to see a blush
Rising through it e're it came;
All his blood should be a flame   30
Quickly fir'd as in beginners
In loves schoole, and yet no sinners.
'Twere to long to speake of all,
What we harmonie doe call
In a body should be there.
Well he should his clothes to weare;
Yet no Taylor help to make him;
Drest, you still for man should take him;
And not thinke h'had eat a stake,
Or were set up in a Brake.   40
Valiant he should be as fire,
Shewing danger more then ire;
Bounteous as the clouds to earth;
And as honest as his Birth.
All his actions to be such,
As to doe nothing too much:
Nor o're-praise, nor yet condemne;
Nor out-valew, nor contemne;
Nor doe wrongs, nor wrongs receave;
Nor tie knots, nor knots unweave;   50
And from basenesse to be free,
As he durst love Truth and me.

    Such a man, with every part,
I could give my very heart;
But of one, if short he came,
I can rest me where I am.

10. ANOTHER LADYES EXCEPTION
PRESENT AT THE HEARING

For his Mind, I doe not care,
That's a Toy, that I could spare:
Let his Title be but great,
His Clothes rich, and band sit neat,
Himselfe young, and face be good,
All I wish is understood.
What you please, you parts may call,
'Tis one good part I'ld lie withall.

III

The Musicall Strife; In a Pastorall Dialogue

Shee

Come with our Voyces, let us warre,
    And challenge all the Spheares,
Till each of us be made a Starre,
    And all the world turne Eares.

Hee

At such a Call, what beast or fowle,
    Of reason emptie is!
What Tree or stone doth want a soule?
    What man but must lose his?

Shee

Mixe then your Notes, that we may prove
    To stay the running floods?   10
To make the Mountaine Quarries move?
    And call the walking woods?

Hee

What need of mee? doe you but sing,
    Sleepe, and the Grave will wake.
No tunes are sweet, nor words have sting,
    But what those lips doe make.

Shee

They say the Angells marke each Deed,
    And exercise below,
And out of inward pleasure feed
    On what they viewing know.   20

Hee

O sing not you then, lest the best
    Of Angels should be driven
To fall againe; at such a feast,
    Mistaking earth for heaven.

Shee

Nay, rather both our soules bee strayn'd
    To meet their high desire;
So they in state of Grace retain'd,
    May wish us of their Quire.

IV

A Song

OH doe not wanton with those eyes,
    Lest I be sick with seeing;
Nor cast them downe, but let them rise,
    Lest shame destroy their being:
O, be not angry with those fires,
    For then their threats will kill me;
Nor looke too kind on my desires,

For then my hopes will spill me;
O, doe not steepe them in thy Teares,
   For so will sorrow slay me;   10
Nor spread them as distract with feares,
   Mine owne enough betray me.

V

In the person of Woman kind

A Song Apologetique

MEN, if you love us, play no more
   The fooles, or Tyrants with your friends,
To make us still sing o're, and o're,
   Our owne false praises, for your ends:
      Wee have both wits, and fancies too,
      And if wee must, let's sing of you.

Nor doe we doubt, but that we can,
   If wee would search with care, and paine,
Find some one good, in some one man;
   So going thorow all your straine: 10
      Wee shall at last, of parcells make
      One good enough for a songs sake.

And as a cunning Painter takes
   In any curious peece you see
More pleasure while the thing he makes
   Then when 'tis made, why so will wee.
      And having pleas'd our art, wee'll try
      To make a new, and hang that by.

VI

Another. In defence of their inconstancie

A SONG

HANG up those dull, and envious fooles
  That talke abroad of Womans change,
We were not bred to sit on stooles,
    Our proper vertue is to range:
      Take that away, you take our lives,
      We are no women then, but wives.

Such as in valour would excell
  Doe change, though man, and often fight,
Which we in love must doe aswell,
  If ever we will love aright.   10
      The frequent varying of the deed,
      Is that which doth perfection breed.

Nor is't inconstancie to change
  For what is better, or to make
(By searching) what before was strange,
    Familiar, for the uses sake;
      The good, from bad, is not descride,
      But as 'tis often vext and tri'd.

And this profession of a store
  In love, doth not alone help forth   20
Our pleasure; but preserves us more
    From being forsaken, then doth worth,
      For were the worthiest woman curst
      To love one man, hee'd leave her first.

VII

A Nymphs Passion

I LOVE, and he loves me againe,
  Yet dare I not tell who;
For if the Nymphs should know my Swaine,
  I feare they'd love him too;
    Yet if it be not knowne,
      The pleasure is as good as none,
For that's a narrow joy is but our owne.

I'le tell, that if they be not glad,
  They yet may envie me:
But then if I grow jealous madde,   10
  And of them pittied be,
    It were a plague 'bove scorne,
      And yet it cannot be forborne,
Unlesse my heart would as my thought be torne.

He is if they can find him, faire,
  And fresh and fragrant too,
As Summers sky, or purged Ayre,
  And lookes as Lillies doe,
    That are this morning blowne,
      Yet, yet I doubt he is not knowne,   20
And feare much more, that more of him be showne.

But he hath eyes so round, and bright,
  As make away my doubt,
Where Love may all his Torches light,
  Though hate had put them out;
    But then t'increase my feares,
      What Nymph so e're his voyce but heares
Will be my Rivall, though she have but eares.

I'le tell no more and yet I love,
  And he loves me; yet no   30
One un-becomming thought doth move
  From either heart, I know;
    But so exempt from blame,
    As it would be to each a fame:
If Love, or feare, would let me tell his name.

VIII

The Houre-glasse

DOE but consider this small dust,
  Here running in the Glasse,
    By Atomes mov'd;
  Could you beleeve, that this,
    The body was
    Of one that lov'd?
And in his Mistresse flame, playing like a flye,
  Turn'd to cinders by her eye?
  Yes; and in death, as life unblest,
    To have't exprest,   10
Even ashes of lovers find no rest.

IX

My Picture Left in Scotland

I NOW thinke, Love is rather deafe, then blind,
  For else it could not be,
      That she,
Whom I adore so much, should so slight me,
  And cast my love behind:

I'm sure my language to her, was as sweet,
And every close did meet
In sentence, of as subtile feet,
As hath the youngest Hee,
That sits in shadow of Apollo's tree.　　10
Oh, but my conscious feares,
That flie my thoughts betweene,
Tell me that she hath seene
My hundreds of gray haires,
Told seven and fortie yeares,
Read so much wast, as she cannot imbrace
My mountaine belly, and my rockie face,
And all these through her eyes, have stopt her eares.

X

Against Jealousie

WRETCHED and foolish Jealousie,
How cam'st thou thus to enter me?
I ne're was of thy kind;
Nor have I yet the narrow mind
To vent that poore desire,
That others should not warme them at my fire:
I wish the Sun should shine
On all mens Fruit, and flowers, as well as mine.

But under the Disguise of love
Thou sai'st, thou only cam'st to prove　　10
What my Affections were.
Think'st thou that love is help'd by feare?
Goe, get thee quickly forth;
Loves sicknesse, and his noted want of worth,
Seeke doubting Men to please;
I ne're will owe my health to a disease.

XI

The Dreame

OR Scorne, or pittie on me take,
I must the true Relation make,
  I am undone to Night;
  Love in a subtile Dreame disguis'd,
  Hath both my heart and me surpriz'd,
Whom never yet he durst t'attempt awake;
Nor will he tell me for whose sake
    He did me the Delight,
      Or Spight,
  But leaves me to inquire,   10
  In all my wild desire
    Of sleepe againe; who was his Aid?
    And sleepe so guiltie and afraid,
As since he dares not come within my sight.

XII

An Epitaph on Master Vincent Corbet

I HAVE my Pietie too, which could
It vent it selfe, but as it would,
Would say as much, as both have done
Before me here, the Friend and Sonne;
For I both lost a friend and Father,
Of him whose bones this Grave doth gather:
Deare Vincent Corbet, who so long
Had wrestled with Diseases strong,
That though they did possesse each limbe,
Yet he broke them, e're they could him,   10
With the just Canon of his life,
A life that knew nor noise, nor strife:

But was by sweetning so his will,
All order, and Disposure, still
His Mind as pure, and neatly kept,
As were his Nourceries; and swept
So of uncleannesse, or offence,
That never came ill odour thence:
And adde his Actions unto these,
They were as specious as his Trees.   20
'Tis true, he could not reprehend;
His very Manners taught t'amend,
They were so even, grave, and holy;
No stubbornnesse so stiffe, nor folly
To licence ever was so light,
As twice to trespasse in his sight,
His lookes would so correct it, when
It chid the vice, yet not the Men.
Much from him I professe I wonne,
And more, and more, I should have done,   30
But that I understood him scant;
Now I conceive him by my want,
And pray who shall my sorrowes read,
That they for me their teares will shed;
For truly, since he left to be,
I feele, I'm rather dead than he!

Reader, whose life, and name, did e're become
   An Epitaph, deserv'd a Tombe:
Nor wants it here through penurie, or sloth,   39
   Who makes the one, so't be first makes both.

XIII

An Epistle to Sir Edward Sacvile,
Now Earle of Dorset

IF Sackvile, all that have the power to doe
Great and good turns, as wel could time them too,
And knew their how, and where: we should have, then
Lesse list of proud, hard, or ingratefull Men.
For benefits are ow'd with the same mind
As they are done, and such returnes they find:
You then whose will not only, but desire
To succour my necessities tooke fire,
Not at my prayers, but your sense; which laid
The way to meet, what others would upbraid; 10
And in the Act did so my blush prevent,
As I did feele it done, as soone as meant:
You cannot doubt, but I who freely know
This Good from you, as freely will it owe;
And though my fortune humble me, to take
The smallest courtesies with thankes, I make
Yet choyce from whom I take them; and would shame
To have such doe me good, I durst not name:
They are the Noblest benefits, and sinke
Deepest in Man, of which when he doth thinke, 20
The memorie delights him more, from whom
Then what he hath receiv'd. Gifts stinke from some,
They are so long a comming, and so hard;
Where any Deed is forc't, the Grace is mard.
 Can I owe thankes, for Curtesies receiv'd
Against his will that doe's 'hem? that hath weav'd
Excuses, or Delayes? or done 'hem scant,
That they have more opprest me, then my want?
Or if he did it not to succour me,
But by meere Chance? for interest? or to free 30
Himselfe of farther trouble, or the weight
Of pressure, like one taken in a streight?

All this corrupts the thankes; lesse hath he wonne,
That puts it in his Debt-booke e're't be done;
Or that doth sound a Trumpet, and doth call
His Groomes to witnesse; or else lets it fall
In that proud manner: as a good so gain'd,
Must make me sad for what I have obtain'd.

    No! Gifts and thankes should have one cheerefull
        face,
So each, that's done, and tane, becomes a Brace.   40
He neither gives, or do's, that doth delay
A Benefit: or that doth throw't away,
No more then he doth thanke, that will receive
Nought but in corners; and is loath to leave,
Lest Ayre, or Print, but flies it: Such men would
Run from the Conscience of it if they could.

    As I have seene some Infants of the Sword
Well knowne, and practiz'd borrowers on their word,
Give thankes by stealth, and whispering in the eare, 49
For what they streight would to the world forsweare;
And speaking worst of those, from whom they went
But then, fist fill'd, to put me off the sent.
Now dam'mee, Sir, if you shall not command
My Sword ('tis but a poore Sword understand)
As farre as any poore Sword i'the Land;
Then turning unto him is next at hand,
Dam's whom he damn'd too, is the veriest Gull,
H'as Feathers, and will serve a man to pull.

    Are they not worthy to be answer'd so,
That to such Natures let their full hands flow,   60
And seeke not wants to succour: but enquire
Like Money-brokers, after Names, and hire
Their bounties forth, to him that last was made,
Or stands to be'n Commission o'the blade?
Still, still, the hunters of false fame apply
Their thoughts and meanes to making loude the cry;
But one is bitten by the Dog he fed,

And hurt seeks Cure; the Surgeon bids take bread,
And spunge-like with it dry up the blood quite:
Then give it to the Hound that did him bite; 70
Pardon, sayes he, that were a way to see
All the Towne-curs take each their snatch at me.
O, is it so? knowes he so much? and will
Feed those, at whom the Table points at still?
I not deny it, but to helpe the need
Of any, is a Great and generous Deed:
Yea, of th'ingratefull: and he forth must tell
Many a pound, and piece will pace one well;
But these men ever want: their very trade
Is borrowing, that but stopt they doe invade 80
All as their prize, turne Pyrats here at Land,
Ha' their Bermudas, and their streights i'th' Strand:
Man out their Boates to th' Temple, and not shift
Now, but command; make tribute, what was gift;
And it is paid'hem with a trembling zeale,
And superstition I dare scarce reveale
If it were cleare, but being so in cloud
Carryed and wrapt, I only am aloud
My wonder! why? the taking a Clownes purse,
Or robbing the poore Market-folkes should nurse 90
Such a religious horrour in the brests
Of our Towne Gallantry! or why there rests
Such worship due to kicking of a Punck!
Or swaggering with the Watch, or Drawer drunke;
Or feats of darknesse acted in Mid-Sun,
And told of with more Licence then th'were done!
Sure there is Misterie in it, I not know,
That men such reverence to such actions show!
And almost deifie the Authors! make
Lowd sacrifice of drinke, for their health-sake 100
Reare Suppers in their Names! and spend whole
    nights
Unto their praise, in certain swearing rites;

133

Cannot a man be reck'ned in the State
Of Valour, but at this Idolatrous rate?
I thought that Fortitude had beene a meane
'Twixt feare and rashnesse: not a lust obscene,
Or appetite of offending, but a skill,
Or Science of discerning Good and Ill.
And you, Sir, know it well to whom I write,
That with these mixtures we put out her light;   110
Her ends are honestie, and publike good!
And where they want, she is not understood.
No more are these of us, let them then goe,
I have the lyst of mine owne faults to know,
Looke too and cure; Hee's not a man hath none,
But like to be, that every day mends one,
And feeles it; Else he tarries by the Beast.
Can I discerne how shadowes are decreast,
Or growne, by height or lownesse of the Sunne?
And can I lesse of substance? When I runne,   120
Ride, saile, am coach'd, know I how farre I have gone,
And my minds motion not? or have I none:
No! he must feele and know, that I will advance:
Men have beene great, but never good by chance,
Or on the sudden. It were strange that he
Who was this Morning such a one, should be
Sydney e're night? or that did go to bed
Coriat, should rise the most sufficient head
Of Christendome? And neither of these know
Were the Rack offer'd them how they came so;   130
'Tis by degrees that men arrive at glad
Profit in ought: each day some little adde,
In time 'twill be a heape; This is not true
Alone in money, but in manners too.
Yet we must more then move still, or goe on,
We must accomplish; 'Tis the last Key-stone
That makes the Arch. The rest that there were put
Are nothing till that comes to bind and shut.

Then stands it a triumphall marke! then Men
Observe the strength, the height, the why, and when,
It was erected; and still walking under   141
Meet some new matter to looke up and wonder!
Such Notes are vertuous men! they live as fast
As they are high; are rooted and will last.
They need no stilts, nor rise upon their toes,
As if they would belie their stature; those
Are Dwarfes of Honour, and have neither weight
Nor fashion; if they chance aspire to height,
'Tis like light Canes, that first rise big and brave,
Shoot forth in smooth and comely spaces; have   150
But few and faire Devisions: but being got
Aloft, grow lesse and streightned; full of knot;
And last, goe out in nothing: You that see
Their difference, cannot choose which you will be.
You know (without my flatt'ring you) too much
For me to be your Indice. Keep you such,
That I may love your Person (as I doe)
Without your gift, though I can rate that too,
By thanking thus the curtesie to life,
Which you will bury, but therein, the strife   160
May grow so great to be example, when
(As their true rule or lesson) either men
Donnor's or Donnee's to their practise shall
Find you to reckon nothing, me owe all.

XIV

An Epistle to Master John Selden

I KNOW to whom I write. Here, I am sure,
Though I am short, I cannot be obscure:
Lesse shall I for the Art or dressing care;
Truth, and the Graces best, when naked are.

Your Booke, my Selden, I have read, and much
Was trusted, that you thought my judgement such
To aske it: though in most of workes it be
A pennance, where a man may not be free,
Rather then Office, when it doth or may
Chance that the Friends affection proves Allay   10
Unto the Censure. Yours all need doth flie
Of this so vitious Humanitie,
Then which there is not unto Studie, a more
Pernitious enemie; we see before
A many of bookes, even good judgements wound
Themselves through favouring what is there not
          found:
But I on yours farre otherwise shall doe,
Not flie the Crime, but the Suspition too:
Though I confesse (as every Muse hath err'd,
And mine not least) I have too oft preferr'd   20
Men, past their termes, and prais'd some names too
          much,
But 'twas with purpose to have made them such.
Since being deceiv'd, I turne a sharper eye
Upon my selfe, and aske to whom? and why?
And what I write? and vexe it many dayes
Before men get a verse: much lesse a Praise;
So that my Reader is assur'd, I now
Meane what I speake: and still will keepe that Vow.
Stand forth my Object, then, you that have beene
Ever at home: yet, have all Countries seene: 30
And like a Compasse keeping one foot still
Upon your Center, doe your Circle fill
Of generall knowledge; watch'd men, manners too,
Heard what times past have said, seene what ours doe:
Which Grace shall I make love too first? your skill,
Or faith in things? or is't your wealth and will
T'instruct and teach? or your unweary'd paine
Of Gathering? Bountie in pouring out againe?

What fables have you vext! what truth redeem'd!
Antiquities search'd! Opinions dis-esteem'd! 40
Impostures branded! and Authorities urg'd!
What blots and errours have you watch'd and purg'd
Records, and Authors of! how rectified
Times, manners, customes! Innovations spide!
Sought out the Fountaines, Sources, Creekes, paths,
 wayes,
And noted the beginnings and decayes!
Where is that nominall marke, or reall rite,
Forme, Act or Ensigne, that hath scap'd your sight!
How are Traditions there examin'd: how
Conjectures retriv'd! And a Storie now 50
And then of times (besides the bare Conduct
Of what it tells us) weav'd in to instruct.
I wonder'd at the richnesse, but am lost,
To see the workmanship so'xceed the cost!
To marke the excellent seas'ning of your Stile!
And manly elocution, not one while
With horrour rough, then rioting with wit!
But to the Subject, still the Colours fit
In sharpnesse of all Search, wisdome of Choise,
Newnesse of Sense, Antiquitie of voyce! 60
 I yeeld, I yeeld, the matter of your praise
Flowes in upon me, and I cannot raise
A banke against it. Nothing but the round
Large claspe of Nature, such a wit can bound.
Monarch in Letters! 'Mongst thy Titles showne
Of others honours, thus, enjoy thine owne;
I first salute thee so; and gratulate
With that thy Stile, thy keeping of thy State,
In offering this thy worke to no great Name,
That would, perhaps, have prais'd, and thank'd the
 same, 70
But nought beyond. He thou hast given it to,
Thy learned Chamber-fellow, knowes to doe

It true respects. He will not only love,
Embrace, and cherish; but he can approve
And estimate thy Paines; as having wrought
In the same Mines of knowledge; and thence brought
Humanitie enough to be a friend,
And strength to be a Champion, and defend
Thy gift 'gainst envie. O how I doe count
Among my commings in, and see it mount,   80
The Graine of your two friendships! Hayward and
Selden! two Names that so much understand!
On whom I could take up, and ne're abuse
The Credit, what would furnish a tenth Muse!
But here's no time, nor place, my wealth to tell,
You both are modest. So am I. Farewell.

XV

An Epistle to a Friend, to perswade him to the Warres

WAKE, friend, from forth thy Lethargie: the Drum
Beates brave, and loude in Europe, and bids come
All that dare rowse: or are not loth to quit
Their vitious ease, and be o'rewhelm'd with it.
It is a call to keepe the spirits alive
That gaspe for action, and would yet revive
Mans buried honour, in his sleepie life:
Quickning dead Nature, to her noblest strife.
All other Acts of Worldlings, are but toyle
In dreames, begun in hope, and end in spoile.   10
Looke on th'ambitious man, and see him nurse
His unjust hopes, with praises begg'd, or (worse)
Bought Flatteries, the issue of his purse,
Till he become both their, and his own curse!
Looke on the false, and cunning man, that loves
No person, nor is lov'd: what wayes he proves

To gaine upon his belly; and at last
Crush'd in the snakie brakes, that he had past!
See, the grave, sower, and supercilious Sir
In outward face, but inward, light as Furre,   20
Or Feathers: lay his fortune out to show
Till envie wound, or maime it at a blow!
See him, that's call'd, and thought the happiest man,
Honour'd at once, and envi'd (if it can
Be honour is so mixt) by such as would
For all their spight be like him if they could:
No part or corner man can looke upon,
But there are objects, bid him to be gone
As farre as he can flie, or follow Day,
Rather then here so bogg'd in vices stay.   30
The whole world here leaven'd with madnesse swells;
And being a thing, blowne out of nought, rebells
Against his Maker; high alone with weeds,
And impious ranknesse of all Sects and seeds:
Not to be checkt, or frighted now with fate,
But more licentious made, and desperate!
Our Delicacies are growne capitall,
And even our sports are dangers! what we call
Friendship is now mask'd Hatred! Justice fled,
And shamefastnesse together! All lawes dead   40
That kept man living! Pleasures only sought!
Honour and honestie, as poore things thought
As they are made! Pride, and stiffe Clownage mixt
To make up Greatnesse! and mans whole good fix'd
In bravery, or gluttony, or coyne,
All which he makes the servants of the Groine,
Thither it flowes; how much did Stallion spend
To have his Court-bred-fillie there commend
His Lace and Starch? And fall upon her back
In admiration, stretch'd upon the rack   50
Of lust, to his rich Suit and Title, Lord?
I, that's a Charme and halfe! She must afford

That all respect; She must lie downe: Nay more,
'Tis there civilitie to be a whore;
Hee's one of blood, and fashion! and with these
The bravery makes, she can no honour leese.
To do't with Cloth, or Stuffes, lusts name might merit,
With Velvet, Plush, and Tissues, it is spirit.

O, these so ignorant Monsters! light, as proud,
Who can behold their Manners, and not clowd-   60
Like upon them lighten? If nature could
Not make a verse; Anger; or laughter would
To see'hem aye discoursing with their Glasse,
How they may make some one that day an Asse,
Planting their Purles, and Curles spread forth like
    Net,
And every Dressing for a Pitfall set
To catch the flesh in, and to pound a Prick;
Be at their Visits, see'hem squemish, sick
Ready to cast, at one, whose band sits ill,
And then, leape mad on a neat Pickardill;   70
As if a Brize were gotten i' their tayle,
And firke, and jerke, and for the Coach-man raile,
And jealous each of other, yet thinke long
To be abroad chanting some baudie song,
And laugh, and measure thighes, then squeake, spring,
    itch,
Doe all the tricks of a saut Lady Bitch;
For t'other pound of sweet-meats, he shall feele
That payes, or what he will. The Dame is steele,
For these with her young Companie shee'll enter,
Where Pittes, or Wright, or Modet would not venter,
And comes by these Degrees, the Stile t'inherit   81
Of woman of fashion, and a Lady of spirit:
Nor is the title question'd with our proud,
Great, brave, and fashion'd folke; these are allow'd
Adulteries now, are not so hid, or strange;
They're growne Commoditie upon Exchange;

He that will follow but anothers wife,
Is lov'd, though he let out his owne for life:
The Husband now's call'd churlish, or a poore
Nature, that will not let his Wife be a whore;   90
Or use all arts, or haunt all Companies
That may corrupt her, even in his eyes.
The brother trades a sister; and the friend
Lives to the Lord, but to the Ladies end.
Lesse must not be thought on then Mistresse: or
If it be thought, kild like her Embrions; for,
Whom no great Mistresse hath as yet infam'd
A fellow of course Letcherie, is nam'd
The Servant of the Serving-woman in scorne,
Ne're came to taste the plenteous Mariage-horne. 100
    Thus they doe talke. And are these objects fit
For man to spend his money on? his wit?
His time? health? soule? will he for these goe throw
Those thousands on his back, shall after blow
His body to the Counters, or the Fleete?
Is it for these that fine man meets the street
Coach'd, or on foot-cloth, thrice chang'd every day,
To teach each suit, he has the ready way
From Hide-Parke to the Stage, where at the last
His deare and borrow'd Bravery he must cast?   110
When not his Combes, his Curling-irons, his Glasse,
Sweet bags, sweet Powders, nor sweet words will passe
For lesse Securitie? O Friend, for these
Is it that man pulls on himselfe Disease?
Surfet? and Quarrell? drinkes the tother health?
Or by Damnation voids it? or by stealth?
What furie of late is crept into our Feasts?
What honour given to the drunkenest Guests?
What reputation to beare one Glasse more?
When oft the Bearer is borne out of dore?   120
This hath our ill-us'd freedome, and soft peace
Brought on us, and will every houre increase.

Our vices doe not tarry in a place,
But being in Motion still (or rather in race)
Tilt one upon another, and now beare
This way, now that, as if their number were
More then themselves, or then our lives could take,
But both fell prest under the load they make.
   I'le bid thee looke no more, but flee, flee friend,
This Præcipice, and Rocks that have no end,   130
Or side, but threatens Ruine. The whole Daʒ
Is not enough now, but the Night's to play:
And whilst our states, strength, body, and mind we
      waste;
Goe make our selves the Usurers at a cast.
He that no more for Age, Cramps, Palsies, can
Now use the bones, we see doth hire a man
To take the box up for him; and pursues
The Dice with glassen eyes, to the glad viewes
Of what he throwes: Like letchers growne content
To be beholders, when their powers are spent.   140
   Can we not leave this worme? or will we not?
Is that the truer excuse? or have we got
In this, and like, an itch of Vanitie,
That scratching now's our best Felicitie?
Well, let it goe. Yet this is better, then
To lose the formes, and dignities of men
To flatter my good Lord, and cry his Bowle
Runs sweetly, as it had his Lordships Soule.
Although, perhaps it has, what's that to me,
That may stand by, and hold my peace? will he   150
When I am hoarse, with praising his each cast,
Give me but that againe, that I must wast
In Sugar Candide, or in butter'd beere,
For the recovery of my voyce? No, there
Pardon his Lordship. Flattry's growne so cheape
With him, for he is followed with that heape
That watch, and catch, at what they may applaud,
As a poore single flatterer, without Baud,

Is nothing, such scarce meat and drinke he'le give,
But he that's both, and slave to boote, shall live,   160
And be belov'd, while the Whores last. O times,
Friend flie from hence; and let these kindled rimes
Light thee from hell on earth: where flatterers, spies,
Informers, Masters both of Arts and lies,
Lewd slanderers, soft whisperers that let blood
The life, and fame-vaynes (yet not understood
Of the poore sufferers); where the envious, proud,
Ambitious, factious, superstitious, lowd
Boasters, and perjur'd, with the infinite more
Prævaricators swarme. Of which the store,   170
(Because th'are every where amongst Man-kind
Spread through the World) is easier farre to find,
Then once to number, or bring forth to hand,
Though thou wert Muster-master of the Land.

Goe quit 'hem all. And take along with thee,
Thy true friends wishes, Colby, which shall be,
That thine be just, and honest, that thy Deeds
Not wound thy conscience, when thy body bleeds;
That thou dost all things more for truth, then glory,
And never but for doing wrong be sory;   180
That by commanding first thy selfe, thou mak'st
Thy person fit for any charge thou tak'st;
That fortune never make thee to complaine,
But what she gives, thou dar'st give her againe;
That whatsoever face thy fate puts on,
Thou shrinke or start not; but be alwayes one;
That thou thinke nothing great, but what is good,
And from that thought strive to be understood.
So, 'live or dead, thou wilt preserve a fame
Still pretious, with the odour of thy name.   190
And last, blaspheme not; we did never heare
Man thought the valianter, 'cause he durst sweare,
No more, then we should thinke a Lord had had
More honour in him, 'cause we'ave knowne him mad:

143

These take, and now goe seeke thy peace in Warre;
Who falls for love of God, shall rise a Starre.

XVI

An Epitaph on Master Philip Gray

READER, stay,
And if I had no more to say,
But here doth lie till the last Day,
All that is left of Philip Gray,
It might thy patience richly pay:
   For, if such men as he could die,
    What suretie of life have thou, and I?

XVII

Epistle to a Friend

THEY are not, Sir, worst Owers, that doe pay
Debts when they can: good men may breake their
   day,
And yet the noble Nature never grudge;
'Tis then a crime, when the Usurer is Judge,
And he is not in friendship. Nothing there
Is done for gaine: If't be 'tis not sincere.
Nor should I at this time protested be,
But that some greater names have broke with me,
And their words too; where I but breake my Band;
I adde that (but) because I understand   10
That as the lesser breach: for he that takes
Simply my Band, his trust in me forsakes,
And lookes unto the forfeit. If you be
Now so much friend, as you would trust in me,

Venter a longer time, and willingly:
All is not barren land, doth fallow lie.
Some grounds are made the richer, for the Rest:
And I will bring a Crop, if not the best.

XVIII

An Elegie

CAN Beautie that did prompt me first to write,
Now threaten, with those meanes she did invite:
Did her perfections call me on to gaze!
Then like, then love; and now would they amaze!
Or was she gracious a-farre off? but neere
A terror? or is all this but my feare?
That as the water makes things, put in't, streight,
Crooked appeare; so that doth my conceipt:
I can helpe that with boldnesse; And love sware,
And fortune once, t'assist the spirits that dare.   10
But which shall lead me on? both these are blind:
Such Guides men use not, who their way would
    find,
Except the way be errour to those ends:
And then the best are, still, the blindest friends!
Oh how a Lover may mistake! to thinke,
Or love, or fortune blind, when they but winke
To see men feare: or else for truth, and State,
Because they would free Justice imitate,
Vaile their owne eyes, and would impartially
Be brought by us to meet our Destinie.   20
If it be thus; Come love, and fortune goe,
I'le lead you on; or if my fate will so,
That I must send one first, my Choyce assignes,
Love to my heart, and fortune to my lines.

XIX

An Elegie

By those bright Eyes, at whose immortall fires
Love lights his torches to inflame desires;
By that faire Stand, your forehead, whence he bends
His double Bow, and round his Arrowes sends;
By that tall Grove, your haire; whose globy rings
He flying curles, and crispeth, with his wings;
By those pure bathes your either cheeke discloses,
Where he doth steepe himselfe in Milke and Roses;
And lastly by your lips, the banke of kisses,
Where men at once my plant, and gather blisses: 10
Tell me (my lov'd Friend) doe you love or no?
So well as I may tell in verse, 'tis so?
You blush, but do not: friends are either none,
(Though they may number bodyes) or but one.
I'le therefore aske no more, but bid you love;
And so that either may example prove
Unto the other; and live patterns, how
Others, in time, may love, as we doe now.
Slip no occasion; As time stands not still,
I know no beautie, nor no youth that will.   20
To use the present, then, is not abuse;
You have a Husband is the just excuse
Of all that can be done him; Such a one
As would make shift, to make himselfe alone,
That which we can, who both in you, his Wife,
His Issue, and all Circumstance of life,
As in his place, because he would not varie,
Is constant to be extraordinarie.

XX

A Satyricall Shrub

A WOMANS friendship! God whom I trust in,
Forgive me this one foolish deadly sin;
Amongst my many other, that I may
No more, I am sorry for so fond cause, say
At fifty yeares, almost, to value it,
That ne're was knowne to last above a fit!
Or have the least of Good, but what it must
Put on for fashion, and take up on trust:
Knew I all this afore? had I perceiv'd,
That their whole life was wickednesse, though
    weav'd   10
Of many Colours; outward fresh, from spots,
But their whole inside full of ends, and knots?
Knew I, that all their Dialogues, and discourse,
Were such as I will now relate, or worse?

. . . Here, something is wanting. . . .

Knew I this Woman? yes; And you doe see,
How penitent I am, or I should be!
Doe not you aske to know her; she is worse
Then all Ingredients made into one curse,
And that pour'd out upon Man-kind can be!
Thinke but the Sin of all her sex, 'tis she!   20
I could forgive her being proud! a whore!
Perjur'd! and painted! if she were no more—,
But she is such, as she might, yet, forestall
The Divell; and be the damning of us all.

XXI

A Little Shrub growing by

ASKE not to know this Man. If fame should speake
His name in any mettall, it would breake.
Two letters were enough the plague to teare
Out of his Grave, and poyson every eare.
A parcell of Court-durt, a heape, a masse
Of all vice hurld together, there he was,
Proud, false, and trecherous, vindictive, all
That thought can adde, unthankfull, the lay-stall
Of putrid flesh alive! of blood, the sinke!
And so I leave to stirre him, lest he stinke.   10

XXII

An Elegie

THOUGH Beautie be the Marke of praise,
    And yours of whom I sing be such
    As not the World can praise too much,
Yet is't your vertue now I raise.

A vertue, like Allay, so gone
    Throughout your forme; as though that move,
    And draw, and conquer all mens love,
This subjects you to love of one.

Wherein you triumph yet: because
    'Tis of your selfe, and that you use   10
    The noblest freedome, not to chuse
Against or Faith, or honours lawes.

But who should lesse expect from you,
In whom alone love lives agen?
By whom he is restor'd to men:
And kept, and bred, and brought up true?

His falling Temples you have rear'd,
The withered Garlands tane away;
His Altars kept from the Decay,
That envie wish'd, and Nature fear'd.   20

And on them burne so chaste a flame,
With so much Loyalties expence
As Love, t'aquit such excellence,
Is gone himselfe into your Name.

And you are he: the Dietie
To whom all Lovers are design'd;
That would their better objects find:
Among which faithfull troope am I.

Who as an off-spring at your shrine,
Have sung this Hymne, and here intreat   30
One sparke of your Diviner heat
To light upon a Love of mine.

Which if it kindle not, but scant
Appeare, and that to shortest view,
Yet give me leave t'adore in you
What I, in her, am griev'd to want.

XXIII

An Ode. To himselfe

WHERE do'st thou carelesse lie
   Buried in ease and sloth?
Knowledge, that sleepes, doth die;
And this Securitie,
   It is the common Moath,
That eats on wits, and Arts, and oft destroyes
     them both.

Are all th'Aonian springs
   Dri'd up? lyes Thespia wast?
Doth Clarius Harp want strings,
That not a Nymph now sings!   10
   Or droop they as disgrac't,
To see their Seats and Bowers by chattring
     Pies defac't?

If hence thy silence be,
   As 'tis too just a cause;
Let this thought quicken thee,
Minds that are great and free,
   Should not on fortune pause,
'Tis crowne enough to vertue still, her owne
     applause.

What though the greedie Frie
   Be taken with false Baytes   20
Of worded Balladrie,
And thinke it Poesie?
   They die with their conceits,
And only pitious scorne, upon their folly
     waites.

Then take in hand thy Lyre,
    Strike in thy proper straine,
With Japhets lyne, aspire
Sols Chariot for new fire,
    To give the world againe:
Who aided him, will thee, the issue of Joves
      braine.   30

And since our Daintie age
    Cannot endure reproofe,
Make not thy selfe a Page,
To that strumpet the Stage,
    But sing high and aloofe,
Safe from the wolves black jaw, and the dull
    Asses hoofe.

XXIV

The mind of the Frontispice to a Booke

FROM Death and darke Oblivion (neere the same)
    The Mistresse of Mans life, grave Historie,
Raising the World to good, or Evill fame,
    Doth vindicate it to Æternitie.
High Providence would so: that nor the good
    Might be defrauded, nor the Great secur'd,
But both might know their wayes are understood,
    And the reward, and punishment assur'd.
This makes, that lighted by the beamie hand
    Of Truth, which searcheth the most hidden
      springs,   10
And guided by Experience, whose streight wand
    Doth mete, whose Line doth sound the depth of
      things:
Shee chearefully supporteth what shee reares;
    Assisted by no strengths, but are her owne

Some note of which each varied Pillar beares,
  By which as proper titles shee is knowne,
Times witnesse, Herald of Antiquitie,
The light of Truth, and life of Memorie.

XXV

An Ode to James Earle of Desmond

WRIT IN QUEENE ELIZABETHS TIME, SINCE LOST,
AND RECOVERED

WHERE art thou, Genius? I should use
  Thy present Aide: Arise Invention,
Wake, and put on the wings of Pindars Muse,
    To towre with my intention
  High, as his mind, that doth advance
Her upright head, above the reach of Chance,
      Or the times envie:
      Cynthius, I applie
My bolder numbers to thy golden Lyre:
      O, then inspire   10
Thy Priest in this strange rapture; heat my braine
      With Delphick fire:
That I may sing my thoughts, in some unvulgar
      straine.

  Rich beame of honour, shed your light
  On these darke rymes; that my affection
May shine (through every chincke) to every sight
    Graced by your Reflection!
  Then shall my Verses, like strong Charmes
Breake the knit Circle of her Stonie Armes,
      That holds your spirit: 20
      And keepes your merit

152

Lock't in her cold embraces, from the view
    Of eyes more true,
Who would with judgement search, searching
    conclude,
    (As prov'd in you)
True noblesse. Palme growes straight, though
    handled ne're so rude!

  Nor thinke your selfe unfortunate,
    If subject to the jealous errors
Of politique pretext, that wryes a State,
    Sinke not beneath these terrors: 30
  But whisper; O glad Innocence
Where only a mans birth is his offence;
    Or the dis-favor,
    Of such as savour
Nothing, but practise upon honours thrall.
    O vertues fall,
When her dead essence (like the Anatomie
    In Surgeons hall)
Is but a Statists theame, to read Phlebotomie.

  Let Brontes, and black Steropes   40
    Sweat at the forge, their hammers beating;
Pyracmon's houre will come to give them ease,
    Though but while mettal's heating:
  And, after all the Ætnean Ire,
Gold, that is perfect, will out-live the fire.
    For fury wasteth,
    As patience lasteth.
No Armour to the mind! he is shot-free
    From injurie,
That is not hurt; not he, that is not hit;   50
    So fooles we see,
Oft scape an Imputation, more through luck, then
    wit.

But to your selfe, most loyall Lord,
  (Whose heart in that bright Sphere flames
      clearest,
Though many Gems be in your bosome stor'd,
    Unknowne which is the Dearest.)
  If I auspitiously devine,
(As my hope tells) that our faire Phœbes shine,
      Shall light those places,
      With lustrous Graces,   60
Where darknesse with her glomie Sceptred hand,
    Doth now command.
O then (my best-best lov'd) let me importune,
    That you will stand,
As farre from all revolt, as you are now from
      Fortune.

XXVI

An Ode

  High spirited friend,
I send nor Balmes, nor Cor'sives to your wound;
    Your fate hath found
A gentler, and more agile hand, to tend
The Cure of that, which is but corporall,
And doubtfull Dayes (which were nam'd Criticall ,)
    Have made their fairest flight,
    And now are out of sight.
Yet doth some wholsome Physick for the mind,
    Wrapt in this paper lie,   10
Which in the taking if you mis-apply,
    You are unkind.

Your covetous hand,
Happy in that faire honour it hath gain'd,
    Must now be rayn'd.
True valour doth her owne renowne command
In one full Action; nor have you now more
To doe, then be a husband of that store.
    Thinke but how deare you bought
    This same which you have caught,   20
Such thoughts wil make you more in love with
    truth:
    'Tis wisdome and that high,
For men to use their fortune reverently,
    Even in youth.

XXVII

An Ode

HELLEN, did Homer never see
Thy beauties, yet could write of thee?
Did Sappho on her seven-tongu'd Lute,
So speake (as yet it is not mute)
Of Phaos forme? or doth the Boy
In whom Anacreon once did joy,
Lie drawne to life, in his soft Verse,
As he whom Maro did rehearse?
Was Lesbia sung by learn'd Catullus?
Or Delia's Graces, by Tibullus?   10
Doth Cynthia, in Propertius song
Shine more, then she the Stars among?
Is Horace his each love so high
Rap't from the Earth, as not to die?
With bright Lycoris, Gallus choice,
Whose fame hath an eternall voice?
Or hath Corynna, by her name
Her Ovid gave her, dimn'd the fame

Of Cæsars Daughter, and the line
Which all the world then styl'd devine? 20
Hath Petrarch since his Laura rais'd
Equall with her? or Ronsart prais'd
His new Cassandra, 'bove the old,
Which all the Fate of Troy foretold?
Hath our great Sydney, Stella set,
Where never Star shone brighter yet?
Or Constables Ambrosiack Muse
Made Dian not his notes refuse?
Have all these done (and yet I misse
The Swan that so relish'd Pancharis) 30
And shall not I my Celia bring,
Where men may see whom I doe sing?
Though I, in working of my song,
Come short of all this learned throng,
Yet sure my tunes will be the best,
So much my Subject drownes the rest.

XXVIII

A Sonnet. To the Noble Lady, the Lady Mary Wroth

I THAT have beene a lover, and could shew it,
    Though not in these, in rithmes not wholly
        dumbe,
    Since I exscribe your Sonnets, am become
A better lover, and much better Poet.
Nor is my Muse, or I asham'd to owe it,
    To those true numerous Graces; whereof some
    But charme the Senses, others over-come
Both braines and hearts; and mine now best doe
        know it:
For in your verse all Cupids Armorie,

His flames, his shafts, his Quiver, and his Bow,   10
His very eyes are yours to overthrow.
But then his Mothers sweets you so apply,
   Her joyes, her smiles, her loves, as readers take
   For Venus Ceston, every line you make.

XXIX

A Fit of Rime against Rime

RIME, the rack of finest wits,
That expresseth but by fits,
            True Conceipt,
Spoyling Senses of their Treasure,
Cosening Judgement with a measure,
            But false weight.
Wresting words, from their true calling;
Propping Verse, for feare of falling
            To the ground.
Joynting Syllabes, drowning Letters,   10
Fastning Vowells, as with fetters
            They were bound!
Soone as lazie thou wert knowne,
All good Poetrie hence was flowne,
            And Art banish'd.
For a thousand yeares together,
All Pernassus Greene did wither,
            And wit vanish'd.
Pegasus did flie away,
At the Wells no Muse did stay,   20
            But bewail'd
So to see the Fountaine drie,
And Apollo's Musique die,
            All light failed!

157

Starveling rimes did fill the Stage,
Not a Poet in an Age,
   Worth crowning;
Not a worke deserving Baies,
Nor a line deserving praise,
   Pallas frowning.   30
Greeke was free from Rimes infection,
Happy Greeke, by this protection,
   Was not spoyled.
Whilst the Latin, Queene of Tongues,
Is not yet free from Rimes wrongs,
   But rests foiled.
Scarce the hill againe doth flourish,
Scarce the world a Wit doth nourish,
   To restore
Phœbus to his Crowne againe;   40
And the Muses to their braine;
   As before.
Vulgar Languages that want
Words, and sweetnesse, and be scant
   Of true measure:
Tyran Rime hath so abused,
That they long since have refused
   Other ceasure.
He that first invented thee,
May his joynts tormented bee,   50
   Cramp'd forever;
Still may Syllabes jarre with time,
Still may reason warre with rime,
   Resting never.
May his Sense, when it would meet
The cold tumor in his feet,
   Grow unsounder,
And his Title be long foole,
That, in rearing such a Schoole,
   Was the founder.   60

XXX

An Epigram on William Lord Burl: Lo: High Treasurer of England

*Presented upon a plate of Gold to his son Rob. E.
of Salisbury, when he was also Treasurer*

IF thou wouldst know the vertues of Man-kind,
Read here in one, what thou in all canst find,
And goe no farther: let this Circle be
Thy Universe, though his Epitome.
Cecill, the grave, the wise, the great, the good,
What is there more that can ennoble blood?
The Orphans Pillar, the true Subjects shield,
The poores full Store-house, and just servants
   field.
The only faithfull Watchman for the Realme,
That in all tempests, never quit the helme,   10
But stood unshaken in his Deeds, and Name,
And labour'd in the worke; not with the fame:
That still was good for goodnesse sake, nor thought
Upon reward, till the reward him sought.
Whose Offices, and honours did surprize,
Rather than meet him: And, before his eyes
Clos'd to their peace, he saw his branches shoot,
And in the noblest Families tooke root
Of all the Land; who now at such a Rate,
Of divine blessing, would not serve a State?   20

XXXI

An Epigram. To Thomas Lo: Elsmere, the last terme he sate Chancellor

FOR A POORE MAN

So justest Lord, may all your Judgements be
Lawes; and no change e're come to one decree:
So, may the King proclaime your Conscience is
Law, to his Law; and thinke your enemies his:
So, from all sicknesse, may you rise to health,
The Care, and wish still of the publike wealth:
So may the gentler Muses, and good fame
Still flie about the Odour of your Name;
As with the safetie, and honour of the Lawes,
You favour Truth, and me, in this mans Cause.   10

XXXII

Another to Him

FOR THE SAME

The Judge his favour timely then extends,
When a good Cause is destitute of friends,
Without the pompe of Counsell; or more Aide,
Then to make falshood blush, and fraud afraid:
When those good few, that her Defenders be,
Are there for Charitie, and not for fee.
Such shall you heare to Day, and find great foes
Both arm'd with wealth, and slander to oppose,
Who thus long safe, would gaine upon the times
A right by the prosperitie of their Crimes;   10
Who, though their guilt, and perjurie they know,
Thinke, yea and boast, that they have done it so

160

As though the Court pursues them on the sent,
They will come of, and scape the Punishment.
When this appeares, just Lord, to your sharp
    sight,
He do's you wrong, that craves you to doe right.

XXXIII

An Epigram to the Councellour that pleaded, and carried the Cause

THAT I, hereafter, doe not thinke the Barre,
The Seat made of a more then civill warre;
Or the great Hall at Westminster, the field
Where mutuall frauds are fought, and no side
    yield;
That, henceforth, I beleeve nor bookes, nor men,
Who 'gainst the Law, weave Calumnies, my
    Benn;
But when I read or heare the names so rife
Of hirelings, wranglers, stitchers-to of strife,
Hook-handed Harpies, gowned Vultures, put
Upon the reverend Pleaders; doe now shut   10
All mouthes, that dare entitle them (from hence)
To the Wolves studie, or Dogs eloquence;
Thou art my Cause: whose manners since I knew,
Have made me to conceive a Lawyer new.
So dost thou studie matter, men, and times,
Mak'st it religion to grow rich by Crimes!
Dar'st not abuse thy wisdome, in the Lawes,
Or skill to carry out an evill cause!
But first dost vexe, and search it! If not sound,
Thou prov'st the gentler wayes, to clense the
    wound,   20
And make the Scarre faire; If that will not be,
Thou hast the brave scorne, to put back the fee!

But in a businesse, that will bide the Touch,
What use, what strength of reason! and how
   much
Of Bookes, of Presidents, hast thou at hand?
As if the generall store thou didst command
Of Argument, still drawing forth the best,
And not being borrowed by thee, but possest.
So comm'st thou like a Chiefe into the Court
Arm'd at all peeces, as to keep a Fort   30
Against a multitude; and (with thy Stile
So brightly brandish'd) wound'st, defend'st! the
   while
Thy Adversaries fall, as not a word
They had, but were a Reed unto thy Sword.
Then com'st thou off with Victorie and Palme,
Thy Hearers Nectar, and thy Clients Balme,
Thy Courts just honour, and thy Judges love.
And (which doth all Atchievements get above)
Thy sincere practise, breeds not thee a fame
Alone, but all thy ranke a reverend Name.   40

XXXIV

An Epigram. To the small Poxe

ENVIOUS and foule Disease, could there not be
One beautie in an Age, and free from thee?
What did she worth thy spight? were there not store
Of those that set by their false faces more
Then this did by her true? She never sought
Quarrell with Nature, or in ballance brought
Art her false servant; Nor, for Sir Hugh Plat,
Was drawne to practise other hue, then that
Her owne bloud gave her: Shee ne're had, nor hath
Any beliefe, in Madam Baud-bees bath,   10

Or Turners oyle of Talck. Nor ever got
Spanish receipt, to make her teeth to rot.
What was the cause then? Thought'st thou in
    disgrace
Of Beautie, so to nullifie a face,
That heaven should make no more; or should amisse
Make all hereafter, had'st thou ruin'd this?
I, that thy Ayme was; but her fate prevail'd:
And scorn'd, thou'ast showne thy malice, but hast
    fail'd.

XXXV

An Epitaph

WHAT Beautie would have lovely stilde,
What manners prettie, Nature milde,
What wonder perfect, all were fil'd,
Upon record in this blest child.
    And. till the comming of the Soule
    To fetch the flesh, we keepe the Rowle.

XXXVI

A Song

Lover

COME, let us here enjoy the shade,
For love in shadow best is made.
Though Envie oft his shadow be,
None brookes the Sun-light worse then he.

Mistres

Where love doth shine, there needs no Sunne,
All lights into his one doth run;

Without which all the world were darke;
Yet he himselfe is but a sparke.

Arbiter

A Sparke to set whole world a-fire,
Who more they burne, they more desire,   10
And have their being, their waste to see;
And waste still, that they still might bee.

Chorus

Such are his powers, whom time hath stil'd,
Now swift, now slow, now tame, now wild;
Now hot, now cold, now fierce, now mild:
The eldest God, yet still a Child.

XXXVII

An Epistle to a Friend

SIR, I am thankfull, first, to heaven, for you;
Next to your selfe, for making your love true:
Then to your love, and gift. And all's but due.

You have unto my Store added a booke,
On which with profit, I shall never looke,
But must confesse from whom what gift I tooke.

Not like your Countrie-neighbours, that commit
Their vice of loving for a Christmasse fit;
Which is indeed but friendship of the spit:

But, as a friend, which name your selfe receave,   10
And which you (being the worthier) gave me leave
In letters, that mixe spirits, thus to weave.

164

Which, how most sacred I will ever keepe,
So may the fruitfull Vine my temples steepe,
And Fame wake for me, when I yeeld to sleepe.

Though you sometimes proclaime me too severe,
Rigid, and harsh, which is a Drug austere
In friendship, I confesse: But deare friend, heare.

Little know they, that professe Amitie,
And seeke to scant her comelie libertie,   20
How much they lame her in her propertie.

And lesse they know, who being free to use
That friendship which no chance but love did chuse,
Will unto Licence that faire leave abuse.

It is an Act of tyrannie, not love
In practiz'd friendship wholly to reprove,
As flatt'ry with friends humours still to move.

From each of which I labour to be free,
Yet if with eithers vice I teynted be,
Forgive it, as my frailtie, and not me.   30

For no man lives so out of passions sway,
But shall sometimes be tempted to obey
Her furie, yet no friendship to betray.

XXXVIII

An Elegie

'Tis true, I'm broke! Vowes, Oathes, and all I had
Of Credit lost. And I am now run madde:
Or doe upon my selfe some desperate ill;
This sadnesse makes no approaches, but to kill.

It is a Darknesse hath blockt up my sense,
And drives it in to eat on my offence,
Or there to sterve it. Helpe, O you that may
Alone lend succours, and this furie stay.
Offended Mistris, you are yet so faire,
As light breakes from you, that affrights despaire,
And fills my powers with perswading joy,   11
That you should be too noble to destroy.
There may some face or menace of a storme
Looke forth, but cannot last in such a forme.
If there be nothing worthy you can see
Of Graces, or your mercie here in me,
Spare your owne goodnesse yet; and be not great
In will and power, only to defeat.
God, and the good, know to forgive, and save.
The ignorant, and fooles, no pittie have.   20
I will not stand to justifie my fault,
Or lay the excuse upon the Vintners vault;
Or in confessing of the Crime be nice,
Or goe about to countenance the vice,
By naming in what companie 'twas in,
As I would urge Authoritie for sinne.
No, I will stand arraign'd, and cast, to be
The Subject of your Grace in pardoning me,
And (Stil'd your mercies Creature) will live more
Your honour now, then your disgrace before.   30
Thinke it was frailtie, Mistris, thinke me man,
Thinke that your selfe like heaven forgive me can;
Where weaknesse doth offend, and vertue grieve,
There greatnesse takes a glorie to relieve.
Thinke that I once was yours, or may be now;
Nothing is vile, that is a part of you:
Errour and folly in me may have crost
Your just commands; yet those, not I be lost.
I am regenerate now, become the child
Of your compassion; Parents should be mild: 40

There is no Father that for one demerit,
Or two, or three, a Sonne will dis-inherit;
That is the last of punishments is meant;
No man inflicts that paine, till hope be spent:
An ill-affected limbe (what e're it aile)
We cut not off, till all Cures else doe faile:
And then with pause; for sever'd once, that's gone,
Would live his glory that could keepe it on:
Doe not despaire my mending; to distrust
Before you prove a medicine, is unjust.   50
You may so place me, and in such an ayre
As not alone the Cure, but scarre be faire.
That is, if still your Favours you apply,
And not the bounties you ha' done, deny.
Could you demand the gifts you gave, againe!
Why was't? did e're the Cloudes aske back their
     raine?
The Sunne his heat, and light, the ayre his dew?
Or winds the Spirit, by which the flower so grew?
That were to wither all, and make a Grave
Of that wise Nature would a Cradle have!   60
Her order is to cherish, and preserve,
Consumptions nature to destroy, and sterve.
But to exact againe what once is given,
Is natures meere obliquitie! as Heaven
Should aske the blood, and spirits he hath infus'd
In man, because man hath the flesh abus'd.
O may your wisdome take example hence,
God lightens not at mans each fraile offence,
He pardons slips, goes by a world of ills,
And then his thunder frights more, then it kills.   70
He cannot angrie be, but all must quake,
It shakes even him, that all things else doth shake.
And how more faire, and lovely lookes the world
In a calme skie; then when the heaven is horl'd
About in Cloudes, and wrapt in raging weather,
As all with storme and tempest ran together.

O imitate that sweet Serenitie
That makes us live, not that which calls to die
In darke, and sullen mornes; doe we not say
This looketh like an Execution day?   80
And with the vulgar doth it not obtaine
The name of Cruell weather, storme, and raine?
Be not affected with these markes too much
Of crueltie, lest they doe make you such.
But view the mildnesse of your Makers state,
As I the penitents here emulate:
He, when he sees a sorrow such as this,
Streight puts off all his Anger, and doth kisse
The contrite Soule, who hath no thought to win
Upon the hope to have another sin   90
Forgiven him; and in that lyne stand I,
Rather then once displease you more, to die,
To suffer tortures, scorne, and Infamie,
What Fooles, and all their Parasites can apply;
The wit of Ale, and Genius of the Malt
Can pumpe for; or a Libell without salt
Produce; though threatning with a coale, or chalke
On every wall, and sung where e're I walke.
I number these as being of the Chore
Of Contumelie, and urge a good man more   100
Then sword, or fire, or what is of the race
To carry noble danger in the face:
There is not any punishment, or paine,
A man should flie from, as he would disdaine.
Then Mistresse, here, here let your rigour end,
And let your mercie make me asham'd t'offend.
I will no more abuse my vowes to you,
Then I will studie falshood, to be true.
O, that you could but by dissection see
How much you are the better part of me;   110
How all my Fibres by your Spirit doe move,
And that there is no life in me, but love.

You would be then most confident, that tho
Publike affaires command me now to goe
Out of your eyes, and be awhile away;
Absence, or Distance, shall not breed decay.
Your forme shines here, here fixed in my heart:
I may dilate my selfe, but not depart.
Others by common Stars their courses run,
When I see you, then I doe see my Sun;   120
Till then 'tis all but darknesse, that I have;
Rather then want your light, I wish a grave.

*XXXIX

An Elegie

To make the Doubt cleare that no Woman's true,
Was it my fate to prove it full in you?
Thought I but one had breath'd the purer Ayre,
And must she needs be false, because she's faire?
It is your beauties Marke, or of your youth,
Or your perfection not to studie truth;
Or thinke you heaven is deafe? or hath no eyes?
Or those it has, winke at your perjuries?
Are vowes so cheape with women? or the matter
Whereof they are made, that they are writ in water;   10
And blowne away with wind? or doth their breath
Both hot and cold at once, threat life and death?
Who could have thought so many accents sweet
Tun'd to our words, so many sighes should meet
Blowne from our hearts, so many oathes and teares
Sprinkled among? All sweeter by our feares,
And the Devine Impression of stolne kisses,
That seal'd the rest, could now prove emptie blisses?
Did you draw bonds to forfeit? Signe, to breake,
Or must we read you quite from what you speake,   20

169

And find the truth out the wrong way? or must
He first desire you false, would wish you just?
O, I prophane! though most of women be,
The common Monster, Love shall except thee,
My dearest Love, how ever jealousie,
With Circumstance might urge the contrarie.
Sooner I'le thinke the Sunne would cease to cheare
The teeming Earth, and that forget to beare;
Sooner that Rivers would run back, or Thames
With ribs of Ice in June would bid his streames: 30
Or Nature, by whose strength the world indures,
Would change her course, before you alter yours:
But, O, that trecherous breast, to whom, weake you
Did trust our counsells, and we both may rue,
Having his falshood found too late! 'twas he
That made me cast you Guiltie, and you me.
Whilst he, black wretch, betray'd each simple word
We spake unto the comming of a third!
Curst may he be that so our love hath slaine,
And wander wretched on the earth, as Cain,   40
Wretched as he, and not deserve least pittie;
In plaguing him let miserie be wittie.
Let all eyes shun him, and he shun each eye,
Till he be noysome as his infamie;
May he without remorse deny God thrice,
And not be trusted more on his soules price;
And after all selfe-torment, when he dyes,
May Wolves teare out his heart, Vultures his eyes,
Swyne eat his Bowels, and his falser Tongue,
That utter'd all, be to some Raven flung,   50
And let his carrion corse be a longer feast
To the Kings Dogs, then any other beast.
Now I have curst, let us our love revive;
In me the flame was never more alive.
I could begin againe to court and praise,
And in that pleasure lengthen the short dayes

Of my lifes lease; like Painters that doe take
Delight, not in made workes, but whilst they make.
I could renew those times, when first I saw
Love in your eyes, that gave my tongue the Law 60
To like what you lik'd, and at Masques, or Playes,
Commend the selfe-same Actors, the same wayes;
Aske how you did? and often with intent
Of being officious, grow impertinent;
All which were such lost pastimes, as in these
Love was as subtly catch'd as a Disease.
But, being got, it is a treasure, sweet,
Which to defend, is harder then to get;
And ought not be prophan'd on either part,
For though 'tis got by chance, 'tis kept by art.   70

XL

An Elegie

THAT Love's a bitter sweet, I ne're conceive
Till the sower Minute comes of taking leave,
And then I taste it. But as men drinke up
In hast the bottome of a med'cin'd Cup,
And take some sirrup after; so doe I,
To put all relish from my memorie
Of parting, drowne it in the hope to meet
Shortly againe: and make our absence sweet.
This makes me, Mistresse, that sometime by stealth
Under another Name, I take your health;   10
And turne the Ceremonies of those Nights
I give, or owe my friends, into your Rites,
But ever without blazon, or least shade
Of vowes so sacred, and in silence made;
For though Love thrive, and may grow up with
    cheare,
And free societie, hee's borne else-where,

P   171

And must be bred, so to conceale his birth,
As neither wine doe rack it out, or mirth.
Yet should the Lover still be ayrie and light,
In all his Actions rarified to spright;   20
Not like a Midas shut up in himselfe,
And turning all he toucheth into pelfe,
Keepe in reserv'd in his Dark-lanterne face,
As if that ex'lent Dulnesse were Loves grace;
No Mistresse no, the open merrie Man
Moves like a sprightly River, and yet can
Keepe secret in his Channels what he breedes
'Bove all your standing waters, choak'd with
    weedes.
They looke at best like Creame-bowles, and you
    soone
Shall find their depth: they're sounded with a
    spoone.   30
They may say Grace, and for Loves Chaplaines
    passe;
But the grave Lover ever was an Asse;
Is fix'd upon one leg, and dares not come
Out with the other, for hee's still at home;
Like the dull wearied Crane that (come on land)
Doth, while he keepes his watch, betray his stand.
Where he that knowes will like a Lapwing flie
Farre from the Nest, and so himselfe belie
To others, as he will deserve the Trust
Due to that one, that doth believe him just.   40
And such your Servant is, who vowes to keepe
The Jewell of your name, as close as sleepe
Can lock the Sense up, or the heart a thought,
And never be by time, or folly brought,
Weaknesse of braine, or any charme of Wine,
The sinne of Boast, or other countermine
(Made to blow up loves secrets) to discover
That Article, may not become your lover:

Which in assurance to your brest I tell,
If I had writ no word, but Deare, farewell.　50

An Elegie

SINCE you must goe, and I must bid farewell,
Heare, Mistresse, your departing servant tell
What it is like: And doe not thinke they can
Be idle words, though of a parting Man;
It is as if a night should shade noone-day,
Or that the Sun was here, but forc't away;
And we were left under that Hemisphere,
Where we must feele it Darke for halfe a yeare.
What fate is this to change mens dayes and houres,
To shift their seasons, and destroy their powers!　10
Alas I ha' lost my heat, my blood, my prime,
Winter is come a Quarter e're his Time,
My health will leave me; and when you depart,
How shall I doe, sweet Mistris, for my heart?
You would restore it? No, that's worth a feare,
As if it were not worthy to be there:
O, keepe it still; for it had rather be
Your sacrifice, then here remaine with me.
And so I spare it. Come what can become
Of me, I'le softly tread unto my Tombe;　20
Or like a Ghost walke silent amongst men,
Till I may see both it and you agen.

XLII

An Elegie

LET me be what I am, as Virgil cold;
As Horace fat; or as Anacreon old;
No Poets verses yet did ever move,
Whose Readers did not thinke he was in love.
Who shall forbid me then in Rithme to bee
As light, and Active as the youngest hee
That from the Muses fountaines doth indorse
His lines, and hourely sits the Poets horse?
Put on my Ivy Garland, let me see
Who frownes, who jealous is, who taxeth me.   10
Fathers, and Husbands, I doe claime a right
In all that is call'd lovely: take my sight
Sooner then my affection from the faire.
No face, no hand, proportion, line, or Ayre
Of beautie; but the Muse hath interest in:
There is not worne that lace, purle, knot or pin,
But is the Poets matter: And he must,
When he is furious, love, although not lust.
But then content, your Daughters and your Wives,
(If they be faire and worth it) have their lives   20
Made longer by our praises. Or, if not,
Wish, you had fowle ones, and deformed got;
Curst in their Cradles, or there chang'd by Elves,
So to be sure you doe injoy your selves.
Yet keepe those up in sackcloth too, or lether,
For Silke will draw some sneaking Songster thither.
It is a ryming Age, and Verses swarme
At every stall; The Cittie Cap's a charme.
But I who live, and have liv'd twentie yeare
Where I may handle Silke, as free, and neere,   30
As any Mercer; or the whale-bone man
That quilts those bodies, I have leave to span:

Have eaten with the Beauties, and the wits,
And braveries of Court, and felt their fits
Of love, and hate: and came so nigh to know
Whether their faces were their owne, or no:
It is not likely I should now looke downe
Upon a Velvet Petticote, or a Gowne,
Whose like I have knowne the Taylors Wife put on
To doe her Husbands rites in, e're 'twere gone   40
Home to the Customer: his Letcherie
Being, the best clothes still to præoccupie.
Put a Coach-mare in Tissue, must I horse
Her presently? Or leape thy Wife of force,
When by thy sordid bountie she hath on,
A Gowne of that, was the Caparison?
So I might dote upon thy Chaires, and Stooles
That are like cloath'd: must I be of those fooles
Of race accompted, that no passion have
But when thy Wife (as thou conceiv'st) is brave? 50
Then ope thy wardrobe, thinke me that poore
   Groome
That from the Foot-man, when he was become
An Officer there, did make most solemne love,
To ev'ry Petticote he brush'd, and Glove
He did lay up, and would adore the shooe,
Or slipper was left off, and kisse it too,
Court every hanging Gowne, and after that,
Lift up some one, and doe, I tell not what.
Thou didst tell me; and wert o'er-joy'd to peepe
In at a hole, and see these Actions creepe   60
From the poore wretch, which though he play'd in
   prose,
He would have done in verse, with any of those
Wrung on the Withers, by Lord Loves despight,
Had he had the facultie to reade, and write!
Such Songsters there are store of; witnesse he
That chanc'd the lace, laid on a Smock, to see,

And straight-way spent a Sonnet; with that other
That (in pure Madrigall) unto his Mother
Commended the French-hood, and Scarlet gowne
The Lady Mayresse pass'd in through the Towne,
Unto the Spittle Sermon. O, what strange   71
Varietie of Silkes were on th'Exchange!
Or in Moore-fields! this other night, sings one;
Another answers, 'Lasse those Silkes are none,
In smiling *L'envoye*, as he would deride
Any Comparison had with his Cheap-side,
And vouches both the Pageant, and the Day,
When not the Shops, but windowes doe display
The Stuffes, the Velvets, Plushes, Fringes, Lace,
And all the originall riots of the place: 80
Let the poore fooles enjoy their follies, love
A Goat in Velvet; or some block could move
Under that cover; an old Mid-wives hat!
Or a Close-stoole so cas'd; or any fat
Bawd, in a Velvet scabberd! I envy
None of their pleasures! nor will aske thee, why
Thou art jealous of thy Wifes, or Daughters Case:
More then of eithers manners, wit, or face!

XLIII

An Execration upon Vulcan

AND why to me this, thou lame Lord of fire,
What had I done that might call on thine ire?
Or urge thy Greedie flame, thus to devoure
So many my Yeares-labours in an houre?
I ne're attempted, Vulcan, 'gainst thy life;
Nor made least line of love to thy loose Wife;
Or in remembrance of thy afront, and scorne,
With Clownes, and Tradesmen, kept thee clos'd in
    horne.

176

'Twas Jupiter that hurl'd thee headlong downe,
And Mars, that gave thee a Lanthorne for a
   Crowne: 10
Was it because thou wert of old denied
By Jove to have Minerva for thy Bride,
That since thou tak'st all envious care and paine,
To ruine any issue of the braine?
Had I wrote treason there, or heresie,
Imposture, witchcraft, charmes, or blasphemie,
I had deserv'd, then, thy consuming lookes,
Perhaps, to have been burned with my bookes.
But, on thy malice, tell me, didst thou spie
Any, least loose, or scurrile paper lie   20
Conceal'd, or kept there, that was fit to be,
By thy owne vote, a sacrifice to thee?
Did I there wound the honours of the Crowne?
Or taxe the Glories of the Church, and Gowne?
Itch to defame the State? or brand the Times?
And my selfe most, in some selfe-boasting Rimes?
If none of these, then why this fire? Or find
A cause before; or leave me one behind.
Had I compil'd from *Amadis de Gaule*,
Th'*Esplandians*, *Arthurs*, *Palmerins*, and all   30
The learned Librarie of Don Quixote;
And so some goodlier monster had begot,
Or spun out Riddles, and weav'd fiftie tomes
Of Logogriphes, and curious Palindromes,
Or pomp'd for those hard trifles Anagrams,
Or Eteostichs, or those finer flammes
Of Egges, and Halberds, Cradles, and a Herse,
A paire of Scisars, and a Combe in verse;
Acrostichs, and Telestichs, on jumpe names,
Thou then hadst had some colour for thy flames,
On such my serious follies; But, thou'lt say,   41
There were some pieces of as base allay,
And as false stampe there; parcels of a Play,
Fitter to see the fire-light, then the day;

Adulterate moneys, such as might not goe:
Thou should'st have stay'd, till publike fame said
　　so.
Shee is the Judge, Thou Executioner:
Or if thou needs would'st trench upon her power,
Thou mightst have yet enjoy'd thy crueltie
With some more thrift, and more varietie:　　50
Thou mightst have had me perish, piece, by piece,
To light Tobacco, or save roasted Geese,
Sindge Capons, or poore Pigges, dropping their
　　eyes;
Condemn'd me to the Ovens with the pies;
And so, have kept me dying a whole age,
Not ravish'd all hence in a minutes rage.
But that's a marke, whereof thy Rites doe boast,
To make consumption, ever where thou go'st;
Had I fore-knowne of this thy least desire
T'have held a Triumph, or a feast of fire,　　60
Especially in paper; that, that steame
Had tickled your large Nosthrill: many a Reame,
To redeeme mine, I had sent in; enough,
Thou should'st have cry'd, and all beene proper
　　stuffe.
The *Talmud*, and the *Alcoran* had come,
With pieces of the *Legend*; The whole summe
Of errant Knight-hood, with the Dames, and
　　Dwarfes;
The charmed Boates, and the inchanted Wharfes,
The Tristrams, Lanc'lots, Turpins, and the Peers,
All the madde Rolands, and sweet Oliveers;　　70
To Merlins Marvailes, and his Caballs losse,
With the Chimæra of the Rosie-Crosse,
Their Seales, their Characters, Hermetique rings,
Their Jemme of Riches, and bright Stone, that
　　brings
Invisibilitie, and strength, and tongues:
The art of kindling the true Coale, by lungs;

With Nicholas Pasquill's, Meddle with your match,
And the strong lines, that so the time doe catch,
Or Captaine Pamphlets horse, and foot; that sallie
Upon th'Exchange, still out of Popes-head-Alley,
The weekly Corrants, with Pauls Seale; and all   81
Th'admir'd discourses of the Prophet Ball:
These, had'st thou pleas'd either to dine, or sup,
Had made a meale for Vulcan to lick up.
But in my Deske, what was there to accite
So ravenous, and vast an appetite?
I dare not say a body, but some parts
There were of search, and mastry in the Arts.
All the old Venusine, in Poetrie,
And lighted by the Stagerite, could spie,   90
Was there made English: with the Grammar too,
To teach some that, their Nurses could not doe,
The puritie of Language; and among
The rest, my journey into Scotland sung,
With all th'adventures; Three bookes not afraid
To speake the fate of the Sicilian Maid
To our owne Ladyes; and in storie there
Of our fift Henry, eight of his nine yeare;
Wherein was oyle, beside the succour spent,
Which noble Carew, Cotton, Selden lent: 100
And twice-twelve-yeares stor'd up humanitie,
With humble Gleanings in Divinitie;
After the Fathers, and those wiser Guides
Whom Faction had not drawne to studie sides.
How in these ruines, Vulcan, thou dost lurke,
All soote, and embers! odious, as thy worke!
I now begin to doubt, if ever Grace,
Or Goddesse, could be patient of thy face.
Thou woo Minerva! or to wit aspire!
'Cause thou canst halt, with us, in Arts, and Fire!
Sonne of the Wind! for so thy mother gone   111
With lust conceiv'd thee; Father thou hadst none:

When thou wert borne, and that thou look'st at
    best,
She durst not kisse, but flung thee from her brest.
And so did Jove, who ne're meant thee his Cup:
No mar'le the Clownes of Lemnos tooke thee up,
For none but Smiths would have made thee a God.
Some Alchimist there may be yet, or odde
Squire of the Squibs, against the Pageant day,
May to thy name a *Vulcanale* say;   120
And for it lose his eyes with Gun-powder,
As th'other may his braines with Quicksilver.
Well-fare the Wise-men yet, on the Banckside,
My friends, the Watermen! They could provide
Against thy furie, when to serve their needs,
They made a Vulcan of a sheafe of Reedes,
Whom they durst handle in their holy-day coates,
And safely trust to dresse, not burne their Boates.
But, O those Reeds! thy meere disdaine of them
Made thee beget that cruell Stratagem,   130
(Which, some are pleas'd to stile but thy madde
    pranck)
Against the Globe, the Glory of the Banke,
Which, though it were the Fort of the whole Parish,
Flank'd with a Ditch, and forc'd out of a Marish,
I saw with two poore Chambers taken in
And raz'd; e're thought could urge, this might have
    beene!
See the worlds Ruines! nothing but the piles
Left! and wit since to cover it with Tiles.
The Brethren, they streight nois'd it out for Newes,
'Twas verily some Relique of the Stewes: 140
And this a Sparkle of that fire let loose
That was lock'd up in the Winchestrian Goose
Bred on the Banck, in time of Poperie,
When Venus there maintain'd the Misterie.
But, others fell, with that conceipt by the eares,
And cry'd, it was a threatning to the beares;

And that accursed ground, the Parish-Garden:
Nay, (sigh'd a Sister) 'twas the Nun, Kate Arden,
Kindled the fire! But, then did one returne,
No Foole would his owne harvest spoile, or burne!
If that were so, thou rather wouldst advance 151
The place, that was thy Wives inheritance.
O no, cry'd all. Fortune, for being a whore,
Scap'd not his Justice any jot the more:
He burnt that Idoll of the Revels too:
Nay, let White-Hall with Revels have to doe,
Though but in daunces, it shall know his power;
There was a Judgement shew'n too in an houre.
Hee is true Vulcan still! He did not spare
Troy, though it were so much his Venus care. 160
Foole, wilt thou let that in example come?
Did she not save from thence, to build a Rome?
And what hast thou done in these pettie spights,
More then advanc'd the houses, and their rites?
I will not argue thee, from those of guilt,
For they were burnt, but to be better built.
'Tis true, that in thy wish they were destroy'd,
Which thou hast only vented, not enjoy'd.
So would'st th'have run upon the Rolls by stealth,
And didst invade part of the Common-wealth, 170
In those Records, which were all Chronicles gone,
Will be remembred by Six Clerkes, to one.
But, say all sixe, Good Men, what answer yee?
Lyes there no Writ, out of the Chancerie,
Against this Vulcan? No Injunction?
No order? no Decree? Though we be gone
At Common-Law: Me thinkes in his despight
A Court of Equitie should doe us right:
But to confine him to the Brew-houses,
The Glasse-house, Dye-fats, and their Fornaces;
To live in Sea-coale, and goe forth in smoake; 181
Or lest that vapour might the Citie choake,

Condemne him to the Brick-kills, or some Hill-
Foot (out in Sussex) to an iron Mill;
Or in small Fagots have him blaze about
Vile Tavernes, and the Drunkards pisse him out;
Or in the Bell-Mans Lanthorne, like a spie,
Burne to a snuffe, and then stinke out, and die:
I could invent a sentence, yet were worse;
But I'le conclude all in a civill curse.   190
Pox on your flameship, Vulcan; if it be
To all as fatall as't hath beene to me,
And to Pauls-Steeple; which was unto us
'Bove all your Fire-workes had at Ephesus,
Or Alexandria; and though a Divine
Losse remaines yet, as unrepair'd as mine.
Would you had kept your Forge, at Ætna still,
And there made Swords, Bills, Glaves, and Armes
    your fill;
Maintain'd the trade at Bilbo; or else-where;
Strooke in at Millan with the Cutlers there;   200
Or stay'd but where the Fryar, and you first met,
Who from the Divels-Arse did Guns beget;
Or fixt in the Low-Countrey's, where you might
On both sides doe your mischiefes with delight;
Blow up, and ruine, myne, and countermyne,
Make your Petards, and Granats, all your fine
Engines of Murder, and receive the praise
Of massacring Man-kind so many wayes.
We aske your absence here, we all love peace,
And pray the fruites thereof, and the increase;   210
So doth the King, and most of the Kings men
That have good places: therefore once agen,
Pox on thee, Vulcan, thy Pandora's pox,
And all the Evils that flew out of her box
Light on thee: Or if those plagues will not doo.
Thy Wives pox on thee, and Bess Braughtons too.

XLIV

A speach according to Horace

WHY yet, my noble hearts, they cannot say,
But we have Powder still for the Kings Day,
And Ord'nance too: so much as from the Tower
T'have wak'd, if sleeping, Spaines Ambassadour,
Old Æsope Gundomar: the French can tell,
For they did see it the last tilting well,
That we have Trumpets, Armour, and great Horse,
Launces, and men, and some a breaking force.
They saw too store of feathers, and more may,
If they stay here, but till Saint Georges Day.   10
All Ensignes of a Warre are not yet dead,
Nor markes of wealth so from our Nation fled,
But they may see Gold-Chaines, and Pearle worne
    then,
Lent by the London Dames, to the Lords men;
Withall, the dirtie paines those Citizens take,
To see the Pride at Court, their Wives doe make:
And the returne those thankfull Courtiers yeeld
To have their Husbands drawne forth to the field,
And comming home, to tell what acts were done
Under the Auspice of young Swynnerton.   20
What a strong Fort old Pimblicoe had beene!
How it held out! how (last) 'twas taken in!
Well, I say thrive, thrive brave Artillerie yard,
Thou Seed-plot of the warre, that hast not spar'd
Powder, or paper, to bring up the youth
Of London, in the Militarie truth,
These ten yeares day; As all may sweare that looke
But on thy practise, and the Posture booke:
He that but saw thy curious Captaines drill,
Would thinke no more of Vlushing, or the Brill: 30
But give them over to the common eare
For that unnecessarie Charge they were.

Well did thy craftie Clerke, and Knight, Sir Hugh
Supplant bold Panton; and brought there to view
Translated Ælian tactickes to be read,
And the Greeke Discipline (with the moderne) shed
So, in that ground, as soone it grew to be
The Cittie-Question, whether Tilly, or he,
Were now the greater Captaine? for they saw
The Berghen siege, and taking in Breda,   40
So acted to the life, as Maurice might,
And Spinola have blushed at the sight.
O happie Art! and wise Epitome
Of bearing Armes! most civill Soldierie!
Thou canst draw forth thy forces, and fight drie
The Battells of thy Aldermanitie;
Without the hazard of a drop of blood:
More then the surfets, in thee, that day stood.
Goe on, increast in vertue, and in fame:
And keep the Glorie of the English name,   50
Up among Nations. In the stead of bold
Beauchamps, and Nevills, Cliffords, Audley's old;
Insert thy Hodges,* and those newer men,
As Stiles, Dike , Ditchfield, Millar, Crips, and Fen:
That keepe the warre, though now't be growne
    more tame,
Alive yet, in the noise; and still the same;
And could (if our great men would let their Sonnes
Come to their Schooles,) show'hem the use of
    Guns,
And there instruct the noble English heires
In Politique, and Militar Affaires;   60
But he that should perswade, to have this done
For education of our Lordings; soone
Should he heare of billow, wind, and storme,
From the Tempestuous Grandlings, who'll informe
Us, in our bearing, that they are thus, and thus,
Borne, bred, allied? what's he dare tutor us?

* Waller
184

Are we by Booke-wormes to be awde? must we
Live by their Scale, that dare doe nothing free?
Why are we rich, or great, except to show
All licence in our lives? What need we know?　　70
More then to praise a Dog? or Horse? or speake
The Hawking language? or our Day to breake
With Citizens? let Clownes, and Tradesmen breed
Their Sonnes to studie Arts, the Lawes, the Creed:
We will beleeve like men of our owne Ranke,
In so much land a yeare, or such a Banke,
That turnes us so much moneys, at which rate
Our Ancestors impos'd on Prince and State.
Let poore Nobilitie be vertuous: Wee,
Descended in a rope of Titles, be　　　　　　80
From Guy, or Bevis, Arthur, or from whom
The Herald will. Our blood is now become
Past any need of vertue. Let them care,
That in the Cradle of their Gentrie are;
To serve the State by Councels, and by Armes:
We neither love the Troubles, nor the harmes.
What love you then? your whore? what study? gate,
Carriage, and dressing? There is up of late
The Academie, where the Gallants meet—
What, to make legs? yes, and to smell most sweet.
All that they doe at Playes. O, but first here　　91
They learne and studie; and then practise there.
But why are all these Irons i'the fire
Of severall makings? helps, helps, t'attire
His Lordship. That is for his Band, his haire
This, and that box his Beautie to repaire;
This other for his eye-browes; hence, away,
I may no longer on these pictures stay,
These Carkasses of honour; Taylors blocks,
Cover'd with Tissue, whose prosperitie mocks　　100
The fate of things: whilst totter'd vertue holds
Her broken Armes up, to their emptie moulds.

XLV

An Epistle to Master Arth: Squib

WHAT I am not, and what I faine would be,
Whilst I informe my selfe, I would teach thee,
My gentle Arthur; that it might be said
One lesson we have both learn'd, and well read;
I neither am, nor art thou one of those
That hearkens to a Jacks-pulse, when it goes.
Nor ever trusted to that friendship yet
Was issue of the Taverne, or the Spit:
Much lesse a name would we bring up, or nurse,
That could but claime a kindred from the purse. 10
Those are poore Ties, depend on those false ends,
'Tis vertue alone, or nothing that knits friends:
And as within your Office, you doe take
No piece of money, but you know, or make
Inquirie of the worth: So must we doe,
First weigh a friend, then touch, and trie him too:
For there are many slips, and Counterfeits.
Deceit is fruitfull. Men have Masques and nets,
But these with wearing will themselves unfold:
They cannot last. No lie grew ever old.   20
Turne him, and see his Threds: looke, if he be
Friend to himselfe, that would be friend to thee.
For that is first requir'd, A man be his owne.
But he that's too-much that, is friend of none.
Then rest, and a friends value understand:
It is a richer Purchase then of land.

XLVI

An Epigram on Sir Edward Coke, when he was Lord Chiefe Justice of England

HE that should search all Glories of the Gowne,
And steps of all rais'd servants of the Crowne,
He could not find, then thee of all that store
Whom Fortune aided lesse, or vertue more.
Such, Coke, were thy beginnings, when thy good
In others evill best was understood:
When, being the Strangers helpe, the poore mans
    aide,
Thy just defences made th'oppressor afraid.
Such was thy Processe, when Integritie,
And skill in thee, now, grew Authoritie;   10
That Clients strove, in Question of the Lawes,
More for thy Patronage, then for their Cause,
And that thy strong and manly Eloquence
Stood up thy Nations fame, her Crownes defence,
And now such is thy stand; while thou dost deale
Desired Justice to the publique Weale
Like Solons selfe; explat'st the knottie Lawes
With endlesse labours, whilst thy learning drawes
No lesse of praise, then readers in all kinds
Of worthiest knowledge, that can take mens minds.
Such is thy All; that (as I sung before)   21
None Fortune aided lesse, or Vertue more.
Or if Chance must, to each man that doth rise,
Needs lend an aide, to thine she had her eyes.

XLVII

An Epistle answering to one that asked to be Sealed of the Tribe of Ben

MEN that are safe, and sure, in all they doe,
Care not what trials they are put unto;
They meet the fire, the Test, as Martyrs would;
And though Opinion stampe them not, are gold.
I could say more of such, but that I flie
To speake my selfe out too ambitiously,
And shewing so weake an Act to vulgar eyes,
Put conscience and my right to compromise.
Let those that meerely talke, and never thinke,
That live in the wild Anarchie of Drinke   10
Subject to quarrell only; or else such
As make it their proficiencie, how much
They'ave glutted in, and letcher'd out that weeke,
That never yet did friend, or friendship seeke
But for a Sealing: let these men protest.
Or th'other on their borders, that will jeast
On all Soules that are absent; even the dead;
Like flies, or wormes, which mans corrupt parts
    fed:
That to speake well, thinke it above all sinne,
Of any Companie but that they are in,   20
Call every night to Supper in these fitts,
And are received for the Covey of Witts;
That censure all the Towne, and all th'affaires,
And know whose ignorance is more then theirs;
Let these men have their wayes, and take their
    times
To vent their Libels, and to issue rimes;
I have no portion in them, nor their deale
Of newes they get, to strew out the long meale.

I studie other friendships, and more one,
Then these can ever be; or else wish none.　　30
What is't to me whether the French Designe
Be, or be not, to get the Val-telline?
Or the States Ships sent forth belike to meet
Some hopes of Spaine in their West-Indian Fleet?
Whether the Dispensation yet be sent,
Or that the Match from Spaine was ever meant?
I wish all well, and pray high heaven conspire
My Princes safetie, and my Kings desire,
But if for honour, we must draw the Sword,
And force back that, which will not be restor'd,　　40
I have a body, yet, that spirit drawes
To live, or fall, a Carkasse in the cause.
So farre without inquirie what the States,
Brunsfield, and Mansfield doe this yeare, my fates
Shall carry me at Call; and I'le be well,
Though I doe neither heare these newes, nor tell
Of Spaine or France; or were not prick'd downe
　　one
Of the late Mysterie of reception,
Although my Fame, to his, not under-heares,
That guides the Motions, and directs the beares.　　50
But that's a blow, by which in time I may
Lose all my credit with my Christmas Clay,
And animated Porc'lane of the Court;
I, and for this neglect, the courser sort
Of earthen Jarres, there may molest me too:
Well, with mine owne fraile Pitcher, what to doe
I have decreed; keepe it from waves, and presse;
Lest it be justled, crack'd, made nought, or lesse:
Live to that point I will, for which I am man,
And dwell as in my Center, as I can,　　60
Still looking too, and ever loving heaven;
With reverence using all the gifts thence given.
'Mongst which, if I have any friendships sent
Such as are square, wel-tagde, and permanent,

Not built with Canvasse, paper, and false lights
As are the Glorious Scenes, at the great sights;
And that there be no fev'ry heats, nor colds,
Oylie Expansions, or shrunke durtie folds,
But all so cleare, and led by reasons flame,
As but to stumble in her sight were shame.   70
These I will honour, love, embrace, and serve:
And free it from all question to preserve.
So short you read my Character, and theirs
I would call mine, to which not many Staires
Are asked to climbe. First give me faith, who know
My selfe a little. I will take you so,
As you have writ your selfe. Now stand, and then,
Sir, you are Sealed of the Tribe of Ben.

XLVIII

The Dedication of the Kings New Cellar
To Bacchus

SINCE, Bacchus, thou art father
Of Wines, to thee the rather
We dedicate this Cellar,
Where new, thou art made Dweller;
And seale thee thy Commission:
But 'tis with a condition,
That thou remaine here taster
Of all to the great Master,
And looke unto their faces,
Their Qualities, and races,   10
That both, their odour take him,
And relish merry make him.
    For, Bacchus, thou art freer
Of cares, and over-seer
Of feast, and merry meeting,
And still begin'st the greeting:

See then thou dost attend him,
Lyæus, and defend him,
By all the Arts of Gladnesse
From any thought like sadnesse.　　　　20
　　So mayst thou still be younger
Then Phœbus; and much stronger
To give mankind their eases,
And cure the Worlds diseases:
　　So may the Muses follow
Thee still, and leave Apollo,
And thinke thy streame more quicker
Then Hippocrenes liquor:
And thou make many a Poet,
Before his braine doe know it;　　　　30
So may there never Quarrell
Have issue from the Barrell;
But Venus and the Graces
Pursue thee in all places,
And not a Song be other
Then Cupid, and his Mother.
That when King James, above here
Shall feast it, thou maist love there
The causes and the Guests too,
And have thy tales and jests too,　　　　40
Thy Circuits, and thy Rounds free
As shall the feasts faire grounds be.
　　Be it he hold Communion
In great Saint Georges Union;
Or gratulates the passage
Of some wel-wrought Embassage:
Whereby he may knit sure up
The wished Peace of Europe:
Or else a health advances,
To put his Court in dances,　　　　50
And set us all on skipping,
When with his royall shipping

The narrow Seas are shadie,
And Charles brings home the Ladie.

Accessit fervor Capiti, Numerusque Lucernis.

XLIX

An Epigram on the Court Pucell

Do's the Court-Pucell then so censure me,
And thinkes I dare not her? let the world see.
What though her Chamber be the very pit
Where fight the prime Cocks of the Game, for wit?
And that as any are strooke, her breath creates
New in their stead, out of the Candidates?
What though with Tribade lust she force a Muse,
And in an Epicæne fury can write newes
Equall with that, which for the best newes goes,
As aerie light, and as like wit as those?   10
What though she talke, and cannot once with them
Make State, Religion, Bawdrie, all a theame?
And as lip-thirstie, in each words expence,
Doth labour with the Phrase more then the sense?
What though she ride two mile on Holy-dayes
To Church, as others doe to Feasts and Playes,
To shew their Tires? to view, and to be view'd?
What though she be with Velvet gownes indu'd,
And spangled Petticotes brought forth to eye,
As new rewards of her old secrecie!   20
What though she hath won on Trust, as many doe,
And that her truster feares her? Must I too?
I never stood for any place: my wit
Thinkes it selfe nought, though she should valew it.
I am no States-man, and much less Divine;
For bawdry, 'tis her language, and not mine.

192

Farthest I am from the Idolatrie
To stuffes and Laces, those my Man can buy.
And trust her I would least, that hath forswore
In Contract twice, what can shee perjure more? 30
Indeed, her Dressing some man might delight,
Her face there's none can like by Candle light:
Not he, that should the body have, for Case
To his poore Instrument, now out of grace.
Shall I advise thee, Pucell? steale away
From Court, while yet thy fame hath some small
    day;
The wits will leave you, if they once perceive
You cling to Lords, and Lords, if them you leave
For Sermoneeres: of which now one, now other,
They say you weekly invite with fits o'th'Mother, 40
And practise for a Miracle; take heed,
This Age would lend no faith to Dorrels Deed;
Or if it would, the Court is the worst place,
Both for the Mothers, and the Babes of grace,
For there the wicked in the Chaire of scorne,
Will cal't a Bastard, when a Prophet's borne.

L

An Epigram. To the Honour'd —— Countesse of ——

THE Wisdome, Madam, of your private Life,
Wherewith this while you live a widowed wife,
And the right wayes you take unto the right,
To conquer rumour, and triumph on spight;
Not only shunning by your act, to doe
Ought that is ill, but the suspition too,
Is of so brave example, as he were
No friend to vertue, could be silent here:

The rather, when the vices of the Time
Are growne so fruitfull, and false pleasures climbe
By all oblique Degrees, that killing height   11
From whence they fall, cast downe with their owne
    weight.
And though all praise bring nothing to your name,
Who (herein studying conscience, and not fame)
Are in your selfe rewarded; yet 'twill be
A cheerefull worke to all good eyes, to see
Among the daily Ruines that fall foule,
Of State, of fame, of body, and of soule,
So great a Vertue stand upright to view,
As makes Penelopes old fable true,   20
Whilst your Ulisses hath ta'ne leave to goe,
Countries, and Climes, manners, and men to know.
Only your time you better entertaine,
Then the great Homers wit, for her, could faine;
For you admit no companie, but good,
And when you want those friends, or neere in
    blood,
Or your Allies, you make your bookes your friend,s
And studie them unto the noblest ends,
Searching for knowledge, and to keep your mind
The same it was inspir'd, rich, and refin'd.   30
These Graces, when the rest of Ladyes view
Not boasted in your life, but practis'd true,
As they are hard, for them to make their owne,
So are they profitable to be knowne:
For when they find so many meet in one,
It will be shame for them, if they have none.

LI

Lord Bacons Birth-day

HAILE, happie Genius of this antient pile!
How comes it all things so about thee smile?
The fire, the wine, the men! and in the midst,
Thou stand'st as if some Mysterie thou did'st!
Pardon, I read it in thy face, the day
For whose returnes, and many, all these pray:
And so doe I. This is the sixtieth yeare
Since Bacon, and thy Lord was borne, and here;
Sonne to the grave wise Keeper of the Seale,
Fame, and foundation of the English Weale.   10
What then his Father was, that since is hee,
Now with a Title more to the Degree;
Englands high Chancellor: the destin'd heire
In his soft Cradle to his Fathers Chaire,
Whose even Thred the Fates spinne round, and
        full,
Out of their Choysest, and their whitest wooll.
    'Tis a brave cause of joy, let it be knowne,
For 'twere a narrow gladnesse, kept thine owne.
Give me a deep-crown'd-Bowle, that I may sing
In raysing him the wisdome of my King.   20

LII

* *A Poeme sent me by Sir William Burlase*

THE PAINTER TO THE POET

To paint thy Worth, if rightly I did know it,
And were but Painter halfe like thee, a Poet;
        Ben, I would show it:

195

But in this skill, m'unskilfull pen will tire,
Thou, and thy worth, will still be found farre higher;
      And I a Lier.
Then, what a Painter's here? or what an eater
Of great attempts! when as his skil's no greater,
      And he a Cheater?
Then what a Poet's here! whom, by Confession   10
Of all with me, to paint without Digression
      There's no Expression.

MY ANSWER. THE POET TO THE PAINTER

WHY? though I seeme of a prodigious wast,
I am not so voluminous, and vast,
But there are lines, wherewith I might b'embrac'd.

'Tis true, as my wombe swells, so my back stoupes,
And the whole lumpe growes round, deform'd, and
   droupes,
But yet the Tun at Heidelberg had houpes.

You were not tied, by any Painters Law
To square my Circle, I confesse; but draw
My Superficies: that was all you saw.

Which if in compasse of no Art it came   10
To be described by a Monogram,
With one great blot, yo'had form'd me as I am.

But whilst you curious were to have it be
An Archetipe, for all the world to see,
You made it a brave piece, but not like me.

O, had I now your manner, maistry, might,
Your Power of handling shadow, ayre, and spright,
How I would draw, and take hold, and delight.

But, you are he can paint; I can but write:
A Poet hath no more but black and white,   20
Ne knowes he flatt'ring Colours, or false light.

Yet when of Friendship I would draw the face,
A letter'd mind, and a large heart would place
To all posteritie; I will write *Burlase*.

LIII

An Epigram. To William,
Earle of Newcastle

WHEN first, my Lord, I saw you backe your horse,
Provoke his mettall, and command his force
To all the uses of the field, and race,
Me thought I read the ancient Art of Thrace,
And saw a Centaure, past those tales of Greece,
So seem'd your horse and you both of a peece!
You shew'd like Perseus upon Pegasus;
Or Castor mounted on his Cyllarus:
Or what we heare our home-borne Legend tell,
Of bold Sir Bevis, and his Arundell: 10
Nay, so your Seate his beauties did endorse,
As I began to wish my selfe a horse:
And surely had I but your Stable seene
Before: I thinke my wish absolv'd had beene.
For never saw I yet the Muses dwell,
Nor any of their houshold halfe so well.
So well! as when I saw the floore, and Roome,
I look'd for Hercules to be the Groome:
And cri'd, away with the Cæsarian bread,
At these Immortall Managers Virgil fed.   20

197

LIV

Epistle to Mr. Arthur Squib

I AM to dine, Friend, where I must be weigh'd
For a just wager, and that wager paid
If I doe lose it: And, without a Tale
A Merchants Wife is Regent of the Scale,
Who, when shee heard the match, concluded
    streight,
An ill commoditie! 'T must make good weight.
So that upon the point, my corporall feare
Is, she will play Dame Justice, too severe;
And hold me to it close; to stand upright
Within the ballance; and not want a mite;   10
But rather with advantage to be found
Full twentie stone; of which I lack two pound:
That's six in silver; now within the Socket
Stinketh my credit, if into the Pocket
It doe not come: One piece I have in store,
Lend me, deare Arthur, for a weeke five more,
And you shall make me good, in weight, and
    fashion,
And then to be return'd; or protestation
To goe out after—till when take this letter
For your securitie. I can no better.   20

LV

To Mr. John Burges

WOULD God, my Burges, I could thinke
Thoughts worthy of thy gift, this Inke,
Then would I promise here to give
Verse, that should thee, and me out-live.

But since the Wine hath steep'd my braine,
I only can the Paper staine;
Yet with a Dye, that feares no Moth,
But Scarlet-like out-lasts the Cloth.

LVI

Epistle. To My Lady Covell

You won not Verses, Madam, you won mee,
When you would play so nobly, and so free,
A booke to a few lynes: but, it was fit
You won them too, your oddes did merit it.
So have you gain'd a Servant, and a Muse:
The first of which I feare, you will refuse;
And you may justly, being a tardie, cold,
Unprofitable Chattell, fat and old,
Laden with Bellie, and doth hardly approach
His friends, but to breake Chaires, or cracke a
    Coach.   10
His weight is twenty Stone within two pound;
And that's made up as doth the purse abound.
Marrie, the Muse is one, can tread the Aire,
And stroke the water, nimble, chast, and faire,
Sleepe in a Virgins bosome without feare,
Run all the Rounds in a soft Ladyes eare,
Widow or Wife, without the jealousie
Of either Suitor, or a Servant by.
Such, (if her manners like you) I doe send:
And can for other Graces her commend,   20
To make you merry on the Dressing stoole,
A mornings, and at afternoones, to foole
Away ill company, and helpe in rime
Your Joane to passe her melancholie time.
By this, although you fancie not the man,
Accept his Muse; and tell, I know you can:

How many verses, Madam, are your Due!
I can lose none in tendring these to you.
I gaine, in having leave to keepe my Day,
And should grow rich, had I much more to pay. 30

LVII

To Master John Burges

FATHER JOHN BURGES,
Necessitie urges
My wofull crie,
To Sir Robert Pie:
And that he will venter
To send my Debentur.
Tell him his Ben
Knew the time, when
He lov'd the Muses;
Though now he refuses   10
To take Apprehension
Of a yeares Pension,
And more is behind:
Put him in mind
Christmas is neere;
And neither good Cheaer,
Mirth, fooling, nor wit,
Nor any least fit
Of gambol, or sport
Will come at the Court,   20
If there be no money,
No Plover, or Coney
Will come to the Table,
Or Wine to enable
The Muse, or the Poet;
The Parish will know it.

Nor any quick-warming-pan helpe him to bed,
If the 'Chequer be emptie, so will be his Head.

LVIII

Epigram, to my Book-seller

THOU, Friend, wilt heare all censures; unto thee
All mouthes are open, and all stomacks free:
Bee thou my Bookes intelligencer, note
What each man sayes of it, and of what coat
His judgement is; If he be wise, and praise,
Thanke him: if other, hee can give no Bayes.
If his wit reach no higher, but to spring
Thy Wife a fit of laughter; a Cramp-ring
Will be reward enough: to weare like those,
That hang their richest jewells i' their nose;   10
Like a rung Beare, or Swine: grunting out wit
As if that part lay for a [   ] most fit!
If they goe on, and that thou lov'st a-life
Their perfum'd judgements, let them kisse thy
    Wife.

LIX

An Epigram. To William,
Earle of Newcastle

THEY talke of Fencing, and the use of Armes,
The art of urging, and avoyding harmes,
The noble Science, and the maistring skill
Of making just approaches how to kill:
To hit in angles, and to clash with time:
As all defence, or offence were a chime!

201

I hate such measur'd, give me mettall'd fire
That trembles in the blaze, but (then) mounts
   higher!
A quick, and dazeling motion! when a paire
Of bodies meet like rarified ayre!   10
Their weapons shot out, with that flame, and
   force,
As they out-did the lightning in the course;
This were a spectacle! A sight to draw
Wonder to Valour! No, it is the Law
Of daring not to doe a wrong is true
Valour! to sleight it, being done to you!
To know the heads of danger! where 'tis fit
To bend, to breake, provoke, or suffer it!
All this (my Lord) is Valour! This is yours!
And was your Fathers! All your Ancestours!   20
Who durst live great, 'mongst all the colds, and
   heates,
Of humane life! as all the frosts, and sweates
Of fortune! when, or death appear'd, or bands!
And valiant were, with, or without their hands.

LX

An Epitaph, on Henry L. La-ware. To the Passer-by

IF, Passenger, thou canst but reade:
Stay, drop a teare for him that's dead,
Henry, the brave young Lord La-ware,
Minerva's and the Muses care!
What could their care doe 'gainst the spight
Of a Disease, that lov'd no light
Of honour, nor no ayre of good?
But crept like darknesse through his blood?

Offended with the dazeling flame
Of Vertue, got above his name?   10
No noble furniture of parts,
No love of action, and high Arts,
No aime at glorie, or in warre,
Ambition to become a Starre,
Could stop the malice of this ill,
That spread his body o're, to kill:
And only, his great Soule envy'd,
Because it durst have noblier dy'd.

LXI

An Epigram

THAT you have seene the pride, beheld the sport,
And all the games of Fortune, plaid at Court;
View'd there the mercat, read the wretched rate
At which there are, would sell the Prince, and
    State:
That scarce you heare a publike voyce alive,
But whisper'd Counsells, and those only thrive;
Yet are got off thence, with cleare mind, and hands
To lift to heaven: who is't not understands
Your happinesse, and doth not speake you blest,
To see you set apart, thus, from the rest,   10
T'obtaine of God, what all the Land should aske?
A Nations sinne got pardon'd! 'twere a taske
Fit for a Bishops knees! O bow them oft,
My Lord, till felt griefe make our stone hearts soft,
And wee doe weepe, to water, for our sinne.
He, that in such a flood, as we are in
Of riot, and consumption, knowes the way
To teach the people, how to fast, and pray,
And doe their penance, to avert Gods rod,
He is the Man, and Favorite of God.   20

LXII

An Epigram. To K. Charles for a 100.
pounds he sent me in my sicknesse. 1629

GREAT CHARLES, among the holy gifts of grace
Annexed to thy Person, and thy place,
'Tis not enough (thy pietie is such)
To cure the call'd Kings Evill with thy touch;
But thou wilt yet a Kinglier mastrie trie,
To cure the Poets Evill, Povertie:
And, in these Cures, do'st so thy selfe enlarge,
As thou dost cure our Evill, at thy charge.
Nay, and in this, thou show'st to value more
One Poet, then of other folke ten score.   10
O pietie! so to weigh the poores estates!
O bountie! so to difference the rates!
What can the Poet wish his King may doe,
But, that he cure the Peoples Evill too?

LXIII

To K. Charles, and Q. Mary. For the losse
of their first-borne, An epigram consolatorie.
1629

WHO dares denie, that all first fruits are due
To God, denies the God-head to be true:
Who doubts, those fruits God can with gaine restore,
Doth, by his doubt, distrust his promise more.
Hee can, he will, and with large int'rest pay,
What (at his liking) he will take away.
Then Royall Charles, and Mary, doe not grutch
That the Almighties will to you is such:

204

But thanke his greatnesse, and his goodnesse too;
And thinke all still the best, that he will doe.　　10
That thought shall make, he will this losse supply
With a long, large, and blest posteritie!
For God, whose essence is so infinite,
Cannot but heape that grace, he will requite.

LXIV

An Epigram. To our great and good K. Charles on his Anniversary Day. 1629

How happy were the Subject! if he knew,
Most pious King, but his owne good in you!
How many times, live long, Charles, would he say,
If he but weigh'd the blessings of this day?
And as it turnes our joyfull yeare about,
For safetie of such Majestie, cry out?
Indeed, when had great Brittaine greater cause
Then now, to love the Soveraigne, and the Lawes?
When you that raigne, are her Example growne,
And what are bounds to her, you make your owne?
When your assiduous practise doth secure　　11
That Faith, which she professeth to be pure?
When all your life's a president of dayes,
And murmure cannot quarrell at your wayes?
How is she barren growne of love! or broke!
That nothing can her gratitude provoke!
O Times! O Manners! Surfet bred of ease,
The truly Epidemicall disease!
'Tis not alone the Merchant, but the Clowne,
Is Banke-rupt turn'd! the Cassock, Cloake, and
　　Gowne　　20
Are lost upon accompt! And none will know
How much to heaven for thee, great Charles, they
　　owe!

LXV

An Epigram on the Princes birth. 1630

AND art thou borne, brave Babe? Blest be thy birth!
That so hath crown'd our hopes, our spring, and
    earth,
The bed of the chast Lilly, and the Rose!
What Month then May, was fitter to disclose
This Prince of flowers? Soone shoot thou up, and
    grow
The same that thou art promis'd, but be slow,
And long in changing. Let our Nephewes see
Thee, quickly come the gardens eye to bee,
And there to stand so. Haste now, envious Moone,
And interpose thy selfe, ('care not how soone)   10
And threat' the great Eclipse. Two houres but runne,
Sol will re-shine. If not, Charles hath a Sonne.
    ... Non displicuisse meretur
    Festinat Cæsar qui placuisse tibi.

LXVI

An Epigram to the Queene, then lying in. 1630

HAILE Mary, full of grace, it once was said,
And by an Angell, to the blessed'st Maid,
The Mother of our Lord: why may not I
(Without prophanenesse) yet, a Poet, cry
Haile Mary, full of honours, to my Queene,
The Mother of our Prince? When was there seene
(Except the joy that the first Mary brought,
Whereby the safetie of Man-kind was wrought)

206

So generall a gladnesse to an Isle,
To make the hearts of a whole Nation smile,   10
As in this Prince? Let it be lawfull, so
To compare small with great, as still we owe
Glorie to God. Then, Haile to Mary! spring
Of so much safetie to the Realme, and King.

LXVII

An Ode, or Song, by all the Muses

IN CELEBRATION OF HER MAJESTIES BIRTH-DAY. 1630·

1. *Clio*.   Up publike joy, remember
        This sixteenth of November,
           Some brave un-common way:
        And though the Parish-steeple
        Be silent, to the people
           Ring thou it Holy-day.

2. *Mel*.   What, though the thriftie Tower
        And Gunnes there, spare to poure
           Their noises forth in Thunder:
        As fearfull to awake   10
        This Citie, or to shake
           Their guarded gates asunder?

3. *Thal*.   Yet, let our Trumpets sound;
        And cleave both ayre and ground,
           With beating of our Drums:
         Let every Lyre be strung,
        Harpe, Lute, Theorbo sprung,
           With touch of daintie thum's!

4. *Eut*.   That when the Quire is full,
        The Harmony may pull   20
           The Angels from their Spheares:
        And each intelligence
        May wish it selfe a sense,
           Whilst it the Dittie heares.

5. *Terp.*   Behold the royall Mary,
           The Daughter of great Harry!
              And Sister to just Lewis!
           Comes in the pompe, and glorie
           Of all her Brothers storie,
              And of her Fathers prowesse!   30

6. *Erat.*   Shee showes so farre above
           The fained Queene of Love,
              This sea-girt Isle upon:
           As here no Venus were;
           But, that shee raigning here,
              Had got the Ceston on!

7. *Calli.*   See, see our active King
           Hath taken twice the Ring
              Upon his pointed Lance:
           Whilst all the ravish'd rout   40
           Doe mingle in a shout,
              Hay! for the flowre of France!

8. *Ura.*   This day the Court doth measure
           Her joy in state, and pleasure;
              And with a reverend feare,
           The Revells, and the Play,
           Summe up this crowned day,
              Her two and twenti'th yeare!

9. *Poly.*   Sweet! happy Mary! All
           The People her doe call!   50
              And this the wombe divine!
           So fruitfull, and so faire,
           Hath brought the Land an Heire!
              And Charles a Caroline!

LXVIII

An Epigram, to the House-hold. 1630

WHAT can the cause be, when the King hath given
His Poet Sack, the House-hold will not pay?
Are they so scanted in their store? or driven
For want of knowing the Poet, to say him nay?
Well, they should know him, would the King but
　grant
His Poet leave to sing his House-hold true;
Hee'ld frame such ditties of their store, and want,
Would make the very Greene-cloth to looke blew:
And rather wish, in their expence of Sack,
So, the allowance from the King to use,　　　　10
As the old Bard, should no Canary lack,
'Twere better spare a Butt, then spill his Muse.
For in the Genius of a Poets Verse,
The Kings fame lives. Go now, denie his teirce.

LXIX

Epigram. To a Friend, and Sonne

SONNE, and my Friend, I had not call'd you so
To mee; or beene the same to you; if show,
Profit, or Chance had made us: But I know
What, by that name, wee each to other owe,
Freedome, and Truth; with love from those begot:
Wise-crafts, on which the flatterer ventures not.
His is more safe commoditie, or none:
Nor dares he come in the comparison.
But as the wretched Painter, who so ill
Painted a Dog, that now his subtler skill　　　10
Was, t'have a Boy stand with a Club, and fright
All live dogs from the lane, and his shops sight,

Till he had sold his Piece, drawne so unlike:
So doth the flattrer, with farre cunning strike
At a Friends freedome, proves all circling meanes
To keepe him off; and how-so-e're he gleanes
Some of his formes, he lets him not come neere
Where he would fixe, for the distinctions feare.
For as at distance, few have facultie
To judge; So all men comming neere can spie,   20
Though now of flattery, as of picture are
More subtle workes, and finer pieces farre,
Then knew the former ages: yet to life,
All is but web, and painting; be the strife
Never so great to get them: and the ends,
Rather to boast rich hangings, then rare friends.

LXX

To the Immortall Memorie, and Friendship of that Noble Paire, Sir Lucius Cary, and Sir H. Morison

The Turne

BRAVE INFANT OF SAGUNTUM, cleare
Thy comming forth in that great yeare,
When the Prodigious Hannibal did crowne
His rage, with razing your immortall Towne.
Thou, looking then about,
E're thou wert halfe got out,
Wise child, did'st hastily returne,
And mad'st thy Mothers wombe thine urne.
How summ'd a circle didst thou leave man-kind
Of deepest lore, could we the Center find!   10

The Counter-turne

Did wiser Nature draw thee back,
From out the horrour of that sack,

Where shame, faith, honour, and regard of right
Lay trampled on; the deeds of death, and night,
Urg'd, hurried forth, and horld
Upon th'affrighted world:
Sword, fire, and famine, with fell fury met;
And all on utmost ruine set;
As, could they but lifes miseries fore-see,
No doubt all Infants would returne like thee?   20

The Stand

For, what is life, if measur'd by the space,
Not by the act?
Or masked man, if valu'd by his face,
Above his fact?
Here's one out-liv'd his Peeres,
And told forth fourescore yeares;
He vexed time, and busied the whole State;
Troubled both foes, and friends;
But ever to no ends:
What did this Stirrer, but die late?   30
How well at twentie had he falne, or stood!
For three of his foure-score, he did no good.

The Turne

Hee entred well, by vertuous parts,
Got up and thriv'd with honest arts:
He purchas'd friends, and fame, and honours then,
And had his noble name advanc'd with men:
But weary of that flight,
Hee stoop'd in all mens sight
To sordid flatteries, acts of strife,
And sunke in that dead sea of life   40
So deep, as he did then death's waters sup;
But that the Corke of Title boy'd him up.

The Counter-turne

Alas, but Morison fell young:
Hee never fell, thou fall'st, my tongue.
Hee stood, a Souldier to the last right end,
A perfect Patriot, and a noble friend,
But most a vertuous Sonne.
All Offices were done
By him, so ample, full, and round,
In weight, in measure, number, sound, 50
As though his age imperfect might appeare,
His life was of Humanitie the Spheare.

The Stand

Goe now, and tell out dayes summ'd up with
 feares,
And make them yeares;
Produce thy masse of miseries on the Stage,
To swell thine age;
Repeat of things a throng,
To shew thou hast beene long,
Not liv'd; for life doth her great actions spell,
By what was done and wrought 60
In season, and so brought
To light: her measures are, how well
Each syllab'e answer'd, and was form'd, how
 faire;
These make the lines of life, and that's her ayre.

The Turne

It is not growing like a tree
In bulke, doth make man better bee;
Or standing long an Oake, three hundred yeare,
To fall a logge, at last, dry, bald, and seare:
A Lillie of a Day,
Is fairer farre, in May, 70
Although it fall, and die that night;
It was the Plant, and flowre of light.

In small proportions, we just beauties see:
And in short measures, life may perfect bee.

The Counter-turne

Call, noble Lucius, then for Wine,
And let thy lookes with gladnesse shine:
Accept this garland, plant it on thy head,
And thinke, nay know, thy Morison's not dead.
Hee leap'd the present age,
Possest with holy rage,   80
To see that bright eternall Day:
Of which we Priests, and Poets say
Such truths, as we expect for happy men,
And there he lives with memorie: and Ben

The Stand

Jonson! who sung this of him, e're he went
Himselfe to rest,
Or taste a part of that full joy he meant
To have exprest,
In this bright Asterisme:
Where it were friendships schisme,   90
(Were not his Lucius long with us to tarry)
To separate these twi-
Lights, the Dioscuri;
And keepe the one halfe from his Harry.
But fate doth so alternate the designe,
Whilst that in heav'n, this light on earth must
    shine.

The Turne

And shine as you exalted are;
Two names of friendship, but one Starre:
Of hearts the union. And those not by chance
Made, or indenture, or leas'd out t'advance   100
The profits for a time.
No pleasures vaine did chime,

Of rimes, or ryots, at your feasts,
Orgies of drinke, or fain'd protests:
But simple love of greatnesse, and of good;
That knits brave minds, and manners, more then
   blood.

The Counter-turne

This made you first to know the Why
You lik'd, then after, to apply
That liking; and approach so one the tother,
Till either grew a portion of the other: 110
Each stiled by his end,
The Copie of his friend.
You liv'd to be the great surnames,
And titles, by which all made claimes
Unto the Vertue. Nothing perfect done,
But as a Cary, or a Morison.

The Stand

And such a force the faire example had,
As they that saw
The good, and durst not practise it, were glad
That such a Law   120
Was left yet to Man-kind;
Where they might read, and find
Friendship, indeed, was written, not in words:
And with the heart, not pen,
Of two so early men,
Whose lines her rowles were, and records,
Who, e're the first downe bloomed on the chin,
Had sow'd these fruits, and got the harvest in.

LXXI

To the Right Honourable, the Lord High Treasurer of England. An Epistle Mendicant. 1631

MY LORD;
Poore wretched states, prest by extremities,
Are faine to seeke for succours, and supplies
Of Princes aides, or good mens Charities.

Disease, the Enemie, and his Ingineeres,
Wants, with the rest of his conceal'd compeeres,
Have cast a trench about mee, now five yeares.

And made those strong approaches, by False
braies,
Reduicts, Halfe-moones, Horne-workes, and such
close wayes,
The Muse not peepes out, one of hundred dayes;

But lyes block'd up, and straightned, narrow'd in,
Fix'd to the bed, and boords, unlike to win   11
Health, or scarce breath, as she had never bin.

Unlesse some saving-Honour of the Crowne,
Dare thinke it, to relieve, no lesse renowne,
A Bed-rid Wit, then a besieged Towne.

LXXII

To the King. On his Birth-day. An Epigram Anniversarie. Novemb. 19, 1632

THIS is King Charles his Day. Speake it, thou
    Towre,
Unto the Ships, and they from tier, to tier,
Discharge it 'bout the Iland, in an houre,
As lowd as Thunder, and as swift as fire.
Let Ireland meet it out at Sea, halfe way,
Repeating all Great Brittain's joy, and more,
Adding her owne glad accents, to this Day,
Like Eccho playing from the other shore;
What Drums, or Trumpets, or great Ord'nance can,
The Poetrie of Steeples, with the Bells,   10
Three Kingdomes Mirth, in light, and aerie man,
Made lighter with the Wine; All noises else,
At Bonefires, Rockets, Fire-workes, with the
    Shoutes
That cry that gladnesse, which their hearts would
    pray,
Had they but grace, of thinking, at these routes,
On th'often comming of this Holy-day:
    And ever close the burden of the Song,
      Still to have such a Charles, but this Charles
      long.

The wish is great; but where the Prince is such,
What prayers (People) can you thinke too much! 20

LXXIII

On the Right Honourable, and Vertuous Lord Weston, L. High Treasurer of England, upon the day, hee was made earle of Portland, 17. Febr. 1632. To the envious

LOOKE up, thou seed of envie, and still bring
Thy faint, and narrow eyes, to reade the King
In his great Actions: view whom his large hand,
Hath rais'd to be the Port unto his Land!
Weston! That waking man! that Eye of State!
Who seldome sleepes! whom bad men only hate!
Why doe I irritate, or stirre up thee,
Thou sluggish spawne, that canst, but wilt not see!
Feed on thy selfe for spight, and shew thy Kind:
To vertue, and true worth, be ever blind.   10
Dreame thou could'st hurt it, but before thou
    wake,
T'effect it; Feele, thou'ast made thine owne heart
    ake.

LXXIV

To the Right Honourable Hierome, L. Weston. An Ode Gratulatorie. For his returne from his Embassie. 1632

SUCH pleasure as the teeming Earth
Doth take in easie Natures birth,
   When shee puts forth the life of ev'ry thing:
And in a dew of sweetest Raine,
Shee lies deliver'd without paine,
   Of the prime beautie of the yeare, the Spring:

The Rivers in their shores doe run;
The Clowdes rack cleare before the Sun,
   The rudest Winds obey the calmest Ayre:
Rare Plants from ev'ry banke doe rise,   10
And ev'ry Plant the sense surprize,
   Because the order of the whole is faire!
The very verdure of her nest,
Wherein she sits so richly drest,
   As all the wealth of Season, there was spread;
Doth show, the Graces, and the Houres
Have multipli'd their arts, and powers,
   In making soft her aromatique bed:
Such joyes, such sweets doth your Returne
Bring all your friends, (faire Lord) that burne   20
   With love, to heare your modestie relate,
The bus'nesse of your blooming wit,
With all the fruit shall follow it,
   Both to the honour of the King and State.
O how will then our Court be pleas'd,
To see great Charles of Travaile eas'd,
   When he beholds a graft of his owne hand,
Shoot up an Olive, fruitfull, faire,
To be a shadow to his Heire,
   And both a strength, and Beautie to his
      Land!   30

LXXV

Epithalamion;

OR, A SONG:

CELEBRATING THE NUPTIALS OF THAT NOBLE
GENTLEMAN, MR. HIEROME WESTON, SON, AND
HEIRE, OF THE LORD WESTON, LORD HIGH
TREASURER OF ENGLAND, WITH THE
LADY FRANCES STUART, DAUGHTER OF ESME
D. OF LENOX DECEASED, AND SISTER OF THE
SURVIVING DUKE OF THE SAME NAME

THOUGH thou hast past thy Summer standing, stay
  A-while with us, bright Sun, and helpe our light;
Thou can'st not meet more Glory, on the way,
  Betweene thy Tropicks, to arrest thy sight,
    Then thou shalt see to day:
      We wooe thee, stay
    And see, what can be seene,
The bountie of a King, and beautie of his Queene!

See, the Procession! what a Holy day
  (Bearing the promise of some better fate)   10
Hath filed, with Caroches, all the way,
  From Greenwich, hither, to Row-hampton gate!
    When look'd the yeare, at best,
      So like a feast?
    Or were Affaires in tune,
By all the Spheares consent, so in the heart of June?

What Beautie of beauties, and bright youths at
          charge
  Of Summers Liveries, and gladding greene;
Doe boast their Loves, and Brav'ries so at large,
  As they came all to see, and to be seene!   20

When look'd the Earth so fine,
　　Or so did shine,
　In all her bloome, and flower;
To welcome home a Paire, and deck the nuptiall
　　　bower?

It is the kindly Season of the time,
　　The Month of youth, which calls all Creatures
　　　forth
To doe their Offices in Natures Chime,
　　And celebrate (perfection at the worth)
　　　Mariage, the end of life,
　　　　That holy strife,   30
　　　And the allowed warre:
Through which not only we, but all our Species are.

Harke how the Bells upon the waters play
　　Their Sister-tunes, from Thames his either side,
As they had learn'd new changes, for the day,
　　And all did ring th'approches of the Bride;
　　　The Lady Frances, drest
　　　　Above the rest
　　　Of all the Maidens faire;
In gracefull Ornament of Garland, Gemmes, and
　　　Haire.   40

See, how she paceth forth in Virgin-white,
　　Like what she is, the Daughter of a Duke,
And Sister: darting forth a dazling light
　　On all that come her Simplesse to rebuke!
　　　Her tresses trim her back,
　　　　As she did lack
　　　Nought of a Maiden Queene,
With Modestie so crown'd, and Adoration seene.

Stay, thou wilt see what rites the Virgins doe!
   The choicest Virgin-troup of all the Land!   50
Porting the Ensignes of united Two,
    Both Crownes, and Kingdomes in their either
        hand;
      Whose Majesties appeare,
        To make more cleare
      This Feast, then can the Day
Although that thou, O Sun, at our intreaty stay!

See, how with Roses, and with Lillies shine,
   (Lillies and Roses, Flowers of either Sexe)
The bright Brides paths, embelish'd more then
        thine
    With light of love, this Paire doth intertexe!   60
      Stay, see the Virgins sow,
        (Where she shall goe)
      The Emblemes of their way.
O, now thou smil'st, faire Sun, and shin'st, as thou
        wouldst stay!

With what full hands, and in how plenteous
        showers
    Have they bedew'd the Earth, where she doth
        tread,
As if her ayrie steps did spring the flowers,
    And all the Ground were Garden, where she led!
      See, at another doore,
        On the same floore,   70
      The Bridegroome meets the Bride
With all the pompe of Youth, and all our Court
        beside.

Our Court, and all the Grandees; now, Sun, looke,
   And looking with thy best Inquirie, tell,
In all thy age of Journals thou hast tooke,

Saw'st thou that Paire, became these Rites so
     well,
    Save the preceding Two?
      Who, in all they doe,
      Search, Sun, and thou wilt find
They are th'exampled Paire, and mirrour of their
     kind.   80

Force from the Phœnix then, no raritie
    Of Sex, to rob the Creature; but from Man
The king of Creatures; take his paritie
    With Angels, Muse, to speake these: Nothing can
      Illustrate these, but they
        Themselves to day,
      Who the whole Act expresse;
All else we see beside, are Shadowes, and goe
     lesse.

It is their Grace, and favour, that makes seene,
    And wonder'd at the bounties of this day: 90
All is a story of the King and Queene!
    And what of Dignitie, and Honour may
      Be duly done to those
        Whom they have chose,
      And set the marke upon
To give a greater Name, and Title to! Their owne!

Weston, their Treasure, as their Treasurer,
    That Mine of Wisdome, and of Counsells deep,
Great Say-Master of State, who cannot erre,
    But doth his Carract, and just Standard keepe
      In all the prov'd assayes,   101
        And legall wayes
      Of Tryals, to worke downe
Mens Loves unto the Lawes, and Lawes to love the
     Crowne.

And this well mov'd the Judgement of the King
   To pay with honours, to his noble Sonne
To day, the Fathers service; who could bring
   Him up, to doe the same himselfe had done.
      That farre-all-seeing Eye
        Could soone espie   110
     What kind of waking Man
He had so highly set; and, in what Barbican.

Stand there; for when a noble Nature's rais'd,
   It brings Friends Joy, Foes Griefe, Posteritie
        Fame;
In him the times, no lesse then Prince, are prais'd,
   And by his Rise, in active men, his Name
      Doth Emulation stirre;
        To th' dull, a Spur
     It is: to th'envious meant
A meere upbraiding Griefe, and tort'ring punish-
        ment.   120

See, now the Chappell opens; where the King
   And Bishop stay, to consummate the Rites:
The holy Prelate prayes, then takes the Ring,
   Askes first, Who gives her (I Charles) then he
        plights
      One in the others hand,
        Whilst they both stand
     Hearing their charge, and then
The Solemne Quire cryes, Joy; and they returne,
        Amen.

O happy bands! and thou more happy place,
   Which to this use, wert built and consecrate! 130
To have thy God to blesse, thy King to grace,
   And this their chosen Bishop celebrate,
      And knit the Nuptiall knot,
        Which Time shall not,

Or canker'd Jealousie,
With all corroding Arts, be able to untie!

The Chappell empties, and thou may'st be gone
  Now, Sun, and post away the rest of day:
These two, now holy Church hath made them one,
  Doe long to make themselves, so, another way:
    There is a Feast behind,   141
      To them of kind,
    Which their glad Parents taught
One to the other, long e're these to light were
      brought.

Haste, haste, officious Sun, and send them Night
  Some houres before it should, that these may
      know
All that their Fathers, and their Mothers might
  Of Nuptiall Sweets, at such a season, owe,
    To propagate their Names,
      And keepe their Fames   150
    Alive, which else would die,
For Fame keepes Vertue up, and it Posteritie.

Th'Ignoble never liv'd, they were a-while
  Like Swine, or other Cattell here on earth:
Their names are not recorded on the File
  Of life, that fall so; Christians know their birth,
    Alone, and such a race,
      We pray may grace
    Your fruitfull spreading Vine,
But dare not aske our wish in Language
      fescennine: 160

Yet, as we may, we will, wish chast desires,
  (The holy perfumes of the Mariage bed)
Be kept alive, those Sweet, and Sacred fires
  Of Love betweene you, and your Lovely-head:

That when you both are old,
    You find no cold
  There; but, renewed, say,
(After the last child borne;) This is our wedding
      day.

Till you behold a race to fill your Hall,
  A Richard, and a Hierome, by their names   170
Upon a Thomas, or a Francis call;
    A Kate, a Frank, to honour their Grand-dames,
      And 'tweene their Grandsires thighes,
        Like pretty Spies,
      Peepe forth a Gemme; to see
How each one playes his part, of the large
      Pedigree.

And never may there want one of the Stem,
  To be a watchfull Servant for this State;
But like an Arme of Eminence, 'mongst them,
    Extend a reaching vertue, early and late: 180
      Whilst the maine tree still found
        Upright and sound,
      By this Sun's Noone sted's made
So great; his Body now alone projects the shade.

They both are slip'd to Bed; Shut fast the Doore,
  And let him freely gather Loves First-fruits.
Hee's Master of the Office; yet no more
    Exacts then she is pleas'd to pay: no suits,
      Strifes, murmures, or delay,
        Will last till day;   190
      Night, and the sheetes will show
The longing Couple, all that elder Lovers know.

LXXVI

The Humble Petition of Poore Ben. To th' Best of Monarchs, Masters, Men, King Charles

... Doth most humbly show it,
To your Majestie your Poet:

That whereas your royall Father,
James the blessed, pleas'd the rather,
Of his speciall grace to Letters,
To make all the Muses debters
To his bountie; by extension
Of a free Poetique Pension,
A large hundred Markes annuitie,
To be given me in gratuitie   10
For done service, and to come:
  And that this so accepted summe,
Or dispenc'd in bookes, or bread,
(For with both the Muse was fed)
Hath drawne on me, from the times,
All the envie of the Rymes,
And the ratling pit-pat-noyse,
Of the lesse-Poetique boyes;
When their pot-guns ayme to hit,
With their pellets of small wit,   20
Parts of me (they judg'd) decay'd,
But we last out, still unlay'd.
  Please your Majestie to make
Of your grace, for goodnesse sake,
Those your Fathers Markes, your Pounds;
Let their spite (which now abounds)
Then goe on, and doe its worst;
This would all their envie burst:

226

And so warme the Poets tongue
You'ld reade a Snake, in his next Song.　　30

LXXVII

To the Right Honourable, the Lord Treasurer of England. An Epigram

If to my mind, great Lord, I had a state,
I would present you now with curious plate
Of Noremberg, or Turkie; hang your roomes
Not with the Arras, but the Persian Loomes.
I would, if price, or prayer could them get,
Send in, what or Romano, Tintaret,
Titian, or Raphael, Michael Angelo
Have left in fame to equall, or out-goe
The old Greek-hands in picture, or in stone.
This I would doe, could I thinke Weston one　　10
Catch'd with these Arts, wherein the Judge is wise
As farre as sense, and onely by the eyes.
But you, I know, my Lord; and know you can
Discerne betweene a Statue, and a Man;
Can doe the things that Statues doe deserve,
And act the businesse, which they paint, or carve.
What you have studied are the arts of life;
To compose men, and manners; stint the strife
Of murmuring Subjects; make the Nations know
What worlds of blessings to good Kings they owe:　20
And mightiest Monarchs feele what large increase
Of sweets, and safeties, they possesse by Peace.
These I looke up at, with a reverent eye,
And strike Religion in the standers-by;
Which, though I cannot as an Architect
In glorious Piles, or Pyramids erect
Unto your honour: I can tune in song
Aloud; and (haply) it may last as long.

LXXVIII

An Epigram to my Muse, the Lady Digby, on her Husband, Sir Kenelme Digby

Tho', happy Muse, thou know my Digby well;
Yet read him in these lines: He doth excell
In honour, courtesie, and all the parts
Court can call hers, or Man could call his Arts.
Hee's prudent, valiant, just, and temperate;
In him all vertue is beheld in State:
And he is built like some imperiall roome
For that to dwell in, and be still at home.
His brest is a brave Palace, a broad Street,
Where all heroique ample thoughts doe meet: 10
Where Nature such a large survey hath ta'en,
As other soules to his dwelt in a Lane:
Witnesse his Action done at Scanderoone;
Upon my Birth-day the eleventh of June;
When the Apostle Barnabee the bright
Unto our yeare doth give the longest light,
In signe the Subject, and the Song will live
Which I have vow'd posteritie to give.
Goe, Muse, in, and salute him. Say he be
Busie, or frowne at first; when he sees thee,   20
He will cleare up his forehead: thinke thou bring'st
Good Omen to him, in the note thou sing'st,
For he doth love my Verses, and will looke
Upon them, (next to Spensers noble booke)
And praise them too. O! what a fame 'twill be?
What reputation to my lines, and me,
When hee shall read them at the Treasurers bord?
The knowing Weston, and that learned Lord
Allowes them? Then, what copies shall be had,
What transcripts begg'd? how cry'd up, and how
   glad   30

Wilt thou be, Muse, when this shall them befall?
Being sent to one, they will be read of all.

LXXIX

New yeares, expect new gifts: Sister, your Harpe,
   Lute, Lyre, Theorbo, all are call'd to day,
Your change of Notes, the flat, the meane, the sharpe,
   To shew the rites, and t'usher forth the way
Of the New Yeare, in a new silken warpe,
     To fit the softnesse of our Yeares-gift: When
     We sing the best of Monarchs, Masters, Men;
For, had we here said lesse, we had sung nothing then.

A NEW-YEARES-GIFT SUNG TO KING CHARLES, 1635

Rector To day old Janus opens the new yeare,
Chori.   And shuts the old. Haste, haste, all loyall
        Swaines,   10
      That know the times, and seasons when
        t'appeare,
        And offer your just service on these plaines;
        Best Kings expect first-fruits of your glad
        gaines.

      1. Pan is the great Preserver of our bounds.
      2. To him we owe all profits of our grounds,
      3. Our milke, 4. Our fells, 5. Our fleeces,
        6. and first Lambs,
      7. Our teeming Ewes, 8. and lustie-mounting
        Rammes.
      9. See where he walkes with Mira by his side.
Chor. Sound, sound his praises loud, and with his
      hers divide.

Shep.   Of Pan wee sing, the best of Hunters, Pan, 20
Chor.   That drives the Hart to seeke unused wayes,
    And in the chase, more then Sylvanus can,
      Heare, O you Groves, and, Hills, resound
        his praise.

Nym.   Of brightest Mira, doe we raise our Song,
Chor.   Sister of Pan, and glory of the Spring:
    Who walkes on Earth as May still went along.
      Rivers, and Vallies, Eccho what wee sing.

Shep.   Of Pan wee sing, the Chiefe of Leaders, Pan,
Chor.   That leades our flocks and us, and calls
      both forth
    To better Pastures then great Pales can: 30
      Heare, O you Groves, and, Hills, resound
        his worth.

Nymp.   Of brightest Mira, is our Song; the grace
Chor.   Of all that Nature, yet, to life did bring;
    And were shee lost, could best supply her
      · place.
      Rivers, and Valleys, Eccho what wee sing.

    1. Where ere they tread th'enamour'd ground,
      The Fairest flowers are alwayes found;
    2. As if the beauties of the yeare
      Still waited on 'hém where they were.
    1. Hee is the Father of our peace;   40
    2. She, to the Crowne, hath brought encrease.
    1. Wee know no other power then his,
      Pan only our great Shep'ard is,
Chorus. Our great, our good. Where one's so drest
    In truth of colours, both are best.

Haste, haste you hither, all you gentler
    Swaines,
That have a Flock, or Herd, upon these
    plaines;
This is the great Preserver of our bounds,
To whom you owe all duties of your grounds;
Your Milkes, your Fells, your Fleeces, and
    first Lambes,   50
Your teeming Ewes, as well as mounting
    Rammes;
Whose praises let's report unto the Woods,
That they may take it eccho'd by the Floods.
    'Tis hee, 'tis hee, in singing hee,
    And hunting, Pan, exceedeth thee.
    Hee gives all plentie, and encrease,
    Hee is the author of our peace.

Where e're he goes upon the ground,
The better grasse, and flowers are found.
To sweeter Pastures lead hee can,   60
Then ever Pales could, or Pan;
Hee drives diseases from our Folds,
The theefe from spoyle, his presence holds.
Pan knowes no other power then his,
This only the great Shep'ard is.
    'Tis hee, 'tis hee, &c.

*LXXX

Faire Friend, 'tis true, your beauties move
    My heart to a respect:
Too little to bee paid with love,
    Too great for your neglect.

I neither love, nor yet am free,
    For though the flame I find

Be not intense in the degree,
   'Tis of the purest kind.

It little wants of love, but paine,
   Your beautie takes my sense,   10
And lest you should that price disdaine,
   My thoughts, too, feele the influence.

'Tis not a passions first accesse
   Readie to multiply,
But like Loves calmest State it is
   Possest with victorie.

It is like Love to Truth reduc'd,
   All the false value's gone,
Which were created, and induc'd
   By fond imagination.   20

'Tis either Fancie, or 'tis Fate,
   To love you more then I;
I love you at your beauties rate,
   Lesse were an Injurie.

Like unstamp'd Gold, I weigh each grace,
   So that you may collect,
Th'intrinsique value of your face,
   Safely from my respect.

And this respect would merit love,
   Were not so faire a sight   30
Payment enough; for, who dare move
   Reward for his delight?

*LXXXI

On the Kings Birth-day

Rowse up thy selfe, my gentle Muse,
  Though now our greene conceits be gray,
And yet once more doe not refuse
  To take thy Phrygian Harp, and play
  In honour of this cheerefull Day:
    Long may they both contend to prove,
    That best of Crownes is such a love.

Make first a Song of Joy, and Love,
  Which chastly flames in royall eyes,
Then tune it to the Spheares above,   10
  When the benignest Stars doe rise,
  And sweet Conjunctions grace the skies.
    Long may, &c.

To this let all good hearts resound,
  Whilst Diadems invest his head;
Long may he live, whose life doth bound
  More then his Lawes, and better led
  By high Example, then by dread.
    Long may, &c.

Long may he round about him see   20
  His Roses, and his Lillies blowne:
Long may his only Deare, and Hee
  Joy in Idæas of their owne,
  And Kingdomes hopes so timely sowne.
    Long may they both contend to prove.
    That best of Crownes is such a love.

LXXXII

To My L. the King, on the Christning His second Sonne James

THAT thou art lov'd of God, this worke is done,
Great King, thy having of a second Sonne:
And by thy blessing, may thy People see
How much they are belov'd of God, in thee;
Would they would understand it! Princes are
Great aides to Empire, as they are great care
To pious Parents, who would have their blood
Should take first Seisin of the publique good,
As hath thy James; cleans'd from originall drosse,
This day, by Baptisme, and his Saviours crosse: 10
Grow up, sweet Babe, as blessed, in thy Name,
As in renewing thy good Grandsires fame;
Me thought, Great Brittaine in her Sea, before,
Sate safe enough, but now secured more.
At land she triumphs in the triple shade,
Her Rose, and Lilly, intertwind, have made.

Oceano secura meo, securior umbris.

LXXXIII

An Elegie on the Lady Jane Pawlet, Marchion: of Winton

WHAT gentle Ghost, besprent with April deaw,
Hayles me, so solemnly, to yonder Yewgh?
And beckning wooes me, from the fatall tree
To pluck a Garland, for her selfe, or mee?
I doe obey you, Beautie! for in death,
You seeme a faire one! O that you had breath,

234

To give your shade a name! Stay, stay, I feele
A horrour in mee! all my blood is steele!
Stiffe! starke! my joynts 'gainst one another knock!
Whose Daughter? ha? Great Savage of the Rock?   10
Hee's good, as great. I am almost a stone!
And e're I can aske more of her shee's gone!
Alas, I am all Marble! write the rest
Thou wouldst have written, Fame, upon my brest:
It is a large faire table, and a true,
And the disposure will be something new,
When I, who would the Poet have become,
At least may beare th'inscription to her Tombe.
Shee was the Lady Jane, and Marchionisse
Of Winchester; the Heralds can tell this.   20
Earle Rivers Grand-Child—serve not formes, good
    Fame,
Sound thou her Vertues, give her soule a Name.
Had I a thousand Mouthes, as many Tongues,
And voyce to raise them from my brazen Lungs,
I durst not aime at that: The dotes were such
Thereof, no notion can expresse how much
Their Carract was! I, or my trump must breake,
But rather I, should I of that part speake!
It is too neere of kin to Heaven, the Soule,
To be describ'd! Fames fingers are too foule   30
To touch these Mysteries! We may admire
The blaze, and splendor, but not handle fire!
What she did here, by great example, well,
T'inlive posteritie, her Fame may tell!
And, calling truth to witnesse, make that good
From the inherent Graces in her blood!
Else, who doth praise a person by a new,
But a fain'd way, doth rob it of the true.
Her Sweetnesse, Softnesse, her fair Curtesie,
Her wary guardes, her wise simplicitie,   40
Were like a ring of Vertues, 'bout her set,
And pietie the Center, where all met.

A reverend State she had, an awfull Eye,
A dazling, yet inviting, Majestie:
What Nature, Fortune, Institution, Fact
Could summe to a perfection, was her Act!
How did she leave the world? with what contempt?
Just as she in it liv'd! and so exempt
From all affection! when they urg'd the Cure
Of her disease, how did her soule assure   50
Her suffrings, as the body had beene away!
And to the Torturers (her Doctors) say,
Stick on your Cupping-glasses, feare not, put
Your hottest Causticks to, burne, lance, or cut:
'Tis but a body which you can torment,
And I, into the world, all Soule, was sent!
Then comforted her Lord! and blest her Sonne!
Chear'd her faire Sisters in her race to runne!
With gladnesse temper'd her sad Parents teares!
Made her friends joyes, to get above their feares! 60
And, in her last act, taught the Standers-by,
With admiration, and applause to die!
Let Angels sing her glories, who did call
Her spirit home, to her originall!
Who saw the way was made it! and were sent
To carry, and conduct the Complement
'Twixt death and life! Where her mortalitie
Became her Birth-day to Eternitie!
And now, through circumfused light, she lookes
On Natures secrets, there, as her owne bookes: 70
Speakes Heavens Language, and discourses free
To every Order, ev'ry Hierarchie!
Beholds her Maker! and, in him, doth see
What the beginnings of all beauties be;
And all beatitudes, that thence doe flow:
Which they that have the Crowne are sure to know!
Goe now, her happy Parents, and be sad
If you not understand, what Child you had,

If you dare grudge at Heaven, and repent
T'have paid againe a blessing was but lent,⠀⠀⠀80
And trusted so, as it deposited lay
At pleasure, to be call'd for, every day!
If you can envie your owne Daughters blisse,
And wish her state lesse happie then it is!
If you can cast about your either eye,
And see all dead here, or about to dye!
The Starres, that are the Jewels of the Night,
And Day, deceasing! with the Prince of light,
The Sunne! great Kings! and mightiest Kingdomes
⠀⠀⠀fall!
Whole Nations! nay, Mankind! the World, with all
That ever had beginning there, to'ave end!⠀⠀⠀91
With what injustice should one soule pretend
T'escape this common knowne necessitie,
When we were all borne, we began to die;
And, but for that Contention, and brave strife
The Christian hath t'enjoy the future life,
Hee were the wretched'st of the race of men:
But as he soares at that, he bruiseth then
The Serpents head: Gets above Death, and Sinne,
And, sure of Heaven, rides triumphing in.⠀⠀⠀100

LXXXIV

Eupheme;

OR, THE FAIRE FAME. LEFT TO POSTERITIE OF THAT
TRULY-NOBLE LADY, THE LADY VENETIA DIGBY,
LATE WIFE OF SIR KENELME DIGBY, KNIGHT:
A GENTLEMAN ABSOLUTE IN ALL NUMBERS;

Consisting of these Ten Pieces.

The Dedication of her Cradle.
The Song of her Descent.

237

The Picture of her Body.
Her Mind.
Her being chosen a Muse.
Her faire Offices.
Her happie Match.
Her hopefull Issue.
Her APOTHEOSIS, or Relation to the Saints.
Her Inscription, or Crowne.

> *Vivam amare voluptas, defunctam Religio.*
> *Stat.*

1. THE DEDICATION OF HER CRADLE

FAIRE FAME, who art ordain'd to crowne
With ever-greene, and great renowne,
Their Heads, that Envy would hold downe
   With her, in shade

Of Death, and Darknesse; and deprive
Their names of being kept alive,
By Thee, and Conscience, both who thrive
   By the just trade

Of Goodnesse still: Vouchsafe to take
This Cradle, and for Goodnesse sake,   10
A dedicated Ensigne make
   Thereof, to Time:

That all Posteritie, as wee,
Who read what the Crepundia bee,
May something by that twilight see
   'Bove rattling Rime.

For, though that Rattles, Timbrels, Toyes,
Take little Infants with their noyse,
As prop'rest gifts, to Girles, and Boyes,
   Of light expence;   20

Their Corrals, Whistles, and prime Coates,
Their painted Maskes, their paper Boates,
With Sayles of silke, as the first notes
      Surprize their sense:

Yet, here are no such Trifles brought,
No cobweb Call's; no Surcoates wrought
With Gold, or Claspes, which might be bought
      On every Stall.

But, here's a Song of her Descent;
And Call to the high Parliament   30
Of Heaven; where Seraphim take tent
      Of ord'ring all.

This, utter'd by an antient Bard,
Who claimes (of reverence) to be heard,
As comming with his Harpe, prepar'd
      To chant her 'gree,

Is sung: as als' her getting up
By Jacobs Ladder, to the top
Of that eternall Port kept ope'
      For such as Shee.   40

2. THE SONG OF HER DESCENT

I SING the just, and uncontrol'd Descent
  Of Dame Venetia Digby, styl'd The Faire:
  For Mind, and Body, the most excellent
That ever Nature, or the later Ayre
  Gave two such Houses as Northumberland,
  And Stanley, to the which shee was Co-heire.
Speake it, you bold Penates, you that stand
  At either Stemme, and know the veines of good
  Run from your rootes; Tell, testifie the grand
Meeting of Graces, that so swell'd the flood   10

Of vertues in her, as, in short, shee grew
    The wonder of her Sexe, and of your Blood.
And tell thou, Alde-legh, None can tell more true
    Thy Neeces line, then thou that gav'st thy Name
    Into the Kindred, whence thy Adam drew
Meschines honour with the Cestrian fame
    Of the first Lupus, to the Familie
    By Ranulph—

        The rest of this Song is lost.

3. THE PICTURE OF THE BODY

SITTING, and ready to be drawne,
What makes these Velvets, Silkes, and Lawne,
Embroderies, Feathers, Fringes, Lace,
Where every lim takes like a face?

Send these suspected helpes, to aide
Some Forme defective, or decay'd;
This beautie, without falshood fayre,
Needs nought to cloath it but the ayre.

Yet something, to the Painters view,
Were fitly interpos'd; so new   10
Hee shall, if he can understand,
Worke with my fancie, his owne hand.

Draw first a Cloud: all save her neck;
And, out of that, make Day to breake;
Till, like her face, it doe appeare,
And Men may thinke, all light rose there.

Then let the beames of that, disperse
The Cloud, and show the Universe;
But at such distance, as the eye
May rather yet adore, then spy.   20

The Heaven design'd, draw next a Spring,
With all that Youth, or it can bring:
Foure Rivers branching forth like Seas,
And Paradise confining these.

Last, draw the circles of this Globe,
And let there be a starry Robe
Of Constellations 'bout her horld;
And thou hast painted beauties world.

But, Painter, see thou doe not sell
A Copie of this peece; nor tell   30
Whose 'tis: but if it favour find,
Next sitting we will draw her mind.

4. THE MIND

PAINTER, yo'are come, but may be gone,
Now I have better thought thereon,
This worke I can performe alone;
And give you reasons more then one.

Not, that your Art I doe refuse:
But here I may no colours use.
Beside, your hand will never hit,
To draw a thing that cannot sit.

You could make shift to paint an Eye,
An Eagle towring in the skye,   10
The Sunne, a Sea, or soundlesse Pit;
But these are like a Mind, not it.

No, to expresse this Mind to sense,
Would aske a Heavens Intelligence;
Since nothing can report that flame,
But what's of kinne to whence it came.

Sweet Mind, then speake your selfe, and say,
As you goe on, by what brave way
Our sense you doe with knowledge fill,
And yet remaine our wonder still.   20

I call you Muse; now make it true:
Hence-forth may every line be you;
That all may say, that see the frame,
This is no Picture, but the same.

A Mind so pure, so perfect fine,
As 'tis not radiant, but divine:
And so disdaining any tryer;
'Tis got where it can try the fire.

There, high exalted in the Spheare,
As it another Nature were,   30
It moveth all; and makes a flight
As circular, as infinite.

Whose Notions when it would expresse
In speech, it is with that excesse
Of grace, and Musique to the eare,
As what it spoke, it planted there.

The Voyce so sweet, the words so faire,
As some soft chime had stroak'd the ayre;
And, though the sound were parted thence,
Still left an Eccho in the sense.   40

But, that a Mind so rapt, so high,
So swift, so pure, should yet apply
It selfe to us, and come so nigh
Earths grossnesse; There's the how, and why.

Is it because it sees us dull,
And stuck in clay here, it would pull
Us forth, by some Celestiall slight
Up to her owne sublimed hight?

Or hath she here, upon the ground,
Some Paradise, or Palace found   50
In all the bounds of beautie fit
For her t'inhabit? There is it.

Thrice happy house, that hast receipt
For this so loftie forme, so streight,
So polisht, perfect, round, and even,
As it slid moulded off from Heaven.

Not swelling like the Ocean proud,
But stooping gently, as a Cloud,
As smooth as Oyle pour'd forth, and calme
As showers, and sweet as drops of Balme.   60

Smooth, soft, and sweet, in all a floud
Where it may run to any good;
And where it stayes, it there becomes
A nest of odorous spice, and gummes.

In action, winged as the wind,
In rest, like spirits left behind
Upon a banke, or field of flowers,
Begotten by that wind, and showers.

In thee, faire Mansion, let it rest,
Yet know, with what thou art possest,   70
Thou entertaining in thy brest,
But such a Mind, mak'st God thy Guest.

*A whole quaternion in the middest of this Poem is lost,
containing entirely the three next pieces of it, and all*

of the fourth (which in the order of the whole, is the eighth) excepting the very end: which at the top of the next quaternion goeth on thus:

But, for you (growing Gentlemen) the happy branches of two so illustrious Houses as these, where from your honour'd Mother is in both lines descended; let me leave you this last Legacie of Counsell; which so soone as you arrive at yeares of mature Understanding, open you (Sir) that are the eldest, and read it to your Brethren, for it will concerne you all alike. Vowed by a faithfull Servant, and Client of your Familie, with his latest breath expiring it.

B. J.

[8.] TO KENELME, JOHN, GEORGE

Boast not these Titles of your Ancestors;
(Brave Youths) th'are their possessions, none of yours:
When your owne Vertues, equall'd have their Names,
'Twill be but faire, to leane upon their Fames;
For they are strong Supporters: But, till then,
The greatest are but growing Gentlemen.
It is a wretched thing to trust to reedes;
Which all men doe, that urge not their owne deeds
Up to their Ancestors; the rivers side,
By which yo'are planted, shews your fruit shall bide:
Hang all your roomes, with one large Pedigree: 11
'Tis Vertue alone, is true Nobilitie.
Which Vertue from your Father, ripe, will fall;
Study illustrious Him, and you have all.

9. ELEGIE ON MY MUSE

The truly honoured Lady, the Lady Venetia Digby;
who living, gave me leave to call her so. Being

Her *APOTHEOSIS*, or Relation to the Saints.

Sera quidem tanto struitur medicina dolori.

'TWERE time that I dy'd too, now shee is dead,
Who was my Muse, and life of all I sey'd,
The Spirit that I wrote with, and conceiv'd.
All that was good, or great in me she weav'd,
And set it forth; the rest were Cobwebs fine,
Spun out in name of some of the old Nine!
To hang a window, or make darke the roome,
Till swept away, th'were cancell'd with a broome!
Nothing, that could remaine, or yet can stirre
A sorrow in me, fit to wait to her!   10
O! had I seene her laid out a faire Corse,
By Death, on Earth, I should have had remorse
On Nature for her: who did let her lie,
And saw that portion of her selfe to die.
Sleepie, or stupid Nature, couldst thou part
With such a Raritie, and not rowse Art
With all her aydes, to save her from the seize
Of Vulture death, and those relentless cleies?
Thou wouldst have lost the Phœnix, had the kind
Beene trusted to thee: not to't selfe assign'd.   20
Looke on thy sloth, and give thy selfe undone,
(For so thou art with me) now shee is gone.
My wounded mind cannot sustaine this stroke,
It rages, runs, flies, stands, and would provoke
The world to ruine with it; in her Fall,
I summe up mine owne breaking, and wish all.
Thou hast no more blowes, Fate, to drive at one:
What's left a Poet, when his Muse is gone?
Sure, I am dead, and know it not! I feele
Nothing I doe; but, like a heavie wheele,   30

Am turned with an others powers. My Passion
Whoorles me about, and to blaspheme in fashion!
I murmure against God, for having ta'en
Her blessed Soule, hence, forth this valley vane
Of teares, and dungeon of calamitie!
I envie it the Angels amitie!
The joy of Saints! the Crowne for which it lives,
The glorie, and gaine of rest, which the place gives!
Dare I prophane, so irreligious bee
To greet, or grieve her soft Euthanasee!   40
So sweetly taken to the Court of blisse,
As spirits had stolne her Spirit, in a kisse,
From off her pillow, and deluded bed;
And left her lovely body unthought dead!
Indeed, she is not dead! but laid to sleepe
In earth, till the last Trumpe awake the Sheepe
And Goates together, whither they must come
To heare their Judge, and his eternall doome;
To have that finall retribution,
Expected with the fleshes restitution.   50
For, as there are three Natures, Schoolemen call
One corporall, only; th'other spirituall,
Like single; so, there is a third, commixt,
Of Body and Spirit together, plac'd betwixt
Those other two; which must be judg'd, or crown'd:
This as it guilty is, or guiltlesse found,
Must come to take a sentence, by the sense
Of that great Evidence, the Conscience!
Who will be there, against that day prepar'd,
T'accuse, or quit all Parties to be heard!   60
O Day of joy, and suretie to the just!
Who in that feast of Resurrection trust!
That great eternall Holy-day of rest,
To Body, and Soule! where Love is all the guest!
And the whole Banquet is full sight of God!
Of joy the Circle, and sole Period!

All other gladnesse, with the thought is barr'd;
Hope hath her end! and Faith hath her reward!
This being thus: why should my tongue, or pen
Presume to interpell that fulnesse, when   70
Nothing can more adorne it, then the seat
That she is in, or, make it more compleat?
Better be dumbe, then superstitious!
Who violates the God-head, is most vitious
Against the Nature he would worship. Hee
Will honour'd be in all simplicitie!
Have all his actions wondred at, and view'd
With silence, and amazement! not with rude,
Dull, and prophane, weake, and imperfect eyes,
Have busie search made in his mysteries!   80
Hee knowes, what worke h'hath done, to call this
     Guest,
Out of her noble body, to this Feast:
And give her place, according to her blood
Amongst her Peeres, those Princes of all good!
Saints, Martyrs, Prophets, with those Hierarchies,
Angels, Arch-angels, Principalities,
The Dominations, Vertues, and the Powers,
The Thrones, the Cherube, and Seraphick bowers,
That, planted round, there sing before the Lamb,
A new Song to his praise, and great *I AM*:   90
And she doth know, out of the shade of Death,
What 'tis t'enjoy an everlasting breath!
To have her captiv'd spirit freed from flesh,
And on her Innocence, a garment fresh
And white, as that, put on: and in her hand
With boughs of Palme, a crowned Victrice stand!
And will you, worthy Sonne, Sir, knowing this,
Put black, and mourning on? and say you misse
A Wife, a Friend, a Lady, or a Love;
Whom her Redeemer, honour'd hath above   100
Her fellowes, with the oyle of gladnesse, bright
In heav'n Empire, and with a robe of light?

Thither, you hope to come; and there to find
That pure, that pretious, and exàlted mind
You once enjoy'd: A short space severs yee,
Compar'd unto that long eternitie,
That shall re-joyne yee. Was she, then, so deare,
When shee departed? you will meet her there,
Much more desir'd, and dearer then before,
By all the wealth of blessings, and the store   110
Accumulated on her, by the Lord
Of life, and light, the Sonne of God, the Word!
There, all the happy soules, that ever were,
Shall meet with gladnesse in one Theatre;
And each shall know, there, one anothers face:
By beatifick vertue of the Place.
There shall the Brother, with the Sister walke,
And Sons, and Daughters, with their Parents talke;
But all of God; They still shall have to say,
But make him All in All, their Theme, that Day:
That happy Day, that never shall see night!   121
Where Hee will be, all Beautie to the Sight;
Wine, or delicious fruits, unto the Taste;
A Musique in the Eares, will ever last;
Unto the Sent, a Spicerie, or Balme;
And to the Touch, a Flower, like soft as Palme.
Hee will all Glory, all Perfection be,
God, in the Union, and the Trinitie!
That holy, great, and glorious Mysterie
Will there revealed be in Majestie!   130
By light, and comfort of spirituall Grace;
The vision of our Saviour, face, to face
In his humanitie! To heare him preach
The price of our Redemption, and to teach
Through his inherent righteousnesse, in death,
The safetie of our soules, and forfeit breath!
What fulnesse of beatitude is here?
What love with mercy mixed doth appeare?

To style us Friends, who were, by Nature, Foes?
Adopt us Heires, by grace, who were of those   140
Had lost our selves? and prodigally spent
Our native portions, and possessed rent;
Yet have all debts forgiven us, and advance
B'imputed right to an inheritance
In h s eternall Kingdome, where we sit
Equall with Angels, and Co-heires of it.
Nor dare we under blasphemy conceive
He that shall be our supreme Judge, should leave
Himselfe so un-inform'd of his elect,
Who knowes the hearts of all, and can dissect   150
The smallest Fibre of our flesh; he can
Find all our Atomes from a point t'a span!
Our closest Creekes, and Corners, and can trace
Each line, as it were graphick, in the face.
And best he knew her noble Character,
For 'twas himselfe who form'd, and gave it her,
And to that forme, lent two such veines of blood
As nature could not more increase the flood
Of title in her! All Nobilitie
(But pride, that schisme of incivilitie)   160
She had, and it became her! she was fit
T'have knowne no envy, but by suffring it!
She had a mind as calme, as she was faire;
Not tost or troubled with light Lady-aire;
But, kept an even gate, as some streight tree
Mov'd by the wind, so comely moved she.
And by the awfull manage of her Eye
She swaid all bus'nesse in the Familie!
To one she said, Doe this, he did it; So
To another, Move; he went; To a third, Go,   170
He run; and all did strive with diligence
T'obey, and serve her sweet Commandements.
She was in one, a many parts of life;
A tender Mother, a discreeter Wife,

A solemne Mistresse, and so good a Friend,
So charitable, to religious end,
In all her petite actions, so devote,
As her whole life was now become one note
Of Pietie, and private holinesse.
She spent more time in teares her selfe to dresse 180
For her devotions, and those sad essayes
Of sorrow, then all pompe of gaudy daies:
And came forth ever cheered, with the rod
Of divine Comfort, when sh'had talk'd with God.
Her broken sighes did never misse whole sense:
Nor can the bruised heart want eloquence:
For, Prayer is the Incense most perfumes
The holy Altars, when it least presumes.
And hers were all Humilitie! they beat
The doore of Grace, and found the Mercy-Seat.
In frequent speaking by the pious Psalmes   191
Her solemne houres she spent, or giving Almes,
Or doing other deeds of Charitie,
To cloath the naked, feed the hungry. Shee
Would sit in an Infirmery, whole dayes
Poring, as on a Map, to find the wayes
To that eternall Rest, where now sh'hath place
By sure Election, and predestin'd grace!
Shee saw her Saviour, by an early light,
Incarnate in the Manger, shining bright   200
On all the world! Shee saw him on the Crosse
Suffring, and dying to redeeme our losse!
Shee saw him rise, triumphing over Death
To justifie, and quicken us in breath!
Shee saw him too, in glory to ascend
For his designed worke the perfect end
Of raising judging, and rewarding all,
The kind of Man, on whom his doome should fall!
All this by Faith she saw, and fram'd a Plea,
In manner of a daily Apostrophe,   210

To him should be her Judge, true God, true Man,
Jesus, the onely gotten Christ! who can
As being Redeemer, and Repairer too
(Of lapsed Nature) best know what to doe,
In that great Act of judgement: which the Father
Hath given wholly to the Sonne (the rather
As being the Sonne of Man) to shew his Power,
His Wisdome, and his Justice, in that houre,
The last of houres, and shutter up of all;
Where first his Power will appeare, by call   220
Of all are dead to life! His Wisdome show
In the discerning of each conscience, so!
And most his Justice, in the fitting parts,
And giving dues to all Mankinds deserts!
In this sweet Extasie, she was rapt hence.
Who reades, will pardon my Intelligence,
That thus have ventur'd these true straines upon;
To publish her a Saint. My Muse is gone.

In pietatis memoriam
quam præstas
Venetiæ tuæ illustrissim:
Marit: dign: Digbeie
Hanc ΑΠΟΘΕΟΣΙΝ, tibi, tuisque sacro.

The Tenth, being her Inscription, or CROWNE, is lost

LXXXV

The Praises of a Countrie Life.
(Horace, Epode 2)

HAPPIE is he, that from all Businesse cleere,
    As the old race of Mankind were,
With his owne Oxen tills his Sires left lands,
    And is not in the Usurers bands:

Nor Souldier-like started with rough alarmes,
   Nor dreads the Seas inraged harmes:
But flees the Barre and Courts, with the proud
   bords,
   And waiting Chambers of great Lords.
The Poplar tall, he then doth marrying twine
   With the growne issue of the Vine;   10
And with his hooke lops off the fruitlesse race,
   And sets more happy in the place:
Or in the bending Vale beholds a-farre
   The lowing herds there grazing are:
Or the prest honey in pure pots doth keepe
   Of Earth, and sheares the tender Sheepe:
Or when that Autumne, through the fields lifts
   round
   His head, with mellow Apples crown'd,
How plucking Peares, his owne hand grafted had,
   And purple-matching Grapes, hee's glad!   20
With which, Priapus, he may thanke thy hands,
   And, Sylvane, thine that keptst his Lands!
Then now beneath some ancient Oke he may,
   Now in the rooted Grasse him lay,
Whilst from the higher Bankes doe slide the
   floods,
   The soft birds quarrell in the Woods,
The Fountaines murmure as the streames doe
   creepe,
   And all invite to easie sleepe.
Then when the thundring Jove his Snow and
   showres
   Are gathering by the Wintry houres;   30
Or hence, or thence, he drives with many a Hound
   Wild Bores into his toyles pitch'd round:
Or straines on his small forke his subtill nets
   For th'eating Thrush, or Pit-falls sets:
And snares the fearfull Hare, and new-come Crane,
   And 'counts them sweet rewards so ta'en.

Who (amongst these delights) would not forget
    Loves cares so evill, and so great?
But if, to boot with these, a chaste Wife meet
    For houshold aid, and Children sweet;   40
Such as the Sabines, or a Sun-burnt-blowse,
    Some lustie quick Apulians spouse,
To deck the hallow'd Harth with old wood fir'd
    Against the Husband comes home tir'd;
That penning the glad flock in hurdles by,
    Their swelling udders doth draw dry:
And from the sweet Tub Wine of this yeare takes,
    And unbought viands ready makes:
Not Lucrine Oysters I could then more prize,
    Nor Turbot, nor bright Golden eyes: 50
If with bright floods, the Winter troubled much,
    Into our Seas send any such:
Th'Ionian God-wit, nor the Ginny hen
    Could not goe downe my belly then
More sweet then Olives, that new gather'd be
    From fattest branches of the Tree:
Or the herb Sorrell, that loves Meadows still,
    Or Mallowes loosing bodyes ill:
Or at the Feast of Bounds, the Lambe then slaine,
    Or Kid forc't from the Wolfe againe.   60
Among these Cates how glad the sight doth come
    Of the fed flocks approaching home!
To view the weary Oxen draw, with bare
    And fainting necks, the turned Share!
The wealthy houshold swarme of bondmen met,
    And 'bout the steeming Chimney set!
These thoughts when Usurer Alphius, now about
    To turne more farmer, had spoke out,
'Gainst th'Ides, his moneys he gets in with paine,
    At th'Calends, puts all out againe.   70

LXXXVI

(Horace.) Ode the First. The Fourth Booke. To Venus

VENUS, againe thou mov'st a warre
Long intermitted, pray thee, pray thee spare:
    I am not such, as in the Reigne
Of the good Cynara I was: Refraine,
    Sower Mother of sweet Loves, forbeare
To bend a man now at his fiftieth yeare
    Too stubborne for Commands, so slack:
Goe where Youths soft intreaties call thee back.
    More timely hie thee to the house,
With thy bright Swans, of Paulus Maximus: 10
    There jest, and feast, make him thine host,
If a fit livor thou dost seeke to toast;
    For he's both noble, lovely, young,
And for the troubled Clyent fyl's his tongue,
    Child of a hundred Arts, and farre
Will he display the Ensignes of thy warre.
    And when he smiling finds his Grace
With thee 'bove all his Rivals gifts take place,
    Hee will thee a Marble Statue make
Beneath a Sweet-wood Roofe, neere Alba Lake: 20
    There shall thy dainty Nostrill take
In many a Gumme, and for thy soft eares sake
    Shall Verse be set to Harpe and Lute,
And Phrygian Hau'boy, not without the Flute.
    There twice a day in sacred Laies,
The Youths and tender Maids shall sing thy praise:
    And in the Salian manner meet
Thrice 'bout thy Altar with their Ivory feet.
    Me now, nor Wench, nor wanton Boy,
Delights, nor credulous hope of mutuall Joy,   30
    Nor care I now healths to propound;
Or with fresh flowers to girt my Temple round.

But, why, oh why, my Ligurine,
Flow my thin teares, downe these pale cheeks of
    mine?
  Or why, my well-grac'd words among,
With an uncomely silence failes my tongue?
  Hard-hearted, I dreame every Night
I hold thee fast! but fled hence, with the Light,
  Whether in Mars his field thou bee,
Or Tybers winding streames, I follow thee.   40

LXXXVII

Ode IX, 3 Booke, to Lydia

Dialogue of Horace, and Lydia

Hor.   Whilst, Lydia, I was lov'd of thee,
    And ('bout thy Ivory neck,) no youth did fling,
      His armes more acceptable free,
    I thought me richer then the Persian King.
Lyd.   Whilst Horace lov'd no Mistres more,
    Nor after Chloe did his Lydia sound;
      In name, I went all names before,
    The Roman Ilia was not more renown'd.
Hor.   'Tis true, I'am Thracian Chloes, I,
    Who sings so sweet, and with such cunning
       plaies,   10
      As, for her, I'l'd not feare to die,
    So Fate would give her life, and longer daies.
Lyd.   And, I am mutually on fire
    With gentle Calais, Thurine Orniths Sonne;
      For whom I doubly would expire,
    So Fates would let the Boy a long thred run.
Hor.   But, say old Love returne should make,
    And us dis-joyn'd force to her brazen yoke,
      That I bright Chloe off should shake;

And to left-Lydia, now the gate stood ope.   20
Lyd.   Though he be fairer then a Starre;
Thou lighter then the barke of any tree,
    And then rough Adria, angrier, farre;
    Yet would I wish to love, live, die with thee.

LXXXVIII

Fragmentum Petron. Arbitr. Translated

DOING, a filthy pleasure is, and short;
And done, we straight repent us of the sport:
Let us not then rush blindly on unto it,
Like lustfull beasts, that onely know to doe it:
For lust will languish, and that heat decay,
But thus, thus, keeping endlesse Holy-day,
Let us together closely lie, and kisse,
There is no labour, nor no shame in this;
This hath pleas'd, doth please, and long will please; never
Can this decay, but is beginning ever.   10

LXXXIX

Epigramma Martialis. Lib. VIII. lxxvii.
Translated

LIBER, of all thy friends, thou sweetest care,
Thou worthy in eternall Flower to fare,
If thou be'st wise, with 'Syrian Oyle let shine
Thy locks, and rosie garlands crowne thy head;
Darke thy cleare glasse with old Falernian Wine;
And heat, with softest love, thy softer bed.
Hee, that but living halfe his dayes, dies such,
Makes his life longer then 'twas given him much.

MISCELLANY

INCLUDING
UNGATHERED VERSE
AND SELECTIONS FROM THE MASQUES
AND PLAYS

To Thomas Palmer

from *The Sprite of Trees and Herbes*

WHEN late (grave Palmer) these thy graffs and flowers
(So well dispos'd by thy auspicious hand)
Weare made the objects to my weaker powers;
I could not but in admiracion stand.
First: thy successe did strike my sence with wonder;
That mongst so manie plants transplanted hether,
Not one but thrives; in spite of stormes and thunder,
Unseason'd Frostes, or the most envyous weather.
Then I admir'd, the rare and prescious use
Thy skill hath made of ranck dispised weedes;   10
Whilst other soules convert to base abuse
The sweetest simples, and most soveraigne seedes.
Next, that which rapt mee, was: I might behold
How lyke the Carbuncle in Aarons brest
The seaven-fold flower of Arte (more rich then gold)
Did sparcle foorth in Center of the rest:
Thus, as a ponderous thinge in water cast
Extendeth circles into infinits,
Still making that the greatest that is last,
Till th'one hath drownd the other in our sightes,   20
So in my braine; the strong impression
Of thy rich labors worlds of thoughts created,
Which thoughts being circumvolvd in gyerlyk
      mocion
Wear spent with wonder as they weare delated,
Till giddie with amazement I fell downe
In a deep trance;* * * * * * * * * *
* * * * * When loe to crowne thy worth
I struggled with this passion that did drowne
My abler faculties; and thus brake foorth:

Palmer, thy travayles well becum thy name,   · 30
And thou in them shall live as longe as Fame.

Dignum laude virum Musa vetat mori.

II

In Authorem. [*Nicholas Breton*]

THOU, that wouldst finde the habit of true passion,
    And see a minde attir'd in perfect straines;
Not wearing moodes, as gallants doe a fashion,
    In these pide times, only to shewe their braines,
Looke here on Bretons worke, the master print:
    Where, such perfections to the life doe rise.
If they seeme wry, to such as looke asquint,
    The fault's not in the object, but their eyes.
For, as one comming with a laterall viewe,
    Unto a cunning piece wrought perspective,   10
Wants facultie to make a censure true:
    So with this Authors readers will it thrive:
Which being eyed directly, I divine,
His proofe their praise will meete, as in this line.

III

Fragments from Englands Parnassus.
1600

1. MURDER (p. 211)

THOSE that in blood such violent pleasure have,
Seldome descend but bleeding to their grave.

2. PEACE (pp. 228–29)

WARRES greatest woes, and miseries increase,
Flowes from the surfets which we take in peace.

3. THE POWER OF GOLD (p. 258)

GOLD is a sutor, never tooke repulse,
It carries Palme with it, (where e're it goes)
Respect, and observation; it uncovers
The knottie heads of the most surly Groomes,
Enforcing yron doores to yeeld it way,
Were they as strong ram'd up as Aetna gates.
It bends the hams of Gossip Vigilance,
And makes her supple feete, as swift as winde.
It thawes the frostiest, and most stiffe disdaine:
Muffles the clearnesse of Election,   10
Straines fancie unto foule Apostacie,
And strikes the quickest-sighted Judgement blinde.
Then why should we dispaire? dispaire? Away:
Where Gold's the Motive, women have no Nay.

IV

Hymn to Diana

from *Cynthias Revells*

QUEENE, and Huntresse, chaste, and faire,
   Now the Sunne is laid to sleepe,
Seated, in thy silver chaire,
   State in wonted manner keepe:
Hesperus intreats thy light,
Goddesse, excellently bright

Earth, let not thy envious shade
    Dare it selfe to interpose;
Cynthias shining orbe was made
    Heaven to cleere, when day did close: 10
Blesse us then with wished sight,
Goddesse, excellently bright.

Lay thy bow of pearle apart,
    And thy cristall-shining quiver;
Give unto the flying hart
    Space to breathe, how short soever:
Thou that mak'st a day of night,
Goddesse, excellently bright.

V

Author ad Librum

GOE little Booke, Goe little Fable
Unto the bright, and amiable
Lucy of Bedford; she, that Bounty
Appropriates still unto that County:
Tell her, his Muse that did invent thee
To Cynthias fayrest Nymph hath sent thee,
And sworne, that he will quite discard thee
If any way she do rewarde thee
But with a Kisse, (if thou canst dare it)
Of her white Hand; or she can spare it.   10

V I

The Phœnix Analysde

Now, after all, let no man
Receive it for a Fable,

If a Bird so amiable,
Do turne into a Woman.

Or (by our Turtles Augure)
　　That Natures fairest Creature,
　　Prove of his Mistris Feature,
But a bare Type and Figure.

Ode Enthousiastike

SPLENDOR! O more then mortall,
For other formes come short all
Of her illustrate brightnesse,
As farre as Sinne's from lightnesse.

Her wit as quicke, and sprightfull
As fire; and more delightfull
Then the stolne sports of Lovers,
When night their meeting covers.

Judgement (adorn'd with Learning)
Doth shine in her discerning,　　　　　　　10
Cleare as a naked vestall
Closde in an orbe of Christall.

Her breath for sweete exceeding
The Phœnix place of breeding,
But mixt with sound, transcending
All Nature of commending.

Alas: then whither wade I,
In thought to praise this Ladie,
When seeking her renowning,
My selfe am so neare drowning?　　　　　　20
263

Retire, and say; Her Graces
Are deeper then their Faces:
Yet shee's nor nice to shew them,
Nor takes she pride to know them.

VIII

Proludium

AN Elegie? no, Muse, it askes a strayne
Too loose, and capringe, for thy stricter vayne.
Thy thoughtes did never melt in amorous fire
Like glasse blowne up and fash'ond by desire.
The skill-full mischiefe of a roving eye
Could ne're make prise of thy white chastitie.
Then, leave these lighter Nombers to light Braynes,
In whome the Flame of every Bewtie raignes,
Such as in lustes wylde Forrest love to range,
Only pursuinge constancie in change.   10
Let these in wanton feete daunce out their Soules:
A farther fury my raysd Spirite controles,
Which rapp's me up to the true Heaven of love,
And conjures all my faculties t'approve
The Glories of it. Now our Muse takes winge,
And now an Epode, to deepe eares, wee singe.

IX

Song

from *Poetaster*

SWELL me a bowle with lustie wine,
Till I may see the plump Lyæus swim
Above the brim:

264

I drinke, as I would wright,
In flowing measure, fill'd with flame, and spright.

x

Song

from *Poetaster*

BLUSH, folly, blush: here's none that feares
The wagging of an asses eares,
Although a woolvish case he weares.
Detraction is but basenesse varlet;
And apes are apes, though cloth'd in scarlet.

x i

Ode. Allegorike

Who saith our Times nor have, nor can
   Produce us a blacke Swan?
    Behold, where one doth swim;
      Whose Note, and Hue,
Besides the other Swannes admiring him,
    Betray it true:
   A gentler Bird, then this,
Did never dint the breast of Tamisis.

Marke, marke, but when his wing he takes,
   How faire a flight he makes!   10
    How upward, and direct!
      Whil'st pleas'd Apollo
Smiles in his Sphære, to see the rest affect,
    In vaine to follow:

This Swanne is onely his,
And Phœbus love cause of his blackenesse is.

He shew'd him first the hoofe-cleft Spring,
 Neere which, the Thespiad's sing;
  The cleare Dircæan Fount
   Where Pindar swamme;   20
The pale Pyrene, and the forked Mount:
   And, when they came
  To brookes, and broader streames,
From Zephyr's rape would close him with his
    beames.

This chang'd his Downe; till this, as white
 As the whole heard in sight,
  And still is in the Brest:
   That part nor Winde,
Nor Sunne could make to vary from the rest,
   Or alter kinde.   30
   'So much doth Virtue hate,
'For stile of rarenesse, to degenerate.

Be then both Rare, and Good; and long
 Continue thy sweete Song.
  Nor let one River boast
   Thy tunes alone;
But prove the Aire, and saile from Coast to
    Coast:
   Salute old Mone,
  But first to Cluid stoope low,
The Vale, that bred thee pure, as her Hills
    Snow.   40

From thence, display thy wing againe
 Over Ierna maine,
  To the Eugenian dale;
   There charme the rout

With thy soft notes, and hold them within Pale
    That late were out.
   'Musicke hath power to draw,
'Where neither Force can bend, nor Feare can
    awe.

Be proofe, the glory of his hand,
   (Charles Montjoy) whose command   50
   Hath all beene Harmony:
    And more hath wonne
Upon the Kerne, and wildest Irishry,
    Then Time hath donne,
   Whose strength is above strength;
And conquers all things, yea it selfe, at length.

Who ever sipt at Baphyre river,
   That heard but Spight deliver
   His farre-admired Acts,
    And is not rap't   60
With entheate rage, to publish their bright tracts?
    (But this more apt
   When him alone we sing)
Now must we plie our ayme; our Swan's on
    wing.

Who (see) already hath ore-flowne
   The Hebrid Isles, and knowne
   The scatter'd Orcades;
    From thence is gon
To utmost Thule: whence, he backes the Seas
    To Caledon,   70
   And over Grampius mountaine,
To Loumond lake, and Twedes blacke-springing
    fountaine.

Haste, Haste, sweete Singer: Nor to Tine,
   Humber, or Owse, decline;

But over Land to Trent:
 There coole thy Plumes,
And up againe, in skies, and aire to vent
 Their reeking fumes;
  Till thou at Tames alight,
From whose prowde bosome, thou began'st thy
   flight.   80

Tames, prowde of thee, and of his Fate
 In entertaining late
 The choise of Europes pride;
  The nimble French;
The Dutch whom Wealth (not Hatred) doth
   divide;
  The Danes that drench
 Their cares in wine; with sure
Though slower Spaine; and Italy mature.

All which, when they but heare a straine
 Of thine, shall thinke the Maine 90
 Hath sent her Mermaides in,
  To hold them here:
Yet, looking in thy face, they shall begin
  To loose that feare;
  And (in the place) envie
So blacke a Bird, so bright a Qualitie.

But should they know (as I) that this,
 Who warbleth *Pancharis*,
 Were Cycnus, once high flying
  With Cupids wing;   100
Though, now by Love transform'd, and dayly
   dying:
  (Which makes him sing
 With more delight, and grace)
Or thought they, Leda's white Adult'rers place

Among the starres should be resign'd
   To him, and he there shrin'd;
   Or Tames be rap't from us
     To dimme and drowne
In heav'n the Signe of old Eridanus:
      How they would frowne!   110
   But these are Mysteries
Conceal'd from all but cleare Propheticke eyes.

It is inough, their griefe shall know
   At their returne, nor Po,
   Iberus, Tagus, Rheine,
     Scheldt, nor the Maas,
Slow Arar, nor swift Rhone; the Loyre, nor
     Seine,
     With all the race
   Of Europes waters can
Set out a like, or second to our Swan.   120

XII

To the Author. Thomas Wright

IN Picture, they which truly understand,
   Require (besides the likenesse of the thing)
   Light, Posture, Height'ning, Shadow, Culloring,
All which are parts commend the cunning hand;
And all your Booke (when it is throughly scan'd)
   Will well confesse; presenting, limiting,
   Each subt'lest Passion, with her source, and spring,
So bold, as shewes your Art you can command.
But now, your Worke is done, if they that view
   The severall figures, languish in suspence,   10
To judge which Passion's false, and which is true,
   Betweene the doubtfull sway of Reason', and sense;

'Tis not your fault, if they shall sense preferre,
Being tould there, Reason cannot, Sense may erre.

XIII

Song

from *The Masque of Beautie*

So beautie on the waters stood,
When love had sever'd earth, from flood!
So when he parted ayre, from fire,
He did with concord all inspire!
And then a motion he them taught,
That elder then himselfe was thought.
Which thought was, yet, the child of earth,
For love is elder then his birth.

XIV

Song

from *The Masque of Beautie*

HAD those, that dwell in error foule,
And hold that women have no soule,
But seene these move; they would have, then,
Said, *Women were the soules of men.*
So they doe move each heart, and eye
With the worlds soule, true harmony.

XV

To the Worthy Author M. John Fletcher

THE wise, and many-headed Bench, that sits
Upon the Life, and Death of Playes, and Wits,
(Compos'd of Gamester, Captaine, Knight, Knight's
    man,
Lady, or Pusil, that weares maske, or fan,
Velvet, or Taffata cap, rank'd in the darke
With the shops Foreman, or some such brave sparke,
That may judge for his six-pence) had, before
They saw it halfe, damd thy whole play, and more,
Their motives were, since it had not to do
With vices, which they look'd for, and came to.   10
I, that am glad, thy Innocence was thy Guilt,
And wish that all the Muses blood were spilt,
In such a Martirdome; To vexe their eyes,
Do crowne thy murdred Poeme: which shall rise
A glorified worke to Time, when Fire,
Or moathes shall eate, what all these Fooles admire.

XVI

Song

from *The Silent Woman*

STILL to be neat, still to be drest,
    As, you were going to a feast;
Still to be pou'dred, still perfum'd:
    Lady, it is to be presum'd,
Though arts hid causes are not found
All is not sweet, all is not sound.

Give me a looke, give me a face,
That makes simplicitie a grace;
Robes loosely flowing, haire as free:
Such sweet neglect more taketh me,   10
Then all th'adulteries of art.
They strike mine eyes, but not my heart.

XVII

Charme

from *The Masque of Queenes*

THE owle is abroad, the bat, and the toad,
  And so is the cat-a-mountayne,
The ant, and the mole sit both in a hole,
  And frog peepes out o'the fountayne;
The dogs, they doe bay, and the timbrels play,
  The spindle is now a turning;
The moone it is red, and the starres are fled,
  But all the skie is a burning:
The ditch is made, and our nayles the spade,
With pictures full, of waxe, and of wooll;   10
Their livers I sticke, with needles quicke;
There lacks but the bloud, to make up the floud.
  Quickly, Dame, then, bring your part in,
Spurre, spurre, upon little Martin,
Merrily, merrily, make him saile,
A worme in his mouth, and a thorne in's taile,
Fire above, and fire below,
With a whip i'your hand, to make him goe.

XVIII

Epitaph

STAY, view this stone: And, if thou beest not such,
Read here a little, that thou mayst know much.
It covers, first, a Virgin; and then, one
That durst be that in Court: a vertu'alone
To fill an Epitaph. But she had more.
She might have claym'd t'have made the Graces
    foure;
Taught Pallas language; Cynthia modesty;
As fit to have encreas'd the harmony
Of Spheares, as light of Starres; She was earthes Eye:
The sole Religious house, and Votary,   10
With Rites not bound, but conscience. Wouldst thou
    All?
She was 'Sell Boulstred. In which name, I call
Up so much truth, as could I it pursue
Might make the Fable of Good Women true.

XIX

To the Right Noble Tom, Tell-Troth of his Travailes, the Coryate of Odcombe, and his Booke now going to Travell

T RIE and trust Roger, was the word, but now
H onest Tom Tell-Troth puts downe Roger. How?
O f travell he discourseth so at large,
M arry, he sets it out at his owne charge;
A nd therein (which is worth his valour too)
S hewes he dares more then Paules Church-yard durst
    do.

273

C ome forth, thou bonnie bouncing booke then,
    daughter
O f Tom of Odcombe, that odde Joviall Author.
R ather his sonne I should have cal'd thee; why?
Y es, thou wert borne out of his travelling thigh   10
A s well as from his braines, and claimest thereby
T o be his Bacchus as his Pallas: bee
E ver his thighes Male then, and his braines Shee.

XX

To the London Reader, on the Odcombian Writer, Polytopian Thomas the Traveller

WHO ever he be, would write a Story at
The height, let him learne of Mr. Tom Coryate;
Who, because his matter in all should be meete,
To his strength, hath measur'd it out with his feet.
And that, say Philosophers, is the best modell.
Yet who could have hit on't but the wise noddell
Of our Odcombian, that literate Elfe?
To line out no stride, but pas'd by himselfe?
And allow you for each particular mile,
By the scale of his booke, a yard of his stile?   10
Which unto all Ages, for his will be knowne,
Since he treads in no other Mans steps but his owne.
And that you may see he most luckily ment
To write it with the selfe same spirit he went,
He sayes to the world, let any man mend it,
In five monthes he went it, in five monthes he pend it.
But who will beleeve this, that chanceth to looke
The Mappe of his journey, and sees in his booke,
France, Savoy, Italy, and Helvetia,
The Low-countries, Germany, and Rhetia   20
There nam'd to be travell'd? For this our Tom saith:
Pies on't, you have his historicall faith.

274

Each leafe of his journall, and line doth unlocke
The truth of his heart there, and tell's what a clocke
He went out at each place, and at what he came in,
How long he did stay, at what signe he did Inne.
Besides, he tried Ship, Cart, Waggon, and Chayre,
Horse, foote, and all but flying in the ayre:
And therefore how ever the travelling nation,
Or builders of Story have oft imputation   30
Of lying, he feares so much the reproofe
Of his foote, or his penne, his braine, or his hoofe,
That he dares to informe you, but somewhat meti-
    culous,
How scabbed, how ragged, and how pediculous
He was in his travaile, how like to be beaten,
For grapes he had gather'd, before they were eaten.
How faine for his venery he was to crie (*Tergum O*)
And lay in straw with the horses at Bergamo,
How well, and how often his shoes too were mended,
That sacred to Odcombe are now there suspended, 40
I meane that one paire, wherewith he so hobled
From Venice to Flushing, were not they well cobled?
Yes. And thanks God in his Pistle or his Booke
How many learned men he have drawne with his
    hooke
Of Latine and Greeke, to his friendship. And seven
He there doth protest he saw of the eleven.
Nay more in his wardrobe, if you will laugh at a
Jest, he saies, *Item* one sute of blacke taffata
Except a dublet, and bought of the Jewes:
So that not them, his scabbes, lice, or the stewes, 50
Or any thing else that another should hide,
Doth he once dissemble, but tels he did ride
In a Cart twixt Montrell and Abbevile.
And being at Flushing enforced to feele
Some want, they say in a sort he did crave:
I writ he onely his taile there did wave;

Which he not denies. Now being so free,
Poore Tom, have we cause to suspect just thee?
No: as I first said, who would write a story at
The height, let him learne of Mr. Tom Coryate. 60

XXI

Satyres Catch

from *Oberon*

BUZ, quoth the blue Flie,
   Hum, quoth the Bee:
Buz, and hum, they crie,
   And so doe wee.
In his eare, in his nose,
   Thus, doe you see?
He eat the dormouse,
   Else it was hee.

XXII

A Speach Presented unto King James at a Tylting in the Behalfe of the Two Noble Brothers Sir Robert and Sir Henrye Rich, now Earles of Warwick and Hollande

Two noble knightes, whome true desire and zeale,
Hath armde att all poyntes, charge mee humblye
   kneele
Unto thee, king of men; their noblest partes
To tender thus, their lives, their loves, their hartes!
The elder of these two, riche hopes Increase,
Presentes a Royall Alter of fayre peace,
And as an ever-lasting Sacrifice

276

His life, his love, his honour, which ne'r dyes,
Hee freely bringes; and on this Alter layes
As true oblations; his Brothers Embleme sayes,   10
Except your Gratious Eye as through a Glass
Made prospective, behould hym, hee must passe
Still that same little poynte hee was; but when
Your Royall Eye which still creates new men
Shall looke, and on hyme soe, then arte's a lyer
Yf from a little sparke hee rise not fier.

XXIII

To his much and worthily esteemed
Friend the Author

WHO takes thy volume to his vertuous hand,
Must be intended still to understand:
Who bluntly doth but looke upon the same,
May aske, *what Author would conceale his name*?
Who reads may roave, and call the passage darke,
Yet may as blind men sometimes hit the marke.
Who reads, who roaves, who hopes to understand,
May take thy volume to his vertuous hand.
Who cannot reade, but onely doth desire
To understand, hee may at length admire.   10

XXIV

To the most Noble, and above his Titles,
Robert, Earle of Somerset

THEY are not those, are present with theyre face,
And clothes, and guifts, that only do thee grace

At these thy Nuptials; but, whose heart, and thought
Do wayte upon thee: and theyre Love not bought.
Such weare true wedding robes, and are true freindes,
That bid, God give thee joy, and have no endes.
Which I do, early, vertuous Somerset,
And pray, thy joyes as lasting bee, as great.
Not only this, but every day of thine,
With the same looke, or with a better, shine.   10
May she, whome thou for spouse, to day, dost take,
Out-bee that *Wife*, in worth, thy freind did make:
And thou to her, that *Husband*, may exalt
Hymens amends, to make it worth his fault.
So, be there never discontent, or sorrow,
To rise with eyther of you, on the morrow.
So, be your Concord, still, as deepe, as mute;
And ev'ry joy, in mariage, turne a fruite.
So, may those Mariage-Pledges, comforts prove:
And ev'ry birth encrease the heate of Love.   20
So, in theyr number, may you never see
Mortality, till you immortall bee.
And when your yeares rise more, then would be told,
Yet neyther of you seeme to th'other old.
That all, that view you then, and late; may say,
Sure, this glad payre were married, but this day.

XXV

To the worthy Author on The Husband

IT fits not onely him that makes a Booke,
To see his worke be good; but that he looke
Who are his Test, and what their judgement is:
Least a false praise do make theyr dotage his.
I do not feele that ever yet I had
The art of uttring wares, if they were bad;

Or skill of making matches in my life:
And therefore I commend unto the *Wife*,
That went before, a *Husband*. Shee, Ile sweare,
Was worthy of a Good one; And this, here,
I know for such, as (if my word will waigh)
Shee need not blush upon the Mariage-Day.

XXVI

To his Friend the Author upon his Richard

WHEN these, and such, their voices have employd;
What place is for my testimony void?
Or, to so many, and so Broad-seales had,
What can one witnesse, and a weake one, add
To such a worke, as could not need theirs? Yet
If Praises, when th'are full, heaping admit,
My suffrage brings thee all increase, to crowne
Thy *Richard*, rais'd in song, past pulling downe.

XXVII

Cylcope's Song

from *Mercury Vindicated from the Alchemists*

SOFT, subtile fire, thou soule of art,
    Now doe thy part
On weaker Nature, that through age is lamed.
    Take but thy time, now she is old,
    And the Sunne her friend growne cold,
She will no more, in strife with thee be named.

Looke, but how few confesse her now,
    In cheeke or browe!

279

From every head, almost, how she is frighted.
   The very age abhorres her so,   10
   That it learnes to speake and goe
As if by art alone it could be righted.

XXVIII

To my truly-belov'd Freind, Mr. Browne: on his Pastorals

SOME men, of Bookes, or Freinds not speaking right,
May hurt them more with praise, then Foes with
   spight.
But I have seene thy worke, and I know thee:
And, if thou list thy selfe, what thou canst bee.
For, though but early in these pathes thou tread,
I find thee write most worthy to be read.
It must be thine owne judgment, yet, that sends
This thy worke forth: that judgment mine commends.
And, where the most reade bookes, on Authors fames,
Or, like our Money-Brokers, take up names   10
On credit, and are cossen'd; see, that thou
By offring not more sureties, then inow,
Hold thyne owne worth unbroke: which is so good
Upon th'Exchange of Letters, as I wou'd
More of our writers would like thee, not swell
With the *how much* they set forth, but th' *how well*.

XXIX

Song

from *The Vision of Delight*

BREAKE, Phant'sie, from thy cave of cloud,
    And spread thy purple wings;
Now all thy figures are allow'd,
    And various shapes of things;
Create of ayrie formes, a streame;
    It must have bloud, and naught of fleame,
    And though it be a waking dreame;
Yet let it like an odour rise
    To all the Sences here,
And fall like sleep upon their eies,   10
    Or musick in their eare.

XXX

Charles Cavendish to his Posteritie

SONNES, seeke not me amonge these polish'd stones:
These only hide part of my flesh, and bones:
Which, did they ne're so neate, or proudly dwell,
Will all turne dust, and may not make me swell.
Let such as justly have out-liv'd all prayse,
Trust in the tombes, their care-full freinds do rsaye;
I made my lyfe my monument, and yours:
To which there's no materiall that endures;
Nor yet inscription like it. Write but that;
And teach your nephewes it to æmulate: 10
It will be matter lowd inoughe to tell
Not when I died, but how I livd. Farewell.

XXXI

To my worthy and honour'd Friend, Mr. George Chapman, on his translation of Hesiods Works and Dayes

WHOSE worke could this be, Chapman, to refine
Olde Hesiods Ore, and give it us; but thine,
Who hadst before wrought in rich Homers Mine?

What treasure hast thou brought us! and what store
Still, still, dost thou arrive with, at our shore,
To make thy honour, and our wealth the more!

If all the vulgar Tongues, that speake this day,
Were askt of thy Discoveries; They must say,
To the Greeke coast thine onely knew the way.

Such passage hast thou found, such Returnes made,
As, now of all men, it is call'd thy Trade: 11
And who make thither else, rob, or invade.

XXXII

Song

from *The Gypsies Metamorphos'd*

THE faery beame upon you,
The starres to glister on you;
    A Moone of light,
    In the noone of night,
Till the Fire-drake hath o're gon you.

282

The wheele of fortune guide you,
The Boy with the bow beside you
　　Runne aye in the way,
　　Till the bird of day,
And the luckier lot betide you.　　　　　10

*XXXIII

Horace, Ode II, 3

REMEMBER, when blinde Fortune knits her brow,
Thy minde be not dejected over-lowe:
Nor let thy thoughts too insolently swell,
Though all thy hopes doe prosper ne'r so well.
For, drink thy teares, with sorrow still opprest,
Or taste pure wine, secure and ever blest,
In those remote, and pleasant shady fields
Where stately Pine and Poplar shadow yeelds,
Or circling streames that warble, passing by;
All will not help, sweet friend: For, thou must die.　10
　The house, thou hast, thou once must leave behind
　　thee,
And those sweet babes thou often kissest kindly:
And when th'hast gotten all the wealth thou can,
Thy paines is taken for another man.
　Alas! what poor advantage doth it bring,
To boast thy selfe descended of a King!
When those, that have no house to hide their heads,
Finde in their grave as warm and easie beds.

XXXIV

On the Author, Worke, and Translator

WHO tracks this Authors, or Translators Pen,
Shall finde, that either hath read Bookes, and Men:
To say but one, were single. Then it chimes,
When the old words doe strike on the new times,
As in this Spanish Proteus; who, though writ
But in one tongue, was form'd with the worlds wit:
And hath the noblest marke of a good Booke,
That an ill man dares not securely looke
Upon it, but will loath, or let it passe,
As a deformed face doth a true glasse.   10
Such Bookes deserve Translators, of like coate
As was the Genius wherewith they were wrote;
And this hath met that one, that may be stil'd
More then the Foster-father of this Child;
For though Spaine gave him his first ayre and Vogue,
He would be call'd, henceforth, the *English-Rogue*,
But that hee's too well suted, in a cloth,
Finer then was his Spanish, if my Oath
Will be receiv'd in Court; If not, would I
Had cloath'd him so. Here's all I can supply   20
To your desert, who'have done it, Friend. And this
Faire Æmulation, and no Envy is;
When you behold me wish my selfe, the man
That would have done that, which you onely can.

XXXV

To the Reader

THIS Figure, that thou here seest put,
It was for gentle Shakespeare cut;

Wherein the Graver had a strife
With Nature, to out-doo the life:
O, could he but have drawne his wit
As well in brasse, as he hath hit
His face; the Print would then surpasse
All, that was ever writ in brasse.
But, since he cannot, Reader, looke
Not on his Picture, but his Booke.   10

XXXVI

To the Memory of my Beloved, the Author, Mr. William Shakespeare: and what he hath left us

To draw no envy (Shakespeare) on thy name,
Am I thus ample to thy Booke, and Fame:
While I confesse thy writings to be such,
As neither Man, nor Muse, can praise too much.
'Tis true, and all mens suffrage. But these wayes
Were not the paths I meant unto thy praise:
For seeliest Ignorance on these may light,
Which, when it sounds at best, but eccho's right;
Or blinde Affection, which doth ne're advance
The truth, but gropes, and urgeth all by chance;   10
Or crafty Malice, might pretend this praise,
And thinke to ruine, where it seem'd to raise.
These are, as some infamous Baud, or Whore,
Should praise a Matron. What could hurt her more?
But thou art proofe against them, and indeed
Above th'ill fortune of them, or the need.
I therefore will begin. Soule of the Age!
The applause! delight! the wonder of our Stage!
My Shakespeare, rise; I will not lodge thee by
Chaucer, or Spenser, or bid Beaumont lye   20

A little further, to make thee a roome:
Thou art a Moniment, without a tombe,
And art alive still, while thy Booke doth live,
And we have wits to read, and praise to give.
That I not mix thee so, my braine excuses;
I meane with great, but disproportion'd Muses:
For, if I thought my judgement were of yeeres,
I should commit thee surely with thy peeres,
And tell, how farre thou didst our Lily out-shine,
Or sporting Kid, or Marlowes mighty line.   30
And though thou hadst small Latine, and lesse
    Greeke,
From thence to honour thee, I would not seeke
For names; but call forth thund'ring Æschilus,
Euripides, and Sophocles to us,
Paccuvius, Accius, him of Cordova dead,
To life againe, to heare thy Buskin tread,
And shake a Stage: Or, when thy Sockes were on,
Leave thee alone, for the comparison
Of all, that insolent Greece, or haughtie Rome
Sent forth, or since did from their ashes come.   40
Triumph, my Britaine, thou hast one to showe,
To whom all Scenes of Europe homage owe.
He was not of an age, but for all time!
And all the Muses still were in their prime,
When like Apollo he came forth to warme
Our eares, or like a Mercury to charme!
Nature her selfe was proud of his designes,
And joy'd to weare the dressing of his lines!
Which were so richly spun, and woven so fit,
As, since, she will vouchsafe no other Wit.   50
The merry Greeke, tart Aristophanes,
Neat Terence, witty Plautus, now not please;
But antiquated, and deserted lye
As they were not of Natures family.
Yet must I not give Nature all: Thy Art,
My gentle Shakespeare, must enjoy a part.

For though the Poets matter, Nature be,
His Art doth give the fashion. And, that he,
Who casts to write a living line, must sweat,
(Such as thine are) and strike the second heat   60
Upon the Muses anvile: turne the same,
(And himselfe with it) that he thinkes to frame;
Or for the lawrell, he may gaine a scorne,
For a good Poet's made, as well as borne.
And such wert thou. Looke how the fathers face
Lives in his issue, even so, the race
Of Shakespeares minde, and manners brightly
     shines
In his well torned, and true-filed lines:
In each of which, he seemes to shake a Lance,
As brandish't at the eyes of Ignorance.   70
Sweet Swan of Avon! what a sight it were
To see thee in our waters yet appeare,
And make those flights upon the bankes of Thames,
That so did take Eliza, and our James!
But stay, I see thee in the Hemisphere
Advanc'd, and made a Constellation there!
Shine forth, thou Starre of Poets, and with rage,
Or influence, chide, or cheere the drooping Stage;
Which, since thy flight from hence, hath mourn'd
     like night,
And despaires day, but for thy Volumes light.   80

XXXVII

Song

from *Neptunes Triumph*

COME, noble Nymphs, and doe not hide
The joyes, for which you so provide:

287

If not to mingle with the men,
What doe you here? goe home agen.
   Your dressings doe confesse,
By what we see, so curious parts
Of Pallas, and Arachnes arts,
   That you could meane no lesse.

Why doe you weare the Silke-wormes toyles;
Or glory in the shell-fish spoyles?   10
Or strive to shew the graines of ore
That you have gather'd on the shore,
   Whereof to make a stocke
To graft the greener Emerald on,
Or any better-water'd stone,
   Or Ruby of the rocke?

Why doe you smell of Ambergris,
Of which was formed Neptunes Neice,
The Queene of Love; unlesse you can,
Like Sea-borne Venus, love a man?   20
   Try, put your selves unto't.
Your lookes, your smiles, and thoughts that
    meet,
Ambrosian hands, and silver feet,
   Doe promise you will do't.

XXXVIII

from
The Touch-stone of Truth

Truth is the triall of it selfe,
   And needs no other touch,
And purer then the purest Gold,
   Refine it ne're so much.
It is the life and light of love,

The Sunne that ever shineth,
And spirit of that speciall Grace,
    That Faith and Love defineth.
It is the warrant of the Word,
    That yeeld's a sent so sweete,   10
As gives a power to Faith, to tread
    All false-hood under feete.
It is the Sword that doth divide,
    The Marrow from the Bone,
And in effect of Heavenly love
    Doth shew the Holy one.
This, blessed Warre, thy blessed Booke
    Unto the world doth prove:
A worthy worke, and worthy well,
    Of the most worthy love.   20

XXXIX

To the Memorye of that most honoured Ladie Jane, Eldest Daughter, to Cuthbert Lord Ogle: and Countesse of Shrewsbury

I COULD begin with that grave forme, *Here lies*,
And pray thee, Reader, bring thy weepinge Eyes
To see who'it is? A noble Countesse, greate,
In blood, in birth, by match, and by her seate;
Religious, wise, chast, loving, gratious, good;
And number Attributes unto a flood:
But every Table in this Church can say,
A list of Epithites: And prayse this way.
No stone in any wall here, but can tell
Such things of every body, and as well.   10
Nay, they will venter ones Descent to hitt,
And Christian name too, with a Heralds witt.
But, I would have, thee, to know something new,
Not usuall in a Lady; and yet true:

289

At least so great a Lady. She was wife
But of one Husband: and since he left life,
But Sorrow, she desir'd no other Friend:
And her, she made her Inmate, to the End,
To call on Sicknes still, to be her Guest,
Whom shee, with Sorrow first did lodge, then feast,
Then entertaine, and as Deaths Harbinger,　　21
So woo'd at last, that he was wonne to her
Importune wish; and by her lov'd Lords side
To lay her here, inclos'd, his second Bride.
Where spight of Death, next Life, for her Loves
　　sake,
This second marriage, will æternall make.

XL

Over the Door at the Entrance into the Apollo

WELCOME all that lead or follow,
To the Oracle of Apollo—
Here he speaks out of his Pottle,
Or the Tripos, his Tower Bottle:
All his Answers are Divine,
Truth it self doth flow in Wine.
Hang up all the poor Hop-Drinkers,
Cries Old Sym, the King of Skinkers;
He the half of Life abuses,
That sits watering with the Muses.　　10
Those dull Girls no good can mean us,
Wine, it is the Milk of Venus,
And the Poet's Horse accounted:
Ply it, and you all are mounted.
'Tis the true Phœbeian Liquor,
Chears the Brains, makes Wit the quicker,

Pays all Debts, cures all Diseases,
And at once three Senses pleases.
Welcome, all that lead or follow,
To the Oracle of Apollo.   20

XLI

To my Chosen Friend, the Learned Translator of Lucan, Thomas May, Esquire

WHEN, Rome, I reade thee in thy mighty paire,
And see both climing up the slippery staire
Of Fortunes wheele by Lucan driv'n about,
And the world in it, I begin to doubt,
At every line some pinn thereof should slacke
At least, if not the generall Engine cracke.
But when again I veiw the parts so peiz'd,
And those in number so, and measure rais'd,
As neither Pompey's popularitie,
Cæsar's ambition, Cato's libertie,   10
Calme Brutus tenor start; but all along
Keepe due proportion in the ample song,
It makes me, ravish'd with just wonder, cry
What Muse, or rather God of harmony
Taught Lucan these true moodes! replyes my sence,
What godds but those of arts, and eloquence?
Phœbus, and Hermes? They whose tongue, or pen
Are still th'interpreters twixt godds, and men!
But who hath them interpreted, and brought
Lucans whole frame unto us, and so wrought,   20
As not the smallest joint, or gentlest word
In the great masse, or machine there is stirr'd?

The selfe same Genius! so the worke will say.
The Sunne translated, or the Sonne of May.

Your true freind in Judgement and Choise,
Ben: Jonson.

XLII

The Vision of Ben. Jonson, on the Muses of his Friend M. Drayton

IT hath beene question'd, Michael, if I bee
A Friend at all; or, if at all, to thee:
Because, who make the question, have not seene
Those ambling visits, passe in verse, betweene
Thy Muse, and mine, as they expect. 'Tis true:
You have not writ to me, nor I to you;
And, though I now begin, 'tis not to rub
Hanch against Hanch, or raise a riming Club
About the towne: this reck'ning I will pay,
Without conferring symboles. This's my day.   10
    It was no Dreame! I was awake, and saw!
Lend me thy voyce, O Fame, that I may draw
Wonder to truth! and have my Vision hoorld,
Hot from the trumpet, round, about the world.
    I saw a Beauty from the Sea to rise,
That all Earth look'd on, and that earth, all Eyes!
It cast a beame as when the chear-full Sun
Is fayre got up, and day some houres begun!
And fill'd an Orbe as circular, as heaven!
The Orbe was cut forth into Regions seaven,   20
And those so sweet, and well-proportion'd parts,
As it had beene the circle of the Arts!
When by thy bright *Ideas* standing by,
I found it pure, and perfect Poesy.

There read I, streight, thy learned *Legends* three,
Heard the soft ayres, between our Swaynes and thee,
Which made me thinke, the old Theocritus,
Or Rurall Virgil come, to pipe to us!
But then, thy'epistolar *Heroick Songs*,
Their loves, their quarrels, jealousies, and wrongs, 30
Did all so strike me, as I cry'd, who can
With us be call'd, the Naso, but this man?
And looking up, I saw Minervas fowle,
Pearch'd over head, the wise Athenian *Owle*:
I thought thee then our Orpheus, that wouldst try
Like him, to make the ayre, one volary:
And I had stil'd thee, Orpheus, but before
My lippes could forme the voyce, I heard that Rore,
And Rouze, the Marching of a mighty force,
Drums against Drums, the neighing of the Horse, 40
The Fights, the Cryes, and wondring at the Jarres
I saw, and read, it was thy *Barons Warres*!
O, how in those, dost thou instruct these times,
That Rebells actions, are but valiant crimes!
And caried, though with shoute, and noyse, confesse
A wild, and an authoriz'd wickednesse!
Say'st thou so, Lucan? But thou scornst to stay
Under one title. Thou hast made thy way
And flight about the Ile, well neare, by this,
In thy admired Periegesis,   50
Or universal circumduction
Of all that reade thy *Poly-Olbyon*.
That read it? that are ravish'd! such was I
With every song, I sweare, and so would dye:
But that I heare, againe, thy Drum to beate
A better cause, and strike the bravest heate
That ever yet did fire the English blood!
Our right in France! if ritely understood.
There, thou art Homer! Pray thee, use the stile
Thou hast deserv'd: And let me reade the while 60

293

Thy Catalogue of Ships, exceeding his,
Thy list of aydes, and force, for so it is:
The Poets act! and for his Country's sake
Brave are the Musters, that the Muse will make.
And when he ships them where to use their Armes,
How do his trumpets breath! What loud alarmes!
Looke, how we read the Spartans were inflam'd
With bold Tyrtæus verse; when thou art nam'd,
So shall our English Youth urge on, and cry
An *Agincourt*, an *Agincourt*, or dye.   70
This booke! it is a Catechisme to fight,
And will be bought of every Lord, and Knight,
That can but reade; who cannot, may in prose
Get broken peeces, and fight well by those.
The miseries of Margaret the Queene
Of tender eyes will more be wept, then seene:
I feele it by mine owne, that over flow,
And stop my sight, in every line I goe.
But then refreshed, with thy *Fayerie Court*,
I looke on *Cynthia*, and *Sirenas* sport,   80
As, on two flowry Carpets, that did rise,
And with their grassie greene restor'd mine eyes.
Yet give mee leave, to wonder at the birth
Of thy strange *Moon-Calfe*, both thy straine of mirth,
And Gossip-got acquaintance, as, to us
Thou hadst brought Lapland, or old Cobalus,
Empusa, Lamia, or some Monster, more
Then Affricke knew, or the full Grecian store!
I gratulate it to thee, and thy Ends,
To all thy vertuous, and well chosen Friends,   90
Onely my losse is, that I am not there:
And, till I worthy am to wish I were,
I call the world, that envies mee, to see
If I can be a Friend, and Friend to thee.

XLIII

Epitaph on Katherine, Lady Ogle

O Zeus kateide chronios eis tas diphtheras.

'TIS a Record in heaven. You, that were
Her Children, and Grand-children, reed it heere!
Transmitt it to your Nephewes, Freinds, Allies,
Tenants, and Servants, have they harts, and eyes,
To veiw the truth and owne it. Doe but looke
With pause upon it; make this page your booke;
Your booke? your volume! Nay, the state, and
    story!
Code, Digests, Pandects of all fæmale glory!

    Diphthera Jovis:—
    Shee was the light (without reflexe
    Upon her selfe) to all her sexe!   10
    The best of Woemen! her whole life
    Was the example of a wife!
    Or of a parent! or a freind!
    All Circles had their spring and end
    In her! and what could perfect bee,
    Or without angles, it was shee!
    All that was solid, in the name
    Of vertue, pretious in the frame:
    Or else Magnetique in the force,
    Or sweet, or various, in the course!   20
    What was proportion, or could bee
    By warrant call'd just Symetry,
    In number, measure, or degree
    Of weight, or fashion, it was shee.
    Her soule possest her fleshes state
    In faire freehould, not an Inmate:
    And when the flesh, here, shut up day,
    Fames heate upon the grave did stay;

And howrely brooding ore the same,
Keeps warme the spice of her good name,   30
Untill the dust retorned bee
Into a Phœnix, which is shee.

For this did Katherine, Ladie Ogle, die
To gaine the Crowne of immortalitye,
Æternities great charter; which became
Her right, by gift, and purchase of the Lambe:
Seal'd, and deliver'd to her, in the sight
Of Angells, and all witnesses of light,
Both Saints, and Martyrs, by her loved Lord.
And this a coppie is of the Record.   40

XLIV

On the Honor'd Poems of his Honored Friend, Sir John Beaumont, Baronet

THIS Booke will live; It hath a Genius: This
Above his Reader, or his Prayser, is.
Hence, then, prophane: Here needs no words expense
In Bulwarkes, Rav'lins, Ramparts, for defense,
Such, as the creeping common Pioners use
When they doe sweat to fortifie a Muse.
Though I confesse a Beaumonts Booke to bee
The Bound, and Frontire of our Poetrie;
And doth deserve all muniments of praise,
That Art, or Ingine, on the strength can raise.   10
Yet, who dares offer a redoubt to reare?
To cut a Dike? or sticke a Stake up, here,
Before this worke? where Envy hath not cast
A Trench against it, nor a Battry plac't?
Stay, till she make her vaine Approches. Then
If, maymed, she come off, 'tis not of men

This Fort of so impregnable accesse,
But higher power, as spight could not make lesse,
Nor flatt'ry! but secur'd by the Authors Name,
Defies, what's crosse to Piety, or good Fame.   20
And like a hallow'd Temple, free from taint
Of Ethnicisme, makes his Muse a Saint.

XLV

To Edward Filmer, on his Musicall Work Dedicated to the Queen. Anno 1629

WHAT charming Peales are these,
That, while they bind the senses, doe so please?
    They are the Marriage-rites
Of two, the choicest Paire of mans delights,
    Musique and Poesie:
French Aire, and English Verse, here wedded lie.
    Who did this Knot compose,
Againe hath brought the Lilly to the Rose;
    And, with their chained dance,
Recelebrates the joyfull Match with France.   10
    They are a School to win
The faire French Daughter to learne English in;
    And, graced with her Song,
To make the Language sweet upon her tongue.

XLVI

A Vision of Beauty

from *The New Inne*

IT was a beauty that I saw
    So pure, so perfect, as the frame
    Of all the universe was lame,

To that one figure, could I draw,
Or give least line of it a law!

A skeine of silke, without a knot!
　A faire march made without a halt!
　A curious forme without a fault!
A printed booke without a blot!
All beauty, and without a spot!　　　　10

XLVII

Ode to Himselfe

Come leave the loathed Stage,
　And the more loathsome Age,
Where pride and impudence in faction knit,
　Usurpe the Chaire of wit:
Inditing and arraigning every day,
　Something they call a Play.
　Let their fastidious vaine
　Commission of the braine,
Runne on, and rage, sweat, censure, and condemn:
They were not made for thee, lesse thou for them.

Say that thou pour'st'hem wheat,　　　　11
　And they would Akornes eat:
'Twere simple fury, still thy selfe to wast
　On such as have no taste:
To offer them a surfeit of pure bread,
　Whose appetites are dead:
　No, give them Graines their fill,
　Huskes, Draffe to drinke, and swill:
If they love Lees, and leave the lusty Wine,
Envy them not, their pallat's with the Swine.　　20

298

No doubt a mouldy Tale,
     Like Pericles, and stale
As the Shrives crusts, and nasty as his Fish,
     Scraps out of every Dish,
Throwne forth and rak'd into the common Tub,
     May keep up the Play Club.
     Broomes sweepings doe as well
     There, as his Masters meale:
For who the relish of these guests will fit,
Needs set them but the Almes-basket of wit.   30

     And much good do't yee then,
     Brave Plush and Velvet men
Can feed on Orts; and safe in your scœne cloaths,
     Dare quit upon your Oathes
The Stagers, and the stage-writes too; your Peers.
     Of stuffing your large eares
     With rage of Commicke socks,
     Wrought upon twenty Blocks;
Which, if they're torne, and foule, and patch'd
          enough,   39
The Gamsters share your gilt, and you their stuffe.

     Leave things so prostitute,
     And take th'Alcaike Lute;
Or thine owne Horace, or Anacreons Lyre;
     Warme thee by Pindars fire:
And though thy Nerves be shrunke, and blood be
          cold,
     Ere years have made thee old,
     Strike that disdainfull heat
     Throughout, to their defeat:
As curious fooles, and envious of thy straine,
May blushing sweare, no Palsi's in thy braine.   50

     But when they heare thee sing
     The glories of thy King;

His zeale to God, and his just awe of men,
    They may be blood-shaken, then
Feele such a flesh-quake to possesse their powers,
    That no tun'd Harpe like ours,
    In sound of Peace or Warres,
    Shall truely hit the Starres
When they shall read the Acts of Charles his Reigne,
And see his Chariot triumph 'bove his Waine.   60

XLVIII

Song

from *Chloridia*

COME forth, come forth, the gentle Spring,
And carry the glad newes, I bring,
    To Earth, our common mother:
It is decreed, by all the Gods,
The Heav'n, of Earth shall have no oddes,
    But one shall love another:

Their glories they shall mutuall make,
Earth looke on Heaven, for Heavens sake;
    Their honours shall be even:
All æmulation cease, and jarres;   10
Jove will have Earth to have her starres
    And lights, no lesse then Heaven.

*XLIX

Another Epigram on the Birth of the Prince

ANOTHER Phœnix, though the first is dead,
A second's flowne from his immortall bed,

To make this our Arabia to be
The nest of an eternall progeny.
Choise Nature fram'd the former but to finde
What error might be mended in Man-kinde:
Like some industrious workmen, which affect
Their first endeavours onely to correct:
So this the building, that the modell was,
The type of all that now is come to passe: 10
That but the shadow, this the substance is,
All that was but a prophesie of this:
And when it did this after birth fore-runne,
'Twas but the morning starre unto this Sunne;
The dawning of this day, when Sol did think,
We having such a light, that he might wink,
And we ne're misse his lustre: nay, so soone
As Charles was borne, he and the pale-fac'd Moon
With envy then did copulate, to try
If such a Birth might be produc'd i'the'sky.   20
What Heavenly favour made a starre appeare,
To bid wise Kings to doe their homage here,
And prove him truely Christian? Long remain
On Earth, sweet Prince, that when great Charles
   shal reign
In Heaven above, our little Charles may be
As great on Earth, because as good as he.

*L

A Paralell of the Prince, to the King

So Peleus, when he faire Thetis got,
As thou thy Sea-Queene; so to him she brought
A blessed Babe, as thine hath done to thee:
His worthiest prov'd of those times, ours may be

301

Of these; his had a Pallas for his guide,
Thy wisdome will as well for ours provide:
His conquered Countries, Cities, Castles, Towers,
A worthy foe; hereafter so may ours.
His all his time, but one Patroclus findes,
But this of ours a world of faithfull friends: 10
His vulnerable in no place but one,
And this of ours (we hope) be hurt of none.
His had his Phœnix, ours no teacher needs,
But the example of thy Life and Deeds.
His Nestor knew, in Armes his fellow was,
But not in yeares, (too soone runne out his Glasse)
Ours, though not Nestor knew, we trust, shall bee
As wise in Armes, as old in yeares as hee.
His after Death had Homer his reviver:
And ours may better merit to live ever,   20
By Deeds farre-passing: but (oh sad dispaire)
No hope of Homer, his wit left no heire.

LI

An Expostulacion with Inigo Jones

MASTER SURVEYOR, you that first begann
From thirty pound in pipkins, to the Man
You are; from them leapt forth an Architect,
Able to talk of Euclide, and correct
Both him and Archimede; damne Architas,
The noblest Ingenyre that ever was!
Controll Ctesibius: overbearing us
With mistooke Names out of Vitruvius!
Drawne Aristotle on us! and thence showne
How much Architectonice is your owne!   10
Whether the buylding of the Stage or Scene!
Or making of the Propertyes it meane?

302

Visors or Anticks? or it comprehend
Something your Surship doth not yet intend!
By all your Titles, and whole style at ones
Of Tyre-man, Mounte-banck and Justice Jones,
I doe salute you! Are you fitted yet?
Will any of these express your place? or witt?
Or are you soe ambitious 'bove your peers!
You would be an Asinigo, by your ears?   20
Why, much good doo't you! Be what beast you will,
You'l be as Langley sayd, an Inigo still.

    What makes your Wretchednes to bray soe loud
In Towne and Court? Are you growne rich? and
    proud?
Your Trappings will not change you. Change your
    mynd.
Noe velvet Sheath you weare, will alter kynde.
A wodden Dagger, is a Dagger of wood
Though gold or Ivory haftes would make it good.
What is the cause you pompe it soe? I aske,
And all men eccho, you have made a Masque.   30
I chyme that too: And I have mett with those
That doe cry up the Machine, and the Showes!
The majesty of Juno in the Cloudes,
And peering forth of Iris in the Shrowdes!
Th'ascent of Lady Fame which none could spy,
Not they that sided her, Dame Poetry,
Dame History, Dame Architecture too,
And Goody Sculpture, brought with much adoe
To hold her up. O Showes! Showes! Mighty Showes!
The Eloquence of Masques! What need of prose   40
Or Verse, or Sense t'express Immortall you?
You are the Spectacles of State! 'Tis true
Court Hieroglyphicks! and all Artes affoord
In the mere perspective of an Inch board!
You aske noe more then certeyne politique Eyes,
Eyes that can pierce into the Misteryes

303

Of many Coulors! read them! and reveale
Mythology there painted on slit deale!
Oh, to make Boardes to speake! There is a taske!
Painting and Carpentry are the Soule of Masque!
Pack with your pedling Poetry to the Stage!   51
This is the money-gett, Mechanick Age!
To plant the Musick where noe eare can reach!
Attyre the Persons as noe thought can teach
Sense, what they are! which by a specious fyne
Terme of the Architects is called Designe!
But in the practisd truth Destruction is
Of any Art, besyde what he calls his!
Whither? oh whither will this Tire-man growe?
His name is *Skeuopoios* wee all knowe,   60
The maker of the Propertyes! in summe
The Scene! the Engyne! but he now is come
To be the Musick Master! Fabler too!
He is, or would be the mayne Dominus doe
All in the Worke! And soe shall still for Ben:
Be Inigo, the Whistle, and his men!
Hee's warme on his feet now, he sayes, and can
Swim without Corke! Why, thank the good Queen
        Anne.
I am too fat t'envy him. He too leane
To be worth Envy. Henceforth I doe meane   70
To pitty him, as smiling at his Feat
Of Lanterne-lerry: with fuliginous heat
Whirling his Whymseys, by a subtilty
Suckt from the Veynes of shop-philosophy.
What would he doe now, gi'ng his mynde that waye
In presentacion of some puppet play!
Should but the king his Justice-hood employ
In setting forth of such a solemne Toye!
How would he firke? like Adam overdooe
Up and about? Dyve into Cellars too,   80
Disguisd? and thence drag forth Enormity?
Discover Vice? Commit Absurdity?

Under the Morall? shewe he had a pate
Moulded or stroakt up to survey a State!
Oh wise Surveyor! wyser Architect!
But wisest Inigo! who can reflect
On the new priming of thy old Signe postes
Reviving with fresh coulors the pale Ghosts
Of thy dead Standards: or (with miracle) see
Thy twice conceyvd, thrice payd for Imagery?   90
And not fall downe before it? and confess
Allmighty Architecture? who noe less
A Goddess is, then paynted Cloth, Deal-boards,
Vermilion, Lake, or Cinnopar affoards
Expression for! with that unbounded lyne
Aymd at in thy omnipotent Designe!
What Poesy ere was painted on a wall
That might compare with thee? what story shall
Of all the Worthyes hope t'outlast thy one,
Soe the Materialls be of Purbeck stone!   100
Lyve long the Feasting Roome. And ere thou burne
Againe, thy Architect to ashes turne!
Whom not ten fyres, nor a Parlyament can
With all Remonstrance make an honest man.

LII

To Inigo, Marquess Would Be,
a Corollary

BUT cause thou hearst the mighty king of Spaine
Hath made his Inigo Marquess, wouldst thou fayne
Our Charles should make thee such? 'Twill not
    become
All kings to doe the self same deeds with some!
Besydes, his Man may merit it, and be
A Noble honest Soule! what's this to thee?

He may have skill and judgment to designe
Cittyes and Temples! thou a Cave for Wyne,
Or Ale! He build a pallace! Thou a shopp
With slyding windowes, and false Lights a top!   10
He draw a Forum, with quadriviall Streets!
Thou paint a Lane, where Thumb the Pygmy meets!
He some Colossus to bestryde the Seas,
From the fam'd Pillars of old Hercules!
Thy Canvas Gyant, at some Channell aymes,
Or Dowgate Torrent falling into Thames,
And stradling shews the Boyes Brown paper fleet,
Yearly set out there, to sayle downe the Street!
Your workes thus differing, troth let soe your style:
Content thee to be Pancridge Earle the while;   20
An Earle of show: for all thy worke is showe:
But when thou turnst a Reall Inigo;
Or canst of truth the least intrenchment pitch,
Wee'll have thee styld the Marquess of New-Ditch.

LIII

To a Freind, an Epigram of Him

Sir Inigo doth feare it as I heare
(And labours to seem worthy of that feare)
That I should wryte upon him some sharp verse,
Able to eat into his bones and pierce
The Marrow! Wretch, I quitt thee of thy paine.
Thou'rt too ambitious: and dost fear in vaine!
The Lybian Lion hunts noe butter flyes,
He makes the Camell and dull Ass his prize.
If thou be soe desyrous to be read,
Seek out some hungry painter, that for bread,   10
With rotten chalk, or Cole upon a wall,
Will well designe thee, to be viewd of all

That sit upon the Comon Draught: or Strand!
Thy Forehead is too narrow for my Brand.

LIV

*To Mr. Jonson upon these Verses

YOUR Verses were commended, as 'tis true,
That they were very good, I meane to you:
For they return'd you, Ben, I have beene told,
The seld seene summe of forty pound in gold.
These Verses then, being rightly understood,
His Lordship, not Ben: Jonson, made them good.

J. E.

TO MY DETRACTOR

MY Verses were commended, thou didst say,
And they were very *good*; yet thou thinkst nay.
For thou objectest, as thou hast beene told,
Th'envy'd returne of forty pound in gold.
Foole, do not rate my rimes; I have found thy vice
Is to make cheape the Lord, the Lines the Price:
But bark thou on; I pitty thee, poore Cur,
That thou shouldst lose thy noise, thy foame, thy slur,
To be knowne what thou art, thou blatent beast;
But writing against me, thou thinkst at least   10
 Inow would write on thee: no, wretch, thy name
Cannot worke out unto it such a Fame:
No man will tarry by thee as he goes
To aske thy name, if he have halfe a nose;
But flye thee like the Pest. Walke not the streete
Out in the Dog-dayes, lest the Killer meet
Thy Noddle with his Club; and dashing forth
Thy dirty brains, men see thy want of worth.

LV

To my Old Faithfull Servant: and (by his continu'd Vertue) my Loving Friend: The Author of this Work, M. Rich. Brome

I HAD you for a Servant, once, Dick Brome;
  And you perform'd a Servants faithfull parts:
Now, you are got into a nearer roome,
  Of Fellowship, professing my old Arts.
And you doe doe them well, with good applause,
  Which you have justly gained from the Stage,
By observation of those Comick Lawes
  Which I, your Master, first did teach the Age.
You learn'd it well; and for it, serv'd your time
  A Prentise-ship: which few doe now a dayes.   10
Now each Court-Hobby-horse will wince in rime;
  Both learned, and unlearned, all write Playes.
It was not so of old: Men tooke up trades
  That knew the Crafts they had bin bred in, right:
An honest Bilbo-Smith would make good blades,
  And the Physician teach men spue, or shite;
The Cobler kept him to his nall; but, now
Hee'll be a Pilot, scarce can guide a Plough.

LVI

* On The Magnetick Lady

... But to advise thee, Ben, in this strict Age,
A Brick-kill's better for thee than a Stage.
Thou better know'st a Groundsil for to lay,
Then lay the Plot or Ground-work of a Play,
And better can'st direct to Cap a Chimney,
Then to converse with Clio, or Polyhimny.

Fall then to work in thy old Age agen,
Take up thy Trug and Trowel, gentle Ben,
Let Plays alone: or if thou needs will write,
And thrust thy feeble Muse into the light;   10
Let Lowen cease, and Taylor scorn to touch
The loathed Stage, for thou hast made it such.

[ALEXANDER GILL.]

BEN JONSON'S ANSWER

Shall the prosperity of a Pardon still
Secure thy railing Rhymes, infamous Gill,
At libelling? Shall no Star-Chamber Peers,
Pillory, nor Whip, nor want of Ears,
All which thou hast incurr'd deservedly:
Nor Degradation from the Ministry,
To be the Denis of thy Father's School,
Keep in thy bawling Wit, thou bawling Fool?
Thinking to stir me, thou hast lost thy End;
I'll laugh at thee, poor wretched Tike; go send 10
Thy blotant Muse abroad, and teach it rather
A Tune to drown the Ballads of thy Father:
For thou hast nought in thee to cure his Fame,
But Tune and Noise, the Eccho of his Shame.
A Rogue by Statute, censur'd to be whipt,
Cropt, branded, slit, neck-stockt; go, you are
    stript.

LVII

To Mrs. Alice Sutcliffe, on her Divine Meditations

WHEN I had read your holy *Meditations*,
And in them view'd th'uncertainty of Life,

The motives, and true Spurres to all good Nations,
The peace of Conscience, and the Godly's strife,
The danger of delaying to Repent,
And the deceipt of pleasures, by Consent,
The comfort of weake Christians, with their warning,
From fearefull back-slides; and the debt we'are in,
To follow Goodnesse, by our owne discerning
Our great reward, th'æternall Crown to win,   10
I sayd, who'had supp'd so deepe of this sweet Chalice,
Must Celia bee, the Anagram of Alice.

LVIII

The Ghyrlond of the Blessed Virgin Marie

HERE, are five letters in this blessed Name,
    Which, chang'd, a five-fold mysterie designe,
The *M.* the Myrtle, *A.* the Almonds clame,
    R. Rose, *I.* Ivy, *E.* sweet Eglantine.

These forme thy Ghyrlond. Whereof Myrtle green,
    The gladdest ground to all the numbred-five,
Is so implexed, and laid in, between,
    As Love, here studied to keep Grace alive.

The second string is the sweet Almond bloome
    Ymounted high upon Selinis crest: 10
As it, alone, (and onely it) had roome,
    To knit thy Crowne, and glorifie the rest.

The third, is from the garden call'd the Rose,
    The Eye of flowers, worthy, for his scent,
To top the fairest Lillie, now, that growes,
    With wonder on the thorny regiment.

310

The fourth is humble Ivy, intersert,
    But lowlie laid, as on the earth asleep,
Preserved, in her antique bed of Vert,
    No faith's more firme, or flat, then, where't doth
        creep.   20

But, that which summes all, is the Eglantine,
    Which, of the field is clep'd the sweetest brier,
Inflam'd with ardor to that mystick Shine,
    In Moses bush, un-wasted in the fire.

Thus, Love, and Hope, and burning Charitie,
    (Divinest graces) are so entermixt,
With od'rous sweets and soft humilitie,
    As if they'ador'd the Head, wheron th'are fixt.

LIX

The Reverse on the Backe Side

THESE Mysteries do point to three more great,
    On the reverse of this your circling crowne,
    All pouring their full showre of graces downe,
The glorious Trinity in Union met.

Daughter, and Mother, and the Spouse of God,
    Alike of kin, to that most blessed Trine,
    Of Persons, yet in Union (One) divine.
How are thy gifts, and graces blaz'd abroad!

Most holy, and pure Virgin, blessed Mayd,
    Sweet Tree of Life, King Davids Strength and
        Tower,   10
    The House of gold, the Gate of heavens power,
The Morning-star, whose light our Fal hath stay'd,

Great Queen of Queens, most mild, most meek,
    most wise,
  Most venerable, Cause of all our joy,
  Whose chearfull look our sadnesse doth destroy,
And art the spotlesse Mirrour to Mans eyes.

The Seat of Sapience, the most lovely Mother,
  And most to be admired of thy Sexe,
  Who mad'st us happy all, in thy reflexe,
By bringing forth God's onely Son, no other,   20

Thou Throne of glory, beauteous as the Moone,
  The rosie Morning, or the rising Sun,
  Who like a Giant hasts his course to run,
Till he hath reach'd his two-fold point of Noone,

How are thy gifts and graces blaz'd abro'd,
  Through all the lines of this circumference,
  T'imprint in all purg'd hearts this virgin sence,
Of being Daughter, Mother, Spouse of God!

LX

To my deare Sonne, and right-learned Friend, Master Joseph Rutter

You looke, my Joseph, I should something say
Unto the world, in praise of your first Play:
And truely, so I would, could I be heard.
You know, I never was of Truth afeard,
And lesse asham'd; not when I told the crowd
How well I lov'd Truth: I was scarce allow'd
By those deepe-grounded, understanding men,
That sit to censure Playes, yet know not when,

Or why to like; they found, it all was new,
And newer, then could please them, by-cause
    trew.   10
Such men I met withall, and so have you.
Now, for mine owne part, and it is but due,
(You have deserv'd it from me) I have read,
And weigh'd your Play: untwisted ev'ry thread,
And know the woofe, and warpe thereof; can tell
Where it runs round, and even: where so well,
So soft, and smooth it handles, the whole piece,
As it were spun by nature, off the fleece:
This is my censure. Now there is a new
Office of Wit, a Mint, and (this is true)   20
Cry'd up of late: Whereto there must be first
A Master-worker call'd, th'old standerd burst
Of wit, and a new made: a Warden then,
And a Comptroller, two most rigid men
For order, and for governing the pixe,
A Say-master, hath studied all the tricks
Of Finenesse, and alloy: follow his hint,
Yo'have all the Mysteries of Wits new Mint,
The valuations, mixtures, and the same
Concluded from a Carract to a dramme.   30

LXI

An Epigram to my Joviall Good Freind Mr. Robert Dover, on his great instauration of his hunting, and dauncing at Cotswold

I CANNOT bring my Muse to dropp Vies
Twixt Cotswold, and the Olimpicke exercise:
But I can tell thee, Dover, how thy Games
Renew the Glories of our blessed Jeames:
How they doe keepe alive his memorie;
With the Glad Countrey, and Posteritie:

How they advance, true Love, and neighbourhood,
And doe both Church, and Common-wealth the
   good,
In spite of Hipocrites, who are the worst
Of Subjects; Let such envie, till they burst.   10

LXII

A Song of Welcome to King Charles

FRESH as the Day, and new as are the Howers,
Our first of fruits, that is the prime of flowers
Bred by your breath, on this low bancke of ours;
   Now, in a garland by the graces knit:
   Upon this obeliske, advanc'd for it,
   We offer as a Circle the most fit
To Crowne the years, which you begin, great
   king,
And you, with them, as Father of our spring.

LXIII

A Song of the Moon

To the wonders of the Peake,
I am come to add, and speake,
Or as some would say to breake
   My mind unto you,
And I sweare by all the light
At my back, I am no spright,
But a very merry wight
   Prest in to se you.

I had somwhat else to say,
But have lost it by the way,   10
314

I shall think on't ere't be day.
  The Moone comends hir
To the merry beards in Hall,
Those turnd up, and those that fall,
Morts, and mirkins that wagg all,
  Tough, foule, or Tender,

And as either newes or mirth
Rise or fall uppon the earth,
She desires of every birth
  Some tast to send hir.   20
Specially the newes of Darby;
For if there, or peace or warr be,
To the Peake it is so hard-by,
  Shee soone will heare it.

If there be a Coockold Major,
That the wife heades for a wager
As the standerd shall engage hir,
  The Moone will beare it.
Though shee chainge as oft as shee,
And of Circle be as free,   30
Or hir quarters lighter bee,
  Yet doe not feare it.

Or if any strife betyde
For the breeches with the bride,
'Tis but the next neighbour ride
  And she is pleased.
Or if't be the Gossipps happ
Each to pawne hir husbands capp,
At Pem Wakers good ale Tapp,
  Hir minde is eased.   40

Or by chance if in their grease
Or theire Ale, they break the peace,

Forfeitinge their drinking lease,
    Shee will not seise it.

LXIV

Ode

Y<small>FF</small> Men, and tymes were nowe
        Of that true Face
As when they both were greate, and both knewe
        howe
    That Fortune to imbrace,
By Cherissheinge the Spirrites that gave their
        greatnesse grace:
        I then could rayse my notes
        Lowd to the wondringe thronge
And better Blason them, then all their Coates,
That were the happie subject of my songe.

Butt, Clownishe pride hath gott   10
        Soe much the starte
Of Civill virtue, that hee now is not
        Nor cann be of desert,
That hath not Countrye impudence enough to
        laughe att Arte,
        Whilest lyke a blaze of strawe,
        Hee dyes with an ill sent,
To every sence, and scorne to those that sawe
Howe soone with a selfe ticklinge hee was spent.

Breake then thie quills, blott out
        Thie long watch'd verse   20
And rather to the Fyre, then to the Rowte
        Their labour'd tunes reherse,
Whose ayre will sooner Hell, then their dull senses
        peirce,

Thou that doest spend thie dayes
  To get thee a leane Face,
And come forth worthie Ivye, or the Bayes,
And in this Age, canst hope no other grace.

Yett: since the bright, and wyse,
  Mynerva deignes
Uppon soe humbled earth to cast hir eyes: 30
  Wee'l rip our richest veynes
And once more stryke the eare of tyme with those
    fresh straynes:
    As shall besides delyght
    And Cunninge of their grownde
Give cause to some of wonnder, some despite,
But unto more dispayre to imitate their sounde.

Throwe, Holye Virgin, then,
  Thie Chrystall sheild
Aboute this Isle, and charme the rounde, as when
  Thou mad'st in open Feild   40
The Rebell Gyantes stoope, and Gorgon Envye
    yeild,
    Cause Reverence, yf not Feare,
    Throughout their generall breastes,
And by their Takeinge, lett it once appeare
Whoe worthie winne, whoe not, to bee wyse Pallas
    guests.

LXV

An Epistle to a Friend

CENSURE, not sharplye then, but mee advise
Before, I wryte more verse, to bee more wyse.

317

Soe ended your Epistle, myne beginns,
Hee that soe Censureth, or adviseth synns,
The emptye Carper, scorne, not Creditt wynns.

I have, with strict advantage of free tyme
O're read, examin'd, try'd, and prov'd your Ryme
As Cleare, and distant, as your selfe from Cryme;

And though your virtue (as becomes it) still
Deignes myne the power to finde, yett want I will   10
Or Malyce to make Faultes, which nowe is skill.

Little knowe they that professe Amitye
And seeke to scant her comelye Libertye,
Howe much they lame hir, in hir propertye:

And lesse they knowe, that being free to use
That Frindshipp, which noe Chaunce, but Love did
    chuse,
Will unto Lycence, that free Leave Abuse:

It is an Acte of Tyranye, not Love,
In Course of Frindshipp, wholie to reprove:
And Flatterye, with Frindes humours still to move. 20

From each of which, I labor to be free,
Yett, yf with eythers vyce, I tainted bee,
Forgive it as my Frayltie, and not mee.

For noe Man Lyves, soe out of passions swaye,
But sometymes shall bee tempted to obaye
Hir Furye, though noe Frindshipp hee betraye.

LXVI

Martial. Epigram *XLVII*, Book *X*

THE Things that make the happier life, are these,
Most pleasant Martial; Substance got with ease,
Not labour'd for, but left thee by thy Sire;
A Soyle, not barren; a continewall fire;
Never at Law; seldome in office gown'd;
A quiet mind; free powers; and body sound;
A wise simplicity; freindes alike-stated;
Thy table without art, and easy-rated:
Thy night not dronken, but from cares layd wast;
No sowre, or sollen bed-mate, yet a Chast;   10
Sleepe, that will make the darkest howres swift-pac't;
Will to bee, what thou art; and nothing more:
Nor feare thy latest day, nor wish therfore.

LXVII

A Speech out of Lucane

JUST and fit actions, Ptolemey, (he saith)
Make many, hurt themselves; a praysed faith
Is her owne scourge, when it sustaines their states
Whom fortune hath deprest; come nere the fates
And the immortall gods; love only those
Whom thou seest happy; wretches flee as foes:
Looke how the starres from earth, or seas from
    flames
Are distant, so is proffitt from just aymes.
The mayne comaund of scepters, soone doth perishe
If it begyn religious thoughts to cherish;   10
Whole armyes fall, swayd by those nyce respects.
It is a lycense to doe ill, protectes

319

Even states most hated, when no lawes resist
The sword, but that it acteth what it list.
Yet ware: thou mayst do all things cruellie:
Not safe; but when thou dost them thoroughlie:
He that will honest be, may quitt the Court,
Virtue, and Soveraigntie, they not consort.
That prince that shames a tyrants name to beare,
Shall never dare do any thing but feare.   20

LXVIII

Song

from *The Sad Shepherd*

THOUGH I am young, and cannot tell,
Either what Death, or Love is well,
Yet I have heard, they both beare darts,
And both doe ayme at humane hearts:
And then againe, I have beene told,
Love wounds with heat, as Death with cold;
So that I feare, they doe but bring
Extreames to touch, and meane one thing.

As in a ruine, we it call
One thing to be blowne up, or fall;   10
Or to our end, like way may have,
By a flash of lightning, or a wave:
So Loves inflamed shaft, or brand,
May kill as soone as Deaths cold hand;
Except Loves fires the vertue have
To fright the frost out of the grave.

NOTES

NOTES ON THE INTRODUC-
TION AND CRITICAL
COMMENTS

1. This biographical sketch draws heavily on the following books and articles for factual material: *Ben Jonson*, edited by C. H. Herford, Percy and Evelyn Simpson, Oxford University Press, 1925–52, Volumes I and XI; Mark Eccles, 'Ben Jonson's Marriage', *Review of English Studies*, XII, 257–72 (1936); Fredson T. Bowers, 'Ben Jonson the Actor', *Studies in Philology*, XXXIV, 393–406 (1937); E. K. Chambers, *The Elizabethan Stage*, Oxford University Press, 1923 (Reprinted 1945); C. J. Sisson, 'Ben Jonson of Gresham College', *Times Literary Supplement*, 21 September 1951, p. 604.

2. See E. K. Chambers, *Elizabethan Stage* (1945), IV, 40; also Herford and Simpson, *Ben Jonson*, XI, 365. Shakespeare's career as an actor is no less a mystery than Jonson's: Heminges and Condell listed Shakespeare at the head of 'the Principall Actors in all these Playes' in the Folio; Jonson included his name as an actor in *Every Man in his Humour* and *Sejanus*; but the roles he played were not stated. Traditions indicate that he was a character actor rather than a leading man: his traditional roles being Adam in *As You Like It*, the Ghost in *Hamlet*, and Falstaff. The role of Horace in *Satiromastix* would be in harmony with the others; but the whole matter is speculative and far beyond proof.

3. William Hazlitt, *Lectures on the Literature of the Age of Elizabeth*, Bohn's Standard Library, London, 1909, p. 177.

4. Hazelton Spencer, *The Art and Life of William Shakespeare*, Harcourt, Brace and Company, New York, 1940, p. 86.

5. 'An Eclogue on the Death of Ben Jonson', *Jonsonus Virbius*, 1638.

6. A. C. Swinburne, *A Study of Ben Jonson*, 1889, pp. 111–12.

7. Willa McClung Evans, *Ben Jonson and Elizabethan Music*, Lancaster, Pennsylvania, 1929, p. 34.

8. Ben Jonson's impact on his own and succeeding ages has made a selection of critical comments an arbitrary matter; there is an embarrassment of riches. Interested readers may consult J. F. Bradley and Joseph Quincy Adams, *The Jonson Allusion Book*, Yale University Press, 1922; Gerald Eades Bentley, *Shakespeare and Jonson*, Chicago, 1945 (two volumes); Herford and Simpson, *Ben Jonson*, XI, 305–569. I have chosen five passages, each by an English poet, each in a different period, each expressing critical respect for Jonson: Dryden, Pope, Coleridge, Swinburne, and T. S. Eliot. Only the first was inevitable.

NOTES ON THE POEMS

Full textual notes are in Herford and Simpson, *Ben Jonson* (hereafter in these notes cited *H&S*). Numerous explanatory notes are in *H&S*, XI, 1–164, and in *The Poems of Ben Jonson*, ed. by B. H. Newdigate, Oxford, 1936. In the present edition textual and explanatory notes have been limited to allow fuller representation of Jonson's text. The basic texts for the poems down to the section *Miscellany* are my copies of the 1616 and 1640 Jonson Folios unless otherwise noted. Poems in *Miscellany* not taken from the Folios will have their sources stated in the notes. Comparison has frequently been made with the 1640 Quarto *Ben Jonson's Execration against Vulcan. With divers epigrams by the same Author...*, and with Newdigate's text and *H&S*. Two earlier editors are sometimes referred to: Peter Whalley (edition in 1756) and William Gifford (edition in 1816, re-edited by F. Cunningham in 1875). Some of the readings in *H&S* are from the 1692 Folio (*F3*).

EPIGRAMMES

Dedication: William Herbert, Earl of Pembroke (1580–1630), was the son of the famous Countess of Pembroke, Sir Philip Sidney's sister. 30–1. Martial, I, letter to the reader: 'Let not Cato enter my theatre, or look if he enters.'

III. 12. *Bucklersbury*] the street of grocers, who needed wrapping paper.

XII. 2. Disreputable quarters in London. 9. *'ssayes* (assays)] tries on.

XIV. William Camden (1551–1623) was Jonson's teacher at Westminster School; he was author of *Britannia*, 1586, *Remaines of a Greater Worke*

Concerning Britaine, 1605, and *Annales Rerum Anglicarum et Hibernicarum, regnante Elizabetha*, 1615.

XVIII. 4. Sir John Davies (1569–1626) and John Weever (1576–1623).

XIX. *Cod*] musk-bag, perfume-bag.

XXII. (1598?) See Introduction.

XXVII. Sir John Roe (1581–1606?) was soldier, poet, and friend of Jonson.

XXVIII. 4. *Rhinocerotes nose*] held haughtily in the air, or curled in a sneer; see Martial, I, iii.

XXXVII. *Cheverill*] flexible kid-leather; figuratively, pliable conscience.

XL. Margaret Ratcliffe (d. 1599) presumably died of grief when her brother Sir Alexander Ratcliffe was killed in Ireland.

XLIII. Robert Cecil, Earl of Salisbury (1563?–1612), was the son of William Cecil, Lord Burleigh (1520–98). Both were able and powerful administrators.

XLV. (1603) 1. *Child of my right hand*] Benjamin. (Listed in Camden's *Remains* in the section 'Usual Christian Names'.)

LI. *H&S* date 1606; Jonson's memory was at fault.

LV. Francis Beaumont (c. 1584–1616) and John Fletcher (1579–1625) exchanged several commendatory poems with Jonson.

LX. William Parker, Baron Mounteagle (1575–1622), was involved in Essex's rebellion and suffered imprisonment. Under James he enjoyed favour, especially after exposing the Gunpowder Plot of 1605 to Salisbury.

LXIII. See *Ep.* XLIII.

LXVI. Sir Henry Cary, Viscount Falkland (c. 1575–1633), was the father of Lucius Cary (see *Und.* LXX). 12. *Broeck*] Broick. *Roor*] the Ruhr.

LXVII. Thomas Howard, Earl of Suffolk (1561–1626), was Lord Chamberlain (1603–14) and Lord Treasurer (1614–19).

LXX. Sir William Roe (1585–1667) was a brother of Sir John Roe. Jonson appeared on his behalf in a Chancery Suit. (*H&S*, I, 223–30.)

LXXIV. Thomas Egerton, Baron Ellesmere (1540?–1617), was Lord Keeper under Elizabeth, Lord Chancellor under James.

LXXVI. Lucy, Countess of Bedford (1581?–1627), was the daughter of the witty Sir John Harington (1561–1612), godson of Queen Elizabeth, and author and translator. The Countess of Bedford took part in several of Jonson's masques. 15. The emblems of the three Fates. *Rock*] distaff.

LXXIX. Elizabeth, Countess of Rutland (1584–1612), was the daughter of Sir Philip Sidney. See *The Forrest* XII and *Und.* L.

LXXXV. Sir Henry Goodyere (d. 1628) was a friend of John Donne.

LXXXVIII. 15. *motion*] puppet-show or puppet.

LXXXIX. Edward Alleyn (1566–1626) was the son-in-law of Philip Henslowe, and after the death of his first wife he married the daughter of John Donne. He acted the title roles in Marlowe's *Tamburlaine*, *Faustus*, and *The Jew of Malta*. See E. K. Chambers, *The Elizabethan Stage*, 1945, II, 296–8.

XC. 17–18. Milo of Crotona's legendary feats included lifting a calf every day until it grew into a bull.

XCI. Sir Horace Vere (1565–1635) was one of England's great soldiers. He saved the Dutch army. He was created Baron Vere of Tilbury. (There were two Veres—so the peerage identifies Horace Vere.) 8. *rellish*] musical note.

XCII. 16. *Mercurius Gallo-Belgicus*] a register of news published in Cologne; English translation was published in 1614. 23–4. James Rime and John Bill were printers and booksellers. (*H&S*.) 25. Giovanni Battista della Porta (1543–1615), Italian physicist, wrote a book on secret writings and cyphers. 30. make not peace, *Gifford*.

XCIII. Sir John Radcliffe (d. 1627) was a second brother of Margaret Radcliffe (Ratcliffe; see *Ep.* XL). He was killed in France. (*H&S*.)

XCIV. See *Ep.* LXXVI.

XCV. Sir Henry Savile (1549–1622) translated four books of Tacitus and inserted *The Ende of Nero and the Beginning of Galba*. He was Provost of Eton.

XCVI. John Donne (1573–1631) and Jonson freely interchanged manuscripts, thereby raising certain problems of authorship. See *Und.* XXXVIII–XLI. 1. *where*] whether. 8. *with the better stone*] in Rome happy days were marked with a white stone.

XCVII. 1. *Motion*] puppet-show. *Fading* or *fadding*] Irish dance. 2. *Captain Pod*] a puppet-showman. *Eltham-thing*] a mechanical show invented by Drebbel. 14. *hath neadd squires*] who has needed pimps.

XCVIII. Sir Thomas Roe (1581–1644) was a collector of coins and manuscripts.

CI. Robert Pooly or Poley was present at Marlowe's death. See J. L. Hotson, *The Death of Christopher Marlowe*, London, 1925; F. S. Boas, *Marlowe and his Circle*, 1929; Mark Eccles, 'Jonson and the Spies', *Review of English Studies*, XIII, 1937; and *H&S*, XI, 21. Parrot is not certainly identified.

CII. See Dedication. 3. to be good *F*] to the good *F3*, *H&S*.

CIII. Mary, Lady Wroth (married 1604), was the daughter of Sir Robert Sidney, niece of Sir Philip. Jonson dedicated *The Alchemist* to her.

CIV. Susan, Countess of Montgomery (1587–1629), was the daughter of Edward de Vere, Earl of Oxford, and wife of Philip Herbert, Earl of Montgomery. She took part in several of Jonson's masques (*H&S*, X, 443).

CVI. Sir Edward Herbert of Cherbury (1583–1648) was author and diplomat.

CVII. 21. The Seigneur de Villeroy and the Marquis de Sillery were French statesmen. 22. B. H. Newdigate suggested Pierre Jeannin, another French statesman, for *Janin*; *H&S* connect the word with the Near East: *cf.* Janissaries.

CVIII. Also printed in the Apologetical Dialogue in *Poetaster*, 1601.

CIX. Sir Henry Nevil (1564?–1615) was imprisoned for a part in Essex's plot.

CX–CXI. These verses were printed in the 1609 edition of *Observations on Cæsar's Commentaries* by Clement Edmonds (1564?–1622).

CXIII. Sir Thomas Overbury (1581–1613) was murdered in the Tower. His death, brought about by Lady Essex, daughter of the Earl of Suffolk, caused a notorious scandal. He was author of *A Wife*, published in 1614.

CXIV. Mistress Philip Sidney (1594–1620) was the daughter of Sir Robert Sidney, niece of Sir Philip.

CXV. *H&S* interpret as attack on Inigo Jones: see X, 689–92. 11. *come from Tripoly*] some indoor sport requiring much activity: *H&S*, X, 42. 27. *old Iniquity*] the comical Vice of the Morality Plays.

CXVI. Sir William Jephson was knighted in 1603. *H&S*.

CXIX. Sir Raph Shelton was one of the voyagers in 'The Famous Voyage' (*Ep.* CXXXIII).

CXX. Salomon Pavy (1589?–1602) was long miscalled Salathiel. See Gerald Eades Bentley, 'A Good Name Lost', *London Times Literary Supplement*, 30 May 1942, p. 276.

CXXI. Benjamin Rudyard (1572–1658) was a poet and politician. (*H&S*.)

CXXV. Sir William Uvedale (fl. 1613–43) was a soldier and financeer.

CXXVII. Esmé Stuart, Lord d'Aubigné (1574–1624), was a generous patron to Jonson, who dedicated *Sejanus* to him.

CXXVIII. See *Ep.* LXX.

CXXIX. *H&S* take this to be another attack on Inigo. 16. Cokely, Pod, and Gue were buffoons or show-men (*H&S*, XI, 28). 17. See *Miscellany* XIX–XX.

CXXX. First printed in *Ayres: by Alphonso Ferrabosco*, London, 1609. Ferrabosco (1567?–1628) composed music for songs and masques by Jonson.

CXXXII. First printed in *Bartas his Devine Weekes and Works Translated*, 1605, by Josuah Sylvester (1563–1618).

CXXXIII. 'On the Famous Voyage.' 5. Sir Raph Shelton: see *Ep.* CXIX. 'The Voyage It Selfe.' 16. Will Kemp, the comedian in Burbage's company. 97. The Paris Garden, near the Globe Theatre, was devoted to bear-baiting. 98. See also *Und.* XLIII, 'An Execration upon Vulcan'. 100. The Lord Mayor's Gally-foist was the state-barge which carried him to Westminster to be sworn in (*H&S*, X, 34). 128. Nicholas Hill (1570?–1610) was a disciple of Democritus in writing on atomic theory. 135. *Tiberts*] cats. 136. Bankes was the trainer of the famous performing horse Morocco. *H&S* point out that Jonson was in error about his fate, for he was still alive in 1625 (XI, 32).

THE FORREST

II. 14. Sir Philip Sidney (1554–86). 19. Barbara Gamage, wife of Sir Robert Sidney (1563–1626).

III. Sir Robert Wroth (1576–1614) was the son-in-law of Sir Robert Sidney. Sir Robert Sidney became Earl of Leicester and spent much time at Penshurst. 46. lend a shade *F*] lent a shade *H&S* after MSS.

v. First printed in *Volpone*, 1605. For discussion of it as translation of Catullus, see *H&S*, II, 386; IX, 718–21.

IX. John Addington Symonds was forestalled by John F. M. Dovaston in *The Monthly Magazine*, 1815, pp. 123–4 in pointing out original passages in the *Epistles* of Philostratus from which this poem was composed: *H&S*, XI, 39.

x. First printed in Robert Chester's *Love's Martyr*, 1601. For a full discussion of this, the following poem, and *Miscellany* VI–VII, see B. H. Newdigate, *The Poems of Ben Jonson*, and *H&S*, XI, 40–2. 17. *Tribade trine*] Lesbian triad, the three Graces.

XII. (See *Ep.* LXXIX.) 93, *Who wheresoere he be...*] here the Folio breaks off with the statement: 'The rest is lost.' At the time of publication of the Folio the wish expressed in the final lines was a mockery, because of the known impotence of the Earl of Rutland (see *H&S*, VIII, 10). The final lines survive in a manuscript and are added to the Folio version in this edition by the courtesy of the Delegates of the Clarendon Press (see *H&S*, VIII, 116).

XIII. Katherine, Lady Aubigny (d. 1627) was the wife of Lord d'Aubigny (see *Ep.* CXXVII).

XIV. Sir William Sidney (1590–1612) was the son of Sir Robert Sidney, nephew of Sir Philip. He was buried at Penshurst.

XV. 1–2. 'The meaning is not—"Can I not think of God without its making me melancholy?" but "Can I not think of God without its being imputed or set down by others to a fit of dejection?" '—A. C. Swinburne, *A Study of Ben Jonson*, 1889, p. 103.

THE UNDER-WOOD

I. 2. 22. Withall *F*] With all *H&S*.

II. 4. Inclusion of this song in *Charis* is somewhat puzzling, as the following poem seems to refer to *Und.* XIX rather than to this piece, part of which is in *The Devil Is an Ass*. 10. Through... through *F*] Thorough... thorough *H&S*.

VI. 9. *Aswell*] 'obsolete way of writing *as well*.' OED.

XI. 6. attempt t'awake *F*] attempt awake *Whalley, Gifford, H&S*.

XII. Vincent Corbet (1540?–1619) was the father of Richard Corbet (1582–1635), bishop and poet.

XIII. Sir Edward Sackville, Earl of Dorset (1591–1652), was the grandson of Thomas Sackville (1536–1608), co-author of *Gorboduc* and *A Mirror for Magistrates*. The 'Epistle' draws heavily on Seneca (*H&S*, XI, 55–7). 83. out of *F*] out *Whalley, Gifford, H&S*. 108. of a discerning *F*] of discerning *Gifford, H&S*. 128. *Coriat*] see *Miscellany* XIX–XX.

XIV. First printed in *Titles of Honor*, 1614, by John Selden (1584–1654). 66. their *F*] thine *H&S* after the text in Selden. 72. Edward Hayward (d. 1658), to whom *Titles of Honor* was dedicated.

XV. 113. 0   for these *F. H&S* suggest *God* omitted for propriety, but give a textual note *Freind* from a manuscript. 132. Nights *F, H&S*. 138. viewers *F*] viewes *Gifford, H&S* after Newcastle Manuscript. 160. both *F*] boote *H&S* after Newcastle MS.

XXIII. 6. and destroyes *F*] and oft destroyes *H&S* after MSS. 9. *Clarius*] Apollo. 10. *Japhets lyne*] Prometheus, son of Iapetus. 30. Minerva.

XXIV. First printed in Sir Walter Raleigh's *History of the World*, 1614; see cut *H&S*, VIII, 177. Folio text is corrupt; the present text is from Raleigh.

XXV. James Fitzgerald, Earl of Desmond (d. 1601),

was imprisoned for almost twenty years; he was released in 1600 (*H&S*, XI, 62). 20. hold *F*] holds *Whalley, Gifford, H&S*. 40–2. Cyclopes who assisted Vulcan.

XXVIII. See *Ep.* CIII.

XXIX. 15. are *F*] Art *Gifford, H&S*.

XXX. See *Ep.* XLIII.

XXXI. See *Ep.* LXIV.

XXXIII. Benn *Whalley, Gifford, H&S*] Sir Anthony Benn (d. 1618).

XXXIV. For accounts of smallpox and Elizabethan beauties, see K. O. Myrick, *Sir Philip Sidney as a Literary Craftsman*, Cambridge, Mass., 1935, pp. 235–6, and *H&S*, XI, 65–6. 7. Sir Hugh Platt wrote *Delightes for Ladies to adorne their persons*, 1602. See *H&S*, XI, 66, and Louis B. Wright, *Middle Class Culture in Elizabethan England*, pp. 595–6. 8. oyle of Talck] a cosmetic whitewash. *H&S* indicate Turner is Anne Turner, who poisoned Overbury; Newdigate suggested her husband, the physician George Turner.

XXXV. Percy Simpson discovered that this epitaph was for Elizabeth Chute (1623–7), daughter of Sir George Chute; he collated the text with the brass tablet in Sonning Church, Berkshire (*H&S*, VIII, 188; XI, 66).

XXXVIII–XLI. The authorship of these four poems has been a controversial subject; see *H&S*, XI, 66–70, for a summary of the problems. Swinburne, Maurice Castelain, and Herford favoured Donne as author of all four; W. D. Briggs and B. H. Newdigate favoured Jonson as author; Percy and Evelyn Simpson assign XXXIX, printed in Donne's works during Jonson's lifetime, to Donne, and the remaining three to Jonson on external and internal evidence. Mrs. Simpson made a convincing case in 'Jonson and Donne', *Review of English Studies*, XV, 1939, 274 ff.

XXXVIII. 14. Such forme *F*] such a forme *Gifford, H&S* after *F3*. 99. *Chore*] chorus. 105. Masters *F*] apparently expanded from Mrs. in the MS. *Mistresse* is substituted wherever this occurs in the poems.

*XXXIX. Donne's 'Expostulation'. 53. receive *F*] revive *H&S*.

XL. 20. ratified *F*] rarefied *H&S* after *F3*. 48. our *F*] your *Gifford, H&S*.

XLII. 37–42. See *The New Inn*, IV, ii–iii. 71. The Spittle Sermon was preached annually in Easter-week near the Hospital of St. Mary, Bishopsgate.

XLIII. Written in 1623, probably in November; see *H&S*, I, 73–4; VIII, 12–14, 202–12; XI, 73–81. See also the Introduction of the present edition. 29–31. *H&S* consider this a double attack: on the chivalric romances and on their translator Antony Munday (1553?–1633). 36. *Eteostichs*] chronograms, recording a date in numeral letters. 37. George Puttenham?, *The Arte of English Poesie* (1589), ed. by Edward Arber, 1869, describes various-shaped verses including the *Pillar* and the *Egge*; Jonson may be exaggerating in the remaining forms. 43. Possibly a draft of *The Staple of News*, performed in 1626. 66. Jacobus de Voragine, *Legenda Aurea*, lives of the saints. 71. *Caballs losse*: loss of secret wisdom or occult power. 72. The Rosicrucians were satirized in *News from the New World*, *Neptune's Triumph*, *The Fortunate Isles*, and *The Staple of News*. 74. *Stone*] Philosophers' Stone. 76. 'Lungs were the unhappy drudges kept by the alchemists to blow their true . . . coal.'—*Gifford-Cunningham*, VIII, 402. 77. *Nicholas Pasquill*] Nicholas Breton. 79. *Captain Pamphlet*] Captain Gainsford, who wrote news sheets (see De Winter, ed., *The Staple of News*, New York, 1905, pp. 142–3, and *H&S*, II, 173–5; XI, 77). 81. *Weekly Corrants*] Nathaniel Butter's *Currant of Newes* (*Modern Language Notes*, XLVI, 1931,

150–3). 82. Newdigate suggested one of Two Puritan divines; *H&S* accept Gifford's suggestion of 'one Ball a Taylor'. 89. Another copy of *The Art of Poetry* survived, or Jonson retranslated the work. 90. Jonson's commentary, based on Aristotle (the Stagirite), did not survive. 91. The *English Grammar* was rewritten. 95–7. W. D. Briggs (*Anglia* XXXVII, 1913, 488–9) quoted the Newcastle MS. of the 'Execration' to explain the 'Sicilian Maid' as Argenis instead of Proserpina:

> ... three bookes not amisse
> Reveald if some can judge, of Argenis
> For our owne Ladyes.

100. Richard Carew (1555–1620) contributed an essay on 'The Excellency of the English Tongue' to Camdens *Remains*. Sir Robert Cotton (1571–1631) was one of Camden's pupils; he was a great book and manuscript collector. See *Und.* XIV for John Selden. 142. 'Anciently the Bankside was a continued row of brothels. ... As the place was within the limits of the Bishop of Winchester's jurisdiction, a person who suffered in venereal combats was opprobriously called a Winchester Goose.'—*Whalley*, VI, 410. 148. *H&S* comment on the reading of the Newcastle MS., 'Venus Nun Kate Arden', that it parodies Marlowe's *Hero and Leander*, I, 45–6. 172. The Six Clerks' Office in Chancery Lane was burned in 1621 (*H&S*, XI, 80). 187–8. See *Ep.* LIX, 'On Spies'. 201. *H&S* give Roger Bacon as the 'Fryar'; B. H. Newdigate suggested Berthold Schwarz, a Franciscan friar, as the more likely candidate. Camden's *Remains* (1870), p. 224, has a passage on Berthold Swarte which strongly supports Newdigate's case. 206. *Granats*] grenades. 216. *H&S*, XI, 81, summarize Aubrey's sketch of Bess Broughton.

XLIV. 4–5. Diego, Count of Gondomar (1567–1626), was ambassador to England 1613–18 and 1620–2. He was notoriously unpopular in England. Middleton satirized him in *A Game at Chess*, 1624. 20 ff. *H&S* identify many of the citizen-soldiers (XI, 83–4). 81. Guy of Warwick and Bevis of Hampton.

XLV. Arthur Squib (fl. 1616–34) was an official at the Exchequer. 5–6. Jack o'clock was a mechanical figure which struck the clock bells; the passage means neither man is a time-server. (*H&S*.)

XLVI. Sir Edward Coke (1552–1634).

XLVII. *H&S* date 1623. 15. *for a Sealing*] as a surety. 48. Inigo Jones helped arrange for the reception of the Infanta in 1623. Jonson, slighted, alludes to Inigo as on a level with puppet-showman or bear-baiter. 62. then *F*] thence *Gifford, H&S*. 65–8. These images of false friendship are drawn from masque-production, with a sharp glance at Inigo. See Allardyce Nicoll, *Stuart Masques and the Renaissance Stage*, 1937.

XLVIII. Inigo Jones supervised the building; see *Misc.*, LII, 8–9. 55. Horace, *Satires*, II, i, 25.

XLIX. According to Drummond the Pucell was Cecilia Bulstrode (1584–1609). See *H&S*, I, 59; II, 356; XI, 87; and *London Times Literary Supplement*, 6 March 1930, p. 187. See also *Misc.* XVIII. 7. *Tribade*] Lesbian. 42. John Dorrel (Darrell) (fl. 1562–1602) was a Puritan preacher who cast out evil spirits.

L. See *For.* XII. 2. where with *F*] wherewith *Gifford, H&S*.

LI. Sir Francis Bacon, Baron Verulam (1561–1626). 1. *antient pile*] York House. 9. *Keeper of the Seale*] Sir Nicholas Bacon (1509–79).

LII. Sir William Burlase (d. 1629) was Sheriff of Buckinghamshire. His portrait of Jonson has not been identified if it survives. (*H&S*, XI, 591–92: Portraits of Jonson.)

LIII. William Cavendish, Earl of Newcastle (1592–1676), is the subject of a biography by his second wife, Margaret Cavendish. See the Introduction of the present text. 7. In the Middle Ages and the Renaissance, both in art and letters, Perseus replaced Bellerophon frequently as the rider of Pegasus, horse or ship. See T. W. Baldwin, 'Perseus Purloins Pegasus', *Philological Quarterly*, XX, 1941, 361–70, and H. Carrington Lancaster, *A History of French Dramatic Literature*, Baltimore, 1932, Part II, p. 680. See *RES.*, N.S. vi (1955). 19–20. Virgil reputedly received an allowance of bread for his knowledge and care of horses in the imperial stables. See A. C. Taylor, 'Virgil and the Bread', *TLS*, 28 August 1937, p. 624, and *H&S*, XI, 90.

LIV. See *Und.* XLV. 12. 278 pounds?

LV. John Burges was a clerk of the Exchequer (*H&S*, I, 236; XI, 90–1).

LVII. 4. Sir Robert Pye (1585–1635) was remembrancer of the Exchequer.

LIX. See *Und.* LIII.

LX. Henry West, Baron De la Ware (1603–28), was the son of Thomas West, Baron De la Ware (1577–1618), colonial governor of Virginia.

LXV. 13. *H&S* point out Jonson's translation of these lines in *The King's Entertainment*: (Martial, *Epigr. Liber*, XXXI.)

> Pardon, if my abruptnesse breed disease;
> He merits not t'offend, that hastes to please.

LXX. Lucius Cary, Viscount Falkland (1610?–43), poet and heroic soldier, contributed the first poem to *Jonsonus Virbius*, 1638. He married the sister of his friend Sir Henry Morrison (1608?–29).

LXXI. The Lord Treasurer was Richard Weston, Earl of Portland (1577–1635). 7–8. Technical terms of military fortifications strengthen the sustained image of the siege. 5. Want, *F*, *H&S*.

LXXV. Hierome, Lord Weston (1605–63), was the son and successor of the Earl of Portland. 11. Cacoches *F*] Caroches *Gifford*, *H&S* after Newcastle MS. 161–2. with chast desires, | (The holy perfumes of the Mariage bed) *F*, *H&S*. The passage is difficult; but my emendation may be unjustified.

LXXVII. See *Und.* LXXI.

LXXVIII. Lady Venetia Digby (1600–33), wife of Sir Kenelm Digby (1603–65), was commemorated in *Eupheme* (*Und.* LXXXIV. Sir Kenelm furnished the printer with the text of the 1640 Folio *Jonson*. 14. *my Birth-day*] earlier texts are divided between *my* and *his*. *H&S*, accepting *my*, now place Jonson's birthday as 11 June 1573. 15. St. Barnabas' Day.

LXXIX. Evelyn Simpson in *Review of English Studies*, XIV, 1938, 175–8, pointed out Jonson's use of portions of *Pan's Anniversary* in this poem. 20–35. The marginal notes distributing passages to singers are not clear in the Folio. I have changed them slightly.

*LXXX. *H&S* attribute to Sidney Godolphin (1610–43), who contributed to *Jonsonus Virbius*. (*H&S*, XI, 450.)

*LXXXI. W. D. Briggs and B. H. Newdigate included this poem in the Jonson canon. Except for its inclusion in the 1640 Folio the external evidence points to Sir Henry Wotton (1568–1639) as the author (*H&S*, XI, 102).

LXXXIII. Lady Jane Pawlet (1607–31) was the wife of John Pawlet (Paulet), Marquis of Winton (1598–1675). See Milton's fine elegy, 'An Epitaph on the Marchioness of Winchester', 1631–2?. 10. Thomas, Viscount Savage of Rock Savage, Cheshire. 25. *dotes*] gifts. 76. they that have the Crowne *F*] the Elect of God *Q*.

LXXXIV. For a brief sketch of Lady Venetia, see *H&S*,

XI, 104. See also *Und.* LXXVIII. *Uxorem enim vivam
amare voluptas est, defunctam religio.* Statius, *Silvae*,
V, preface. *1.* 14. *Crepundia*] child's rattle, but here
apparently *infantile toys*. 26. *Call's*] cauls. 31. *take
tent*] take heed, take care. *2.* 1. *uncontrol'd*] undis-
puted. 13–18. For the ancestral Audleys, Chesters,
and Stanleys see *H&S*, XI, 105–6. *3.* 9. The Painter
may have been Van Dyck, who painted an allegori-
cal portrait of Lady Venetia now in Windsor Castle.
13–28. Two prose descriptions in *The Masque of
Beauty* clarify this projected painting:

'SPLENDOR. In a robe of flame colour, naked
brested; her bright hayre loose flowing: She was
drawn in a circle of clouds, her face, and body
breaking through; and in her hand a branch, with
two Roses, a white, and a red.... PERFECTIO. In a
Vesture of pure Golde, a wreath of Gold upon her
head. About her bodie the Zodiacke, with the
Signes....'

9. Sera quidem... Statius, *Silvae*, V, i (*Epicedion in
Priscillam*), 16. 2. *sey'd*] attempted. 18. *cleies*] claws
(AS. *clea* nom. sing.). 85. St. Thomas Aquinas quotes
Dionysius the Areopagite and Pope Gregory as the
chief authorities on the angelic hierarchy. 229–32.
Adapted from Statius' preface, substituting Digby
for Abascantus, Venetia for Priscilla.

MISCELLANY

Most of the poems in this collection appear in *Ungathered Verse*, *H&S*, VIII, 360–423, and in *Drift-
wood* in Newdigate's *Poems of Ben Jonson*, pp. 241–
306. In addition, selected lyrics from the plays and
masques and a few doubtful pieces are added. Those
pieces which appear in *Ungathered Verse* carry two
numbers: *Misc.* and *U.V.* in the notes.

I. (*U.V.* I.) This book of emblems, 1598–9, is in manuscript in the British Museum (Additional MS. 18040). Camden apparently encouraged the author. 15. the *trivium* and the *quadrivium*. 32. Horace, *Odes*, iv, viii, 28.

II. (*U.V.* II). From Nicholas Breton, *Melancholike Humours*, 1600.

III. (*U.V.* III).

V. (*Inscriptions*, II.) Inserted in a copy of *The Fountaine of Selfe-Love, or Cynthias Revels*. 1601.

VI. (*U.V.* IV.) From Robert Chester, *Loves Martyr*. 1601.

VII. (*U.V.* V.) From the same. See *The Forrest* x, xi.

VIII. From a manuscript in the Folger Library. See *For*. x.

XI. (*U.V.* VI.) From Hugh Holland, *Pancharis: The first Booke*, 1603. See the Introduction, p. xli.

XII. (*U.V.* VII.) From Thomas Wright, *The Passions of the minde in generall*, 1604.

XV. (*U.V.* VIII.) From John Fletcher, *The Faithfull Shepherdesse*, n.d. (1609–10?).

XVIII. (*U.V.* IX.) 'Epitaph on Cecilia Bulstrode', from the holograph in the Library of Harvard University. See *Und.* XLIX. 14. Note the Chaucerian reference.

XIX. (*U.V.* XI.) From *Coryats Crudities*, 1611. Thomas Coryate (1577?–1617) was a noted traveller and buffoon. 1. Proverbial for, 'Trust a plain man'.

XX. (*U.V.* XII.) From *Coryats Crambe*, 1611. 22. *Pies*] pize. 37. *Tergum O*] O my back! *H&S*, XI, 134.

XXI. 5–6. The two young satyrs who sing the catch are trying to rouse two sylvans by tickling their ears and noses with straws or hairs.

XXII. (*U.V.* XVI.) From MS. Ashmole 38, Bodleian Library. 1613.

XXIII. (*U.V.* XVII.) From John Stephens, *Cinthias*

Revenge, 1613. 4. The work appeared anonymously, but was later claimed (*H&S*, XI, 136–8).

XXIV. (*U.V.* XVIII.) From the holograph in a copy of the 1640 Folio in the British Museum. Somerset was married in 1613. 14. *freind*] Overbury.

XXV. (*U.V.* XX.) From *The Husband*, 1614. 8. *Wife*] Overbury's poem.

XXVI. (*U.V.* XIX.) From Christopher Brooke, *The Ghost of Richard the Third*, 1614.

XXVIII. (*U.V.* XXI.) From W. Browne, *Britannia's Pastorals. The Second Booke*. 1616.

XXX. (*U.V.* XXII.) From the Newcastle Manuscript (Harleian MS. 4955, British Museum). Charles Cavendish (15??–1619) was the father of William Cavendish, Earl of Newcastle. See *Und.* LIII, LIX, and Introduction, p. xxxiv.

XXXI. (*U.V.* XXIII.) *The Georgicks of Hesiod, By George Chapman*, 1618. The relationship of Jonson and Chapman (1560–1634) suffered a reversal after this date (see *H&S*, X, 692–7; XI, 406–12). Chapman apparently sided with Inigo Jones in the long quarrel.

*XXXIII. (*H&S, Poems Ascribed to Jonson*, XXI.) From John Ashmore, *Certain Selected Odes of Horace, Englished*, 1621. *H&S*, VIII, 451, present the reasons for considering this spurious. However, although the piece is 'at variance with Jonson's theory and practice of translation', it is no more free than several of his adaptations of classical poems; and there is no evidence that the author rather than the editor considered it an 'Englishing'. The late Joseph Quincy Adams and James G. McManaway of The Folger Shakespeare Library, who called the poem to my attention, considered the genuineness of the poem highly likely.

XXXIV. (*U.V.* XXIV.) From James Mabbe (1572–1642?), *The Rogue: or the Life of Guzman de*

Alfarache. Written in Spanish by Matheo Aleman.
London, 1622.

XXXV. (*U.V.* XXV.) From *Mr. William Shake-speares Comedies, Histories, and Tragedies*, 1623.

XXXVI. (*U.V.* XXVI.) From the same. 19–21. *H&S* quote William Basse's 'Elegy on Shakespeare', requesting Chaucer, Spenser, and Beaumont to move closer together and make room for Shakespeare. 35. Pacuvius (220–130 B.C.) and Accius (170–94 B.C.) were not only praised by Jonson's favourite Horace, but also were praised and quoted freely by his favourites Cicero and Quintilian; neither of the tragedians survives except in fragments of quoted verse. Seneca (4? B.C.–65 A.D.), 'him of Cordova', was the most vital classical influence on Elizabethan tragedy. 58–62. See Jonson's translation of Horace's *Art of Poetry*, 625–8.

XXXVIII. (*U.V.* XXVII.) From Jas. Warre, *The Touchstone of Truth*, 1630. *H&S* have some doubt as to Jonson's authorship of this piece.

XXXIX. (*U.V.* XXVIII.) Lady Jane Ogle (d. 1625) was the wife of Edward, Earl of Shrewsbury, and aunt of William Cavendish, Earl of Newcastle. This poem is from the Newcastle MS. (Harleian 4955).

XL. (*H&S, Leges Convivales.*) From the Jonson Folio of 1692. *H&S* print from the original panel in Glyn, Mills and Company's Bank, No. 1, Fleet Street. 8. Simon Wadlow (d. 1627) was keeper of the Devil Tavern; the Apollo room was on the first floor.

XLI. (*U.V.* XXIX.) From Thomas May, *Lucan's Pharsalia: or The Civill Warres of Rome, betweene Pompey the great, and Julius Caesar*, 1627. Thomas May (1595–1650) also translated Virgil and Martial in part. 24. *Sonne of May*] Mercury, son of Maia: see Hermes in lines 16–17.

XLII. (*U.V.* XXX.) From *The Battaile of Agincourt*

[*and other works*]. *By Michaell Drayton Esquire.*
1627. For the relationship between Jonson and
Drayton (1563–1631), see *H&S*, XI, 147–9. Of
especial interest is the contention of J. W. Hebel,
editor of the Shakespeare Head *Drayton*, that
Jonson's poem is not praise at all, but rather satire.
Cf. *Misc.* XXXVI:

> Or crafty Malice, might pretend this praise,
> And thinke to ruine, where it seem'd to raise.

This interpretation certainly arouses scepticism:
Jonson's praise may be a bit enthusiastic, but it is no
more exaggerated than that in innumerable other
commendatory verses. 23 *ff.* Newdigate and *H&S*
list the works of Drayton to which Jonson refers:
Idea. The Shepheards Garland, 1593; *Peirs Gaveston,
Matilda*, and *The Tragicall Legend of Robert Duke
of Normandy*, printed together in 1596; *Englands
Heroicall Epistles*, 1597; *The Owle*, 1604; *The
Barrons Wars in the raigne of Edward the second*,
1603; *Poly-Olbion*, 1622; and in the 1627 volume:
*The Battaile of Agincourt, The Miseries of Queene
Margarite, Nimphidia, the Court of Fayrie, The
Quest of Cinthia, The Shepheards Sirena, The Moone-
Calfe, Elegies upon sundry occasions*.

XLIII. (*U.V.* XXXI.) Katherine, Lady Ogle (d. 1629),
was the wife of Charles Cavendish and mother of
William Cavendish, Earl of Newcastle. The *Epitaph*
is from the Newcastle MS. (Harleian 4955). *H&S*
give the translation of the motto: 'In the fulness of
time Zeus observes the records.' (From Zenobius,
Proverbs, 4, 11) *H&S*, XI, 150.

XLIV. (*U.V.* XXXII.) From *Bosworth-field: with a
taste of the Variety of other Poems, left by Sir John
Beaumont, Baronet, deceased: Set forth by his Sonne,
Sir John Beaumont, Baronet.* 1629. The elder Sir
John Beaumont (1583–1627) was the brother of

Francis Beaumont; the younger contributed an elegy to *Jonsonus Virbius*.

XLV. (*U.V.* XXXIII.) First printed in *French Court-Aires*, 1629; printed in the 1640 Folio as *Epigram* CXXIX, from which the present text is taken. 14. Jonson used this quotation from Chaucer in *The New Inn* and *A Challenge at Tilt* (*H&S*, X, 303).

XLVII. From *Ben: Jonson's Execration against Vulcan.* 1640. (The Quarto). *H&S* print from a revised text in Ashmole MS. 38 of the Bodleian, and include the 'Ode' with *The New Inn*. 27. Broomes sweepings *Q*] There, sweepings *H&S*. Although the spirit is better, the verse loses all point with the omission of the reference to Richard Brome (fl. 1614–52), Jonson's servant and apprentice in comedy. See *Misc.* LV. Brome's dramatic abilities were by no means contemptible.

*XLIX. From the same. (*H&S* print as *Poems Ascribed to Jonson*, I.) The attribution in the 1640 Quarto seems reasonable to me, especially in view of the alchemic imagery in 17–20: see J. M. Manly, *Canterbury Tales By Geoffrey Chaucer*, New York, 1928, p. 653: 'The alchemists called gold "sol" and silver "luna", and spoke of them as the father and mother of the elixir or philosopher's stone.'

*L. (*Poems Ascribed to Jonson*, II.) Also from the 1640 Quarto. *H&S* believe this piece probably by Thomas Freeman.

LI. (*U.V.* XXXIV.) This and the following two poems are taken from Lord Ellesmere's copy of Jonson's manuscript by *H&S*. I have expanded the abbreviations. For discussion of Jonson and Jones, see *H&S*, X, 689–92, and J. Alfred Gotch, *Inigo Jones*, London, 1928. For the Masque, see *H&S*, II, 249–334; X, 404–45; Allardyce Nicoll, *Stuart Masques and the Renaissance Stage*, London, 1937; Allan H. Gilbert, *The Symbolic Persons in the Masques of*

INDEX OF FIRST LINES